City of Westminster College

116698

KU-724-583

EXAM REVISION NOTES

WITHDRAWN

AS/A-LEVEL

Nuffield Economics & Business Studies

Gerald Wood

Philip Allan Updates
Market Place
Deddington
Oxfordshire
OX15 0SE

Orders

Bookpoint Ltd, 130 Milton Park, Abingdon, Oxfordshire, OX14 4SB
tel: 01235 827720
fax: 01235 400454
e-mail: uk.orders@bookpoint.co.uk
Lines are open 9.00 a.m.–5.00 p.m., Monday to Saturday, with a 24-hour message answering service. You can also order through the Philip Allan Updates website:
www.philipallan.co.uk

© Philip Allan Updates 2003

All rights reserved; no part of this publication may be reproduced, stored in a retrieval system, or transmitted, in any form or by any means, electronic, mechanical, photocopying, recording or otherwise without either the prior written permission of Philip Allan Updates or a licence permitting restricted copying in the United Kingdom issued by the Copyright Licensing Agency Ltd, 90 Tottenham Court Road, London W1T 4LP.

ISBN-13: 978-0-86003-752-1
ISBN-10: 0-86003-752-5

Printed in Spain

CITY OF WESTMINSTER COLLEGE
MAIDA VALE LEARNING CENTRE
WITHDRAWN
DATE....3..4..08
BARCODE...116698.
CLASS NO.....650 WBO

Philip Allan Updates' policy is to use papers that are natural, renewable and recyclable products and made from wood grown in sustainable forests. The logging and manufacturing processes are expected to conform to the environmental regulations of the country of origin.

Contents

THE A2 SPECIFICATION (Units 4–6)

Core content: competitiveness (Unit 4)

The options (Unit 5)

Coursework and past paper practice

Introduction

The publication of this revision guide fulfils one of my long-standing ambitions. The Nuffield Economics and Business Studies A-level has been running since the mid-1990s and has been an outstanding success. With a strong emphasis on hands-on learning by the student, it has proved very popular. And by integrating two closely related subjects, it has played a key role in broadening sixth-form studies.

How to use this guide: AS students

The AS course contains three units. Units 1 and 2 are tested by final examination; Unit 3 by coursework. All the content you need is covered in the first 16 chapters of this book, with Chapters 17 and 18 providing past paper practice and coursework advice.

Within each of the 16 chapters there are normally two units, Unit 1 for the Unit 1 examination; and Unit 2 for the Unit 2 examination. Most students sit both examinations together in the summer. If this is what you are doing, it makes sense to revise both Units together by simply going through each chapter in turn. If, however, you are sitting the Unit 1 examination in January, then you only need to revise the Unit 1 sections of Chapters 1 to 16 for the Unit 1 exam.

How to use this guide: A-level students

The second year of the course also contains three Units. Unit 4 is assessed by a final examination containing pre-release material. The content is covered in Chapters 19 to 24. Unit 5 is also assessed by final examination. Its three Options (every student has to answer questions from two of them) are covered in Chapters 25 to 27. Unit 6 is the coursework component and is discussed together with past paper practice in Chapters 28 and 29.

However, A-level students are also expected to know the AS material when they sit their A2 assessment in Units 4 to 6. For this reason, you will find that Chapters 19 to 29 of this guide make frequent reference back to the earlier, AS chapters. These should be revised as well before you sit your final examination.

Appeals, resits and 'banking': a word of advice

Under the new-style A-levels first sat in 2002, three issues concerning examination tactics have arisen. The recommendations given below are the author's advice as of January 2003. However, the world of examinations is changing faster than ever before, and students are always well advised to seek up-to-date information from their teachers.

Appeals It is possible to appeal the result of any unit. The examination board, Edexcel, will (for a fee) do a remark. However, under new arrangements from 2002, appeals may result in marks going down as well as up. This is no idle threat: the author is already aware of instances where students have been marked down. You are, therefore, strongly recommended to seek the advice of your teachers before appealing any result.

Resits It is also possible to resit any unit once. If you do, the higher mark is the one that counts — whether you scored the higher mark at your first or second attempt. Given that A-level students have to revise the AS work anyway before sitting their A2 units, there is a strong argument for saying that A2 students should resit Units 1 and 2 if they have not done so already. Such an approach cannot reduce your grade and may well improve it. All you have to lose is the examination fee and the half day spent resitting the Units. In 2002, half the author's A-level students went up a grade as a result of resitting Units 1 and 2. The only clear instance the author can see for not resitting is if the student has done so well first time round that further improvement is very unlikely. The same argument could also apply to Unit 4. If you sit it in January, why not resit it in the summer?

Banking It is possible for a student to 'bank' an AS level before proceeding to the full A-level. This means that the AS level has been awarded, and the mark cannot subsequently be changed unless all three units (including the coursework) are resat. There is at present no clear balance of advantage in either banking or not banking. Students should, therefore, seek the advice of their institutions.

This guide is offered in the hope of making a good course even better.

Additional sources of information

Books
- Nancy Wall (ed.), *The Nuffield Economics and Business Students' Book* (Longman), is the full-length textbook produced specifically for this course.
- Nancy Wall (ed.), *The Complete A–Z Economics and Business Studies Handbook* (Hodder and Stoughton), provides a full-length dictionary for students who wish to look up technical terms in some detail.

Websites
www.edexcel.org.uk is the website of the examining board, containing up-to-date news for students and teachers. You can order the specification and past papers through this portal. The AS specification is no. 8128. The A-level specification is no. 9128.

www.google.com is the top search engine for anything and everything.

www.bized.ac.uk is the national website for economics and business teachers and students with good cross-references elsewhere.

www.tutor2u.net is a website focusing on revision articles for sixth-form students of economics, business and politics.

www.philipallan.co.uk is an educational resource provider with a wide range of conferences and magazines suitable for students of this course.

www.geraldwood.com is the author's own website dedicated to further material useful for this course.

Acknowledgements

My thanks first of all to Philip Cross and Penny Fisher at Philip Allan Updates for managing the publishing aspect of this book so professionally. Thank you too, to Edexcel for permission to reproduce two examination questions in Chapter 17.

A special thank you to Brian Ellis, the Chief Examiner of this course, who read the whole manuscript with great care and came up with numerous ways of improving it. The responsibility for any remaining mistakes is, of course, my own.

And finally, my thanks to my wife, Mohini, and our children Geraldine, Jessica, Naomi, Matthew and Lydia — who, for many long hours, had to put up with my much reduced contribution to family life while this book was being written. This book is dedicated to them, with my love and gratitude.

Gerald Wood
Newcastle-upon-Tyne

The AS specification
Units 1–3

Chapter 1
Supply and demand

At the end of this unit, you should be able to:

1 Explain the difference between economics and business studies.

2 Describe economic agents and stakeholders.

3 Describe inputs and specialisation.

4 Use supply/demand diagrams to illustrate and explain how prices change and industries expand and contract.

Introduction to economics and business studies

A biologist gathers his students round him on the East African savannah. 'This is a fascinating ecosystem to study,' he claims. 'Every animal species uses its particular characteristics to key into the features of its surroundings that will enable it to survive. So the elephant's vast bulk condemns it to a ceaseless search for food, while its size ensures the security from predators that it needs to graze without interruption. The dingo is too small to bring down an antelope, so it hunts in packs. A few run directly towards the target antelope, while others fan out. If the antelope changes the direction of its flight, it will lose ground to the dingoes that originally set off in that direction. It has been calculated that 1,000 antelope are needed to support a pack of 20 dingoes, while an antelope needs around 4 acres of grazing to itself. Can you now work out the maximum numbers of dingoes that the 200,000 acre Mara Masai reserve is capable of supporting?'

Meanwhile, on the other side of the hill a lion gathers her cubs around her. 'It's like this,' she says. 'The best chance of getting dinner is to go for the weakest animal. See that group over there? The one in the middle with white hair — the one making the funny sounds — that's the one to go for. Remember, creep round until you're spotted — then sprint for the old one!'

This tale illustrates the difference between economics and business studies. Economics seeks to explain why resource use is as it is. It looks for theoretical explanations to account for the financial world that we observe. It then tries to work out what the government should be doing to make the system work better, rather like a biologist might advise on wildlife management. The subject was originally called 'political economy' to emphasise its links with government. It is still the case that by far the biggest employer of economists is the government.

By contrast, business studies is a 'how to' subject. Rather than standing outside the business world looking in, business studies adopts the position of participant. Given that the world is as it is, how can it best be exploited to enable the business to achieve its financial objectives?

Economics as an academic subject has been around since the mid-eighteenth century, and in secondary schools since the 1950s. Most economists were at first mathematicians, who used their mathematical understanding to understand business. Business studies as a formal discipline is only a century old, and was first introduced into UK schools as recently as the late 1960s. It is now the most popular university subject, while economics is increasingly seen as an option within business studies.

Economic agents

One useful way of looking at the world from the economist's point of view is to group people into decision-making units, known as **economic agents**. Every **household** is an economic agent. Its members make joint decisions about how to spend their money. In this capacity they are known as **consumers**. They also need to decide how to go about earning money in the first place. Every **firm** is also an economic agent. Its owners make decisions about what to sell, and for how much. From the **turnover** the firm gets, it subtracts its expenses — its **costs** — to arrive at its financial surplus, or **profit**. In doing so, it will have to keep the wider **community** on its side, and have regard to the interests of its suppliers, workers and other **stakeholders**.

Firms and households are essentially collections of private individuals. Together they are known as the **private sector**, even if the company is known as a 'public limited company' or 'plc' for short. By contrast, the **government**, which rules the country, and all its branches is known as the **public sector**. So, for example, civil servants, members of the armed forces or the NHS and most schoolteachers are together referred to as 'public sector workers'.

GLOSSARY

community, society: people living within a defined area
consumer, customer: buyer of output, commonly a household
costs (private costs, total costs): all expenses incurred by a firm in its activities
economic agent: person or organisation making financial decisions
firm: collection of inputs organised for output
government, central government: the organisation that rules a territory
household: person(s) under one roof, consumers
private sector: all firms and households
profit ('net' or 'true'), before tax: company income, after deducting all costs
public sector: government bodies, local, national and EU
stakeholder: person or organisation with an interest in a firm's behaviour
turnover, sales, total revenue: money value of a firm's sales

Inputs

A student of both economics and business studies will be interested in all three groups of economic agents outlined above. However, in your course, there is relatively less emphasis on the household, which is also studied in psychology, sociology and home economics. There is relatively more emphasis on the firm, which does, of course, lie at the heart of business studies.

One way of looking at what any firm, or company, does is to say it uses **inputs** to produce **output**. Inputs, also known as 'factors of production', can be conveniently grouped into four types. There is the **labour**, the work of company employees. Then there are the offices, factories and materials with which they work, collectively known as **capital** or **'physical capital'** to distinguish it from 'financial capital' or money. The capital and workers

have to be located on **land**. And the whole business has to be organised by risk-taking individuals who put up the cash. These 'entrepreneurs' provide **enterprise**, the fourth input.

We might ask why workers are organised into firms at all, rather than workers simply working for themselves individually. While such self-employment is increasingly common in the UK, it remains the case that in many industries **productivity** is much higher if **specialisation** takes place; and specialisation often works best if a number of workers provide different skills while working under one roof, for the same organisation.

GLOSSARY

capital (physical), capital stock: all man-made inputs
enterprise: combining inputs to produce output
inputs, factors of production: resources, elements that go into output
labour, work: effort aimed at production
land: the input consisting of all natural resources
output, product: the good or service offered for sale
productivity of labour: output per person per time period
specialisation, division of labour: focus on one particular product or task

Supply and demand (1)

'We're responding to supply and demand,' says the trader who has just increased **prices** to the horror of his customers. Whether prices (or people's wages) are raised or lowered, whether factories or offices are opened, closed or relocated — 'supply and demand' is a powerful way of explaining such events.

Supply and demand is the first example of a **model** — an abstraction that simplifies reality in an attempt to explain it. This particular model is extraordinarily powerful and is closely identified with the whole subject of economics. Adam Smith first described it as an **invisible hand** in the foundation book of economics, *Inquiry into the Nature and Causes of the Wealth of Nations* (1776). The Nuffield A-level course does not spend much time on abstract models, preferring a more hands-on, descriptive approach. However, this model is so fundamental to the whole of economics that it is worth getting to grips with it.

In essence, it is very simple. Consumers with money **demand** goods. The cheaper the goods are, the more consumers want to buy them. This fact can be illustrated with a **demand curve**, which plots the overall demand for a product against a range of prices. The curve has a negative gradient, indicating that the higher the price is, the lower demand will be, and vice versa. An example of a demand curve is shown in Figure 1.1.

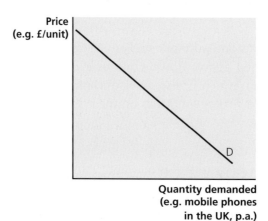

Figure 1.1
A demand curve

It is important to note that this curve communicates the information: 'when the price is low, demand is high' — not the other way round. Thus, price is the *independent variable* and demand is the *dependent variable*. Confusion often arises because in supply and demand diagrams the independent variable (i.e. the price) is on the y-axis, whereas in mathematics the y-axis is commonly used for the dependent variable.

On the other side of the **market** where goods are **exchanged**, firms **supply** goods. Not surprisingly, the higher the price their goods command, the more they will wish to sell — and the more companies will wish to enter the market. This fact can be illustrated with a **supply curve**, which plots the industry's supply of a product against a range of prices. In this case, the curve has a positive gradient, indicating that the higher the price is, the greater the supply will be. This is illustrated in Figure 1.2.

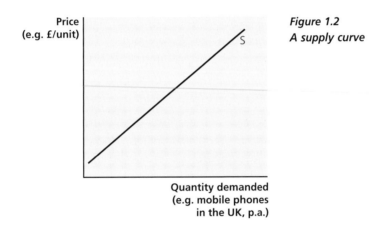

Figure 1.2
A supply curve

If these two graphs are superimposed on top of each other, the result is Figure 1.3. You will notice there is one, and only one, price at which the quantity supplied and quantity demanded are equal. This is known as the market-clearing price. The market 'clears', meaning that every unit of the product that is supplied is also demanded. There is no unsold **surplus**. Equally, every unit that is demanded is matched with a unit supplied. There are no dissatisfied customers and there is no **shortage**.

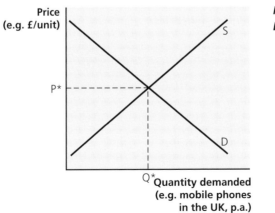

Figure 1.3
Demand and supply

The market-clearing price is also known as the **equilibrium price** (or P* for short) because the price is in a state of rest. In the absence of shortages that would push the price up or surpluses that would push it down, there is no reason for the price to change.

At this equilibrium price, the quantity demanded and the quantity supplied are equal. This quantity is called the **equilibrium quantity** (or Q*).

GLOSSARY

demand curve (D): demand plotted against different prices
demand, effective demand: the desire for and ability to buy a product
equilibrium price, 'clearing' price (P*): price at which supply equals demand
equilibrium quantity (Q*): quantity supplied and demanded at P*
exchange: swapping of goods by barter or by money
invisible hand: metaphor for the efficiency of the free market
market: arrangement by which buyers and sellers meet
model, paradigm: simplification enabling reality to be better understood
price: amount at which a product changes hands
shortage: excess of demand over supply
supply: willingness to offer a good for sale
supply curve (S): supply plotted against different price levels
surplus: excess of supply over demand

Supply and demand (2)

Our analysis so far gives an explanation for prices, but not for why prices might change. We know from everyday observation that many prices change on a daily basis. When so many prices appear to be volatile (i.e. unstable), this seems to be in conflict with the idea of an *equilibrium* price — a price that could be described as being in a state of rest.

The explanation for this is that the supply and demand curves frequently change position, giving rise to a new equilibrium every time one of them shifts. For while demand and supply curves show how demand and supply are influenced by the price of the product, they say nothing about the host of other, non-price factors that might have an influence. If these non-price factors change, then either the demand or the supply curve will shift position. These 'non-price factors' are known as **non-price determinants of demand** and **non-price determinants of supply** respectively.

Looking first at the demand curve, **disposable income** will obviously influence demand. For the vast majority of goods, an increase in disposable income will cause an increase in demand. This is illustrated in Figure 1.4.

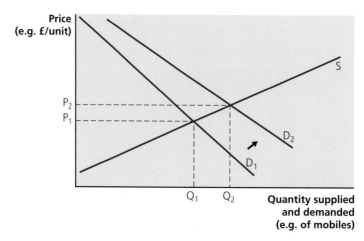

Figure 1.4 An outward shift (increase) in demand

The curve D_2 shows a greater demand for mobile phones than the curve D_1. The equilibrium quantity of mobiles rises from Q_1 to Q_2, while the greater demand also increases the price at which it sells from P_1 to P_2. Manufacturers and retailers will be happy. They work longer hours to produce and sell larger amounts, which they can sell at higher prices. Consumers grumble; it costs more to switch to mobile telephony.

A *reduction* in disposable income would have the opposite effect. Both prices and quantities in the industry would fall.

The other main non-price determinants of demand are:
- *The price of* **substitutes**. Supposing fixed lines (a substitute for mobiles) became more expensive. Mobiles would become relatively more attractive, shifting the demand curve for mobiles outwards.
- *The price of* **complements**. People who buy mobile phones also buy mobile phone calls. The two goods are complementary. If the price of the calls goes down, the mobile phones themselves will again become more attractive, shifting their demand curve outwards.
- **Tastes**. The decision to buy a mobile phone will not only depend on a straightforward calculation of the total costs and convenience of mobile telephony relative to fixed lines. Fashion, the habits of our friends and of opinion-formers, and our own self-image will all play a part too. These influences on our personal preferences are summarised in the word 'tastes'. If our tastes change in favour of mobile phones, then their demand curve will shift outwards.

Equally, a reduction in the price of substitutes, or an increase in the price of complements, or an adverse change in tastes will shift the demand curve inwards. Further non-price determinants of demand are explained in Unit 2 of this chapter. You should be able to illustrate any of these changes with a diagram similar to Figure 1.4, showing the demand curve shifting either inwards or outwards.

However, a shift in the demand curve cannot explain *both* the enormous increase in quantities sold of mobiles *and* the significant reductions in their price. For if the demand curve had shifted outwards, prices should have gone up; and if it had shifted inwards, sales would have gone down. In recent years, neither of these has happened, rather the opposite.

The explanation is that the supply curve has shifted, due to changes in non-price determinants of supply. A company's willingness to supply depends essentially on two things: the price at which it can sell, and what it costs the company to make the product. These 'costs of production' constitute non-price determinants of supply. Costs of production depend in turn on three major variables:
- *The cost of inputs.* If labour, land or physical capital can be hired more cheaply, costs will fall.
- *The productivity of those inputs.* If, for example, advances in technology enable every worker to assemble more mobiles over the course of a shift, the cost of each mobile will fall.
- *Any production taxes imposed on the company.* Petrol costs garages more to supply every time the chancellor increases petrol duty.

If costs fall, the supply curve shifts downwards, leading to an increase in the equilibrium quantity and a reduction in the equilibrium price, as in Figure 1.5.

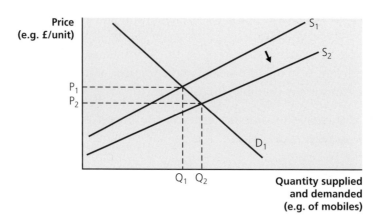

Figure 1.5 An outward shift (increase) in supply

This is called an 'outward shift' in supply. Firms are prepared to supply more, even at the lower price now on offer. Reduced costs will preserve their profits; indeed, profits may actually rise as lower prices lead to higher volumes being sold. In these circumstances, consumers are happy too — it's costing less to get connected.

The theory of **price determination** provided by supply and demand curves is, then, a powerful way of explaining both prices and the expansion or contraction of individual industries. But prices are also interesting in themselves. A rising price encourages consumers to ask whether they can get by with less of the product. The **opportunity cost** of buying it is rising, so perhaps there is a substitute that they could consider. The same rising price tells the entrepreneur, 'There are profits to be made here if your own costs have not risen. You could undercut existing competitors and still make a healthy profit.'

It is prices that operate the invisible hand of the market, ensuring that the quantities of the thousands of different goods produced are an accurate reflection both of the desires of consumers and of the costs of production faced by their suppliers.

GLOSSARY

complements: two goods that are consumed together, e.g. cars and petrol
disposable income: take-home pay plus state benefits
non-price determinants of demand: influences on demand other than price
non-price determinants of supply: influences on supply other than price
opportunity cost: value of the next best alternative forgone
price determination, theory of: theory used to explain price levels
substitutes: two goods that are alternatives for each other, e.g. petrol and diesel
tastes: personal preferences for any particular good

UNIT 2

At the end of this unit, you should be able to:

1 Explain and illustrate the effects of changes in non-price determinants of supply and demand.

2 Explain the concept of allocative (Pareto) efficiency and how the price mechanism helps society to achieve it.

3 Describe income elasticity of demand (IED), work out IED values and explain how IED is used.

4 Describe price elasticity of demand (PED), work out PED values and explain how PED is used.

Further non-price determinants of demand

In Unit 1 it was seen that changes in incomes, tastes and the prices of complements and substitutes can all shift demand curves. Such factors are called 'non-price determinants of demand'. Other examples include:

- *Population growth.* A general increase in population will increase the demand for virtually every good. One reason why isolated islands are often among the poorest countries in the world is that they lack the population to sustain a variety of firms.
- *Change in the age structure.* One of the most significant changes in demand in the UK over the past 20 years has been the rapid increase in the retired population, and particularly the over-80s. Opening up old people's homes has become a significant business opportunity.
- *Change in income distribution.* The rapid rise in UK unemployment in the 1970s and 1980s led to new business opportunities for discount stores such as Kwik Save. In the relatively prosperous 1990s, Kwik Save's share price slumped. High unemployment levels also provide opportunities for bed-and-breakfast enterprises to accommodate homeless families at the expense of the local authority.
- *Change in social habits.* The enormous increase in the number of working mothers with young children over the past decade has increased the demand for all sorts of child-care: after-school clubs, holiday clubs, all-day crèches and nurseries, child-minders and au pairs.
- *Change in cultural trends.* A decline in organised religion, and a change in the law, has opened the way for a new market in 'wedding venues'. A 'back-to-nature' movement has led to a whole new market in organic produce.
- *Change in regional trends.* Different regions may have their own speciality foods, be interested in different sports, have distinct architectural styles and be dominated by different industries. They may have their own music and language. These all create regional patterns of demand, which will change over time.
- *Advertising and promotion.* This non-price determinant of demand is different from the ones listed previously in that it is directly under the control of the individual business. Clearly, successful advertising will shift the demand curve outwards. For more on this, see Chapter 4.

The price mechanism

The typical supply/demand diagram shows four pieces of information: the supply curve, the demand curve, the equilibrium quantity (Q*) and the equilibrium price (P*). Yet how many of these four pieces of information are widely known?

The supply and demand curves themselves are pure theory: they show how much firms *might* supply, and how much consumers *might* demand at a range of price levels. In most cases, they can only be guessed at. As for Q*, some limited information may be available through market research.

But the one figure that every buyer and every seller in any market knows is, of course, the price. From the humblest street market in an African village to the aerospace industry of the developed world, most buyers have a shrewd idea of what constitutes a bargain and most sellers have an equally shrewd idea of how much they can get away with charging.

And, surprisingly, the price is the very thing they *need to know*. Take, for example, estate agents in an area that has become popular due to a local school experiencing rapid improvement. The estate agents may not know this, but they notice that houses in the area

start selling more quickly than usual and at the offered price. Following the estate agents' rule 'If buyers pay the asking price, you're not asking enough', they increase their prices. At the increased price, some people who were thinking of moving decide not to. Perhaps they do not need the school or perhaps they can't afford the prices. At the same time, people in the area who were thinking of selling are encouraged to do so. The price they can now get will enable them to buy something rather bigger elsewhere than they had previously anticipated. Meanwhile, builders realise there are profits to be made in the area. Those with planning permission start to build. Others seek planning permission in the area.

Thus the price increase performs a vital function: it reduces the increased demand caused by the popular school while at the same time increasing the supply of housing. Supply will equal demand once again at a new, higher price. This example of the **price mechanism** is repeated literally thousands of times every day in an almost infinite variety of contexts. When this process takes place on a large scale, either creating a new industry or virtually wiping out an existing one, the process is known as **structural change**.

Prices are said to be a **signalling mechanism**, a means by which shifts in demand and supply curves are communicated to buyers and sellers. Sometimes it is *profits* that are said to be the signalling mechanism. There is obviously a close connection between the price a company can charge and the profits it can make.

Provided the price mechanism works effectively, industries expand if demand expands or supply expands. Equally, they contract if demand contracts or supply contracts. The result is that every industry tends towards exactly the size it should be, relative to every other industry. Inputs are thus allocated between industries in correct proportion. This idea is known as **allocative** (or **Pareto**) **efficiency** because resources (i.e. inputs) are distributed between industries in such a way that the total benefit everyone derives from the nation's GDP is as big as possible.

But there are occasions when the price mechanism fails to work its magic. These examples of **market failure** are looked at again in Chapters 9 and 10.

GLOSSARY

allocative (Pareto) efficiency: optimal relative size of different industries
market failure: failure of the free-market mechanism
price mechanism: method of matching demand with supply
signalling mechanism: communication device (e.g. prices and profits)
structural change in an economy: change in the relative size of industries

The sensitivity of demand to changes in income: income elasticity of demand (IED)

So far a variety of factors have been listed that influence a firm's willingness to supply goods and a consumer's willingness to buy them, but no attempt has been made to quantify these influences. This section shows how to measure the degree to which demand for any product will change in response to the general level of incomes.

The basic idea is to measure the proportionate change in demand relative to the proportionate change in income. So if a 1% increase in incomes led to a 0.5%, 1% or 2% increase in demand for clothes, then the **income elasticity of demand** (IED) of clothes would be 0.5, 1, or 2 respectively. The formula is:

$$\text{IED of good X} = \frac{\text{\% change in demand for good X}}{\text{\% change in income}}$$

If you set the percentage change in income at 1, then the percentage change in demand for good X becomes its IED. This leads to the definition of IED as: the percentage change in demand for a good following a 1% increase in income.

GLOSSARY

income elasticity of demand: responsiveness of demand to changes in income

What determines the likely value of IED?

The more essential a good is, the lower will be its IED. This is because almost all households, regardless of income, buy essential goods. Luxury goods, on the other hand, have high values for IED. As people become richer, demand for these products rises rapidly.

There are some goods whose IED is actually negative — demand for them falls as income rises. These are called **inferior goods**. They include services such as bus transport, which the poor use more than the rich. Goods with a positive IED (the vast majority) are called **normal goods**.

Normal goods can be split into two categories. First, there are **necessities** like food for which demand rises more slowly than income; their IED lies between 0 and 1. Necessities are called **income-inelastic goods**, meaning that demand is only moderately responsive to income changes. Second, there are **luxuries** like holidays for which demand rises faster than income; their IED is greater than 1. Such luxuries are called **income-elastic goods**, meaning that demand is more responsive to changes in income than the average. Table 1.1 summarises the terminology.

What happens to demand when incomes rise	Value of IED	Description of good	
Demand falls	Negative	Inferior	
Demand rises less than proportionately	Between 0 and 1	Normal	Necessity, income inelastic
Demand rises more than proportionately	Greater than 1		Luxury, income elastic

Table 1.1 Terminology for income elasticity of demand

Examples of the IED for common goods sold in the UK are given in Table 1.2. You should be able to work out which of these goods are inferior, which are normal and necessities, and which are normal and luxuries.

Good	IED	Good	IED
Coal	−2.0	Alcohol	1.1
Bread	−0.5	Overseas travel	1.1
Tobacco	−0.5	Consumer durables	1.5
Lighting	0.3	Services	1.8
Food	0.5	Recreational goods	2.0
Vegetables	0.9	Wine and spirits	2.6

Table 1.2 Income elasticities of demand

 **Introduction to economics**

GLOSSARY

income-elastic good: good whose income elasticity of demand is greater than 1
income-inelastic good: good whose income elasticity of demand lies between 0 and 1
inferior good: good whose income elasticity of demand is negative
luxury: good whose income elasticity of demand is greater than 1
necessity: good whose income elasticity of demand lies between 0 and 1
normal good: good whose income elasticity is positive

What is IED used for?

The main use to which IED is put is as an aid to predicting the speed at which markets are likely to grow. If, for example, it is known that the IED for cross-Channel journeys is 2, and that long-term income growth in the EU runs at 2% p.a., then the IED formula can be used to predict a growth in cross-Channel journeys of 4% p.a. The Channel Tunnel was built on the basis of such predictions. When construction started in 1985, there were insufficient cross-Channel journeys to support the business concept. But it was built on the (correct) assumption that the number of such journeys would grow rapidly.

However, it should be obvious that IED is only *one* piece of analysis out of the many variables that a company considering an investment project would have to bear in mind. For example, a market might be growing at 4% p.a., but if your particular company lost market share, then it might not grow at all. Or (as in the case of Eurotunnel) costs might be so much greater than anticipated that, even if the revenue forecasts prove accurate, the company still makes a loss. The whole area of **investment appraisal** is considered in Chapter 7.

GLOSSARY

investment appraisal: analysis of potential investments

The sensitivity of demand to changes in price: price elasticity of demand (PED)

The idea here is essentially the same as for IED, except in this case the responsiveness of demand to changes in *price* is measured. If a 1% increase in the price of clothes led to a 0.5%, 1% or 2% reduction in their demand, then the **price elasticity of demand (PED)** for clothes would be –0.5, –1 or –2 respectively. The formula is:

$$\text{PED of good X} = \frac{\%\ \text{change in demand for good X}}{\%\ \text{change in price}}$$

As before, if you set the percentage change in price at 1, the percentage change in demand for good X becomes its PED. This leads to the definition of PED as: the percentage change in demand for a good following a 1% increase in its price.

Strictly speaking, it is the change in the *real* price that should be considered. If a firm increases the prices of its goods at the end of the year by 3% when inflation is itself 3% p.a., the firm's price increase will not have any impact on demand. The real price increase is, of course, zero.

A good for which the proportionate change in demand is less than the proportionate change in price is called a **price-inelastic good**. Where the proportionate change in demand is greater than the proportionate change in price, the product is called a **price-elastic good**. Table 1.3 summarises the terminology.

What happens to demand when prices rise	Value of IED	Description of good
Demand falls less than proportionately	Between 0 and −1	Price inelastic
Demand falls more than proportionately	More negative than −1	Price elastic

Table 1.3 Terminology for price elasticity of demand

Table 1.4 shows which goods have price-elastic demand, and which have price-inelastic demand.

Good	PED		Good	PED
Bread	−0.2		Entertainment	−1.4
Public transport	−0.4		Expenditure abroad	−1.6
Food	−0.5		Cars	−2.1
Alcohol	−0.8		Restaurant meals	−2.6
Beer	−1.0		Hats	−3.0
Marijuana (USA)	−1.0			

Table 1.4 Price elasticities of demand

What determines the likely value of PED?

There is only one main determinant of PED for any good: the availability of substitutes. The more substitutes a good has, the less likely people are to buy it if its price goes up. So the city-centre sandwich bar has to be very careful before it increases its prices. Substitutes, in the form of competitors, lurk on every corner. But the motorway service station or the train selling identical sandwiches charges two or three times more. The weary traveller has no realistic substitutes to the single company selling food and drink.

GLOSSARY

> **price elastic, elastic demand:** product whose price elasticity of demand is more negative than −1
> **price elasticity of demand:** responsiveness of demand to changes in price
> **price inelastic, inelastic demand:** product whose price elasticity of demand is between 0 and −1

What is PED used for?

For the business, the message of PED is clear. Prices can only be safely increased if there are no close substitutes. Advertising, branding, niche marketing, new product development — indeed any unique selling proposition — are all designed to bring the company to a situation where it can safely increase its prices. The differentiation that it seeks to achieve eliminates any close substitute.

For the economist, the message is rather different. A company whose products have no substitutes at all is called a monopoly. It will be tempted to exploit its monopoly position by charging prices far in excess of costs. These issues will be dealt with in Chapter 9.

Chapter 2
Data interpretation and the national income accounts

UNIT 1

At the end of this unit, you should be able to:

1 Understand simple national income accounts.

2 Explain the difference between real and nominal figures for national income.

3 Appreciate why published national income accounts are inevitably inaccurate.

4 Explain the significance of percentage changes.

The national income

The **national income** measures the value of *everything* a country produces over a year. First developed in the USA in the 1940s to help plan the war effort, it is also known as **gross domestic product** or GDP. If divided by the population to give GDP per head, the figure can be used to compare the **standard of living** in different countries once the figures have been converted into a common currency. And provided that allowance is made for the changing value of money (see 'What is money worth?' below), it can also be used to work out the rate at which an economy is growing. This is discussed further in Chapter 12.

The national income accounts provide considerably more detail than a simple total. That total is broken down in three main ways:

- *By industry.* Every firm is allocated to an industry, and the **value added** of each one of them is added together to give an industry total. In the simplified version below, the industries themselves have been merged into the **primary**, **secondary** and **tertiary** sectors. This way of breaking down the national income total is known as the 'output approach'.

- *By who gets paid for producing that output.* This is known as the 'income approach', and the simplest way of organising the information is to add together all the **wages** of employees and all the profits of owners.

- *By who is the final buyer of the output.* In this 'expenditure approach', buyers are grouped by what sort of economic agent they are. So household purchases are called **consumption** (C); firms' purchases are **investment** (I) and government purchases (including **local government**) are called **government spending** (G). Purchases of UK-produced goods by people living overseas are counted separately as **exports** (X). Lastly, we have to subtract all those purchases by UK residents of goods that the UK did not actually produce: that is, we subtract **imports** (M).

All three ways of classifying the National Income should arrive at the same total, as illustrated in Table 2.1.

Output approach		Income approach		Expenditure approach	
Primary sector	38	Wages	643	Consumption	655
Secondary sector	244	Profits	276	Government spending	191
Tertiary sector	706	Self-employed	69	Investment	164
				Exports	269
				(Imports)	(291)
Total GDP	**988**	**Total GDP**	**988**	**Total GDP**	**988**

Source: The Blue Book; UK National Income Accounts, 2002

Table 2.1 UK national income accounts, 2001 (£bn)

GLOSSARY

consumption (C): final expenditure by households

exports (X): sale of goods to other countries

government spending (G): expenditure by the public sector

gross domestic product (GDP): money value of a country's output, national income

imports (M): purchase of goods from overseas

investment (physical), (I): additions to the capital stock

local government: city and county authorities, part of the public sector

national income (NI): money value of a country's annual output, GDP

primary sector: extractive industries (e.g. agriculture)

secondary sector: manufacturing and construction industries

standard of living (S. of L.): average level of economic well-being in a country

tertiary sector: service industries, around 75% of UK output

value added: turnover minus purchases from other firms

wage, wage level: price of hiring labour

Are the figures accurate?

The ability to interpret data is a crucial skill, both for the successful completion of this course and more generally as a life skill for everyone. In the rest of Unit 1, we look at some of the key issues.

Firstly, are the figures accurate? The historian A. J. P. Taylor once wrote, 'If you ask the questions "Who first said so?" and "What opportunity did they have for knowing?" you will find that much of history simply disappears.' Economic data may be inaccurate due to simple error.

Alternatively, figures may be deliberately falsified in pursuit of some objective. For example, a poor country may wish to exaggerate its population in order to reduce its headline figure for GDP per head, and therefore qualify for international aid. As Table 2.2 shows, the differences in GDP per head from one country to another are very wide.

Country	GDP per head,1997 (US$)	Country	GDP per head,1997 (US$)
Luxembourg	30,863	Kenya	1,190
Brunei	29,773	Burundi	630
USA	29,010	Ethiopia	510
Japan	24,070	Sierra Leone	410
UK	20,730		

Source: Nuffield Economics and Business database, 2000.

Table 2.2 GDP per head: selected countries, 1997

Of course, it is not only economic data that is prone to distortion by its collectors. The use of league tables for A-level results has led to many schools refusing to allow weak candidates to sit their exams, or entering them as private candidates so that poor results are not recorded under the school's name.

What do the figures include — and omit?

The figures that go into the national income accounts are largely made up from the government's tax records. The Inland Revenue aims to collect details of taxable wages and profits from every person and company that has an obligation to pay.

However, much productive activity is never taxed. Those earning under around £4,000 a year do not have to pay tax at all, so significant amounts of part-time work go unrecorded. Then there are the people housekeeping, growing vegetables and caring for the young, the old and the sick within their own households on an unpaid basis. And then there are those operating within the **black economy** — those who should pay taxes but manage to avoid them. All these examples are illustrations of the **informal economy**. The work done is just as real, just as useful, as identical tasks that come to the government's notice, yet because the sums involved are unknown they do not appear in the accounts. In the UK, the black economy alone is estimated to be around 15% of the **formal economy**, the sector that appears in official GDP.

> **GLOSSARY**
>
> **black economy:** activity on which taxes are illegally avoided
> **formal economy, formal activity:** activity on which taxes are paid
> **informal economy:** activity that is untaxed, legally or illegally

What is money worth? Real and nominal values

Data that are expressed in cash units need particular care when the figures are being interpreted. This is because it is not always clear what money is worth. The underlying difficulty is inflation — the general increase in the price level over time — which erodes the value of the money that people use. When national income data figures have been adjusted for inflation so that the recorded increases represent actual increases in output, the figures are called **real** national income. These are the figures that you will normally see. If the figures have not been adjusted, the data are called **nominal** or **money** or **current** national income.

> **GLOSSARY**
>
> **nominal (money, current):** data that have not been adjusted for inflation
> **real:** data that have been adjusted to take account of inflation

How to recognise change: percentages

While it is useful to know whether a country's real national income 'rose' or 'fell' from one year to the next, it is not possible to attach much significance to such **time series** without knowing by *how much* the variable changed. And here, the important piece of information is likely to be the **percentage** change. For example, an increase in the UK's real national income of £2 billion in 1992 sounds less impressive when rephrased as an

increase of 0.3%, from £724 billion to £726 billion. The formula for working out the percentage change from figure 'a' to figure 'b' is:

$$\% \text{ change from a to b} = \frac{(b - a) \times 100}{a}$$

Sometimes, the percentage changes are so much more important than the actual figures that the percentage changes are alone recorded. This is particularly true of the price level. How fast prices are increasing (i.e. the inflation rate) is often of more interest than some difficult-to-define measure of what goods, on average, actually cost. Equally, the rate at which GDP increases (i.e. the economic growth rate) is often of more interest than its overall level.

This general principle has wide applicability. School reports typically dwell as much on a student's rate of improvement (or decline) as they do on the actual level of attainment.

GLOSSARY

percentage: fraction expressed in hundredths
time series: variable plotted over successive time periods

UNIT 2

At the end of this unit, you should be able to:

1 Explain the purpose of index numbers.

2 Describe a trend.

3 Identify cause and effect.

How to recognise change: index numbers

One commonly used way of expressing percentage changes is **index numbers**. Each figure is recorded *as a percentage of the value of some other figure*. Commonly used in time series, the year to which all other figures are compared is known as the **base year**. Index numbers are essential when measuring changes in complex variables. Imagine you wanted to describe how a stock market was moving. It would be impossible to describe briefly every share price movement. Instead, the stock market index tells us what has happened to *average* share price movements. The best-known share price indices include the 100 major shares on the London stock market — the *FTSE 100 index*. The equivalents in New York and Tokyo are known as the *Dow Jones* and the *Nikkei* respectively.

Another very common use of indices is to record the average movement of prices in the shops — known as 'retail prices'. Again, it would be impossible to describe clearly every price movement. Instead, an average price movement is recorded every month, and then published as the **retail price index** (RPI). This figure is of great significance. Many benefits, such as pensions, are linked to the value of the RPI. And inflation is measured by looking at the percentage change between the RPI in the current month and the RPI this time last year.

GLOSSARY

base year: the year on which an index number is based
index number: number expressed as a percentage of another
retail price index (RPI): an index of consumer price movements

How to recognise income distribution: deciles

It is possible to divide a population into ten groups of equal size based on their income. These groups are known as **deciles**. In societies of very unequal income (e.g. most of South America), the highest decile (i.e. the richest 10%) might earn 50% of all income, and the lowest decile only 2%. In the more equal societies of Scandinavia, the equivalent figures are nearer 35% and 5%.

It is equally possible to divide a population into fifths (known as 'quintiles'), or into hundredths (centiles). The division of a population into groups of equal size has a wide applicability. For example, new parents are given graphs showing the 1st and 99th centile of baby boys' and girls' height and weight over the first few months of life. The idea is that as long as their baby develops within these boundaries, it is likely to be physically healthy.

GLOSSARY

deciles, tenths: classification of a population into ten same-size groups

A major source of UK data: the census

Since 1801, the UK government has conducted a decennial (= every 10 years) census of the entire population. The last one took place in April 2001. Unlike every other form of market research, the national census is compulsory. You can be fined or sent to prison for failing to fill it in. The questions seek to discover **population trends**, numbers of people, their ages, locations, incomes and jobs. This information is used to help plan government schools and hospitals — but it is also available to commercial companies. *Individual* details that would enable you to be personally identified are, however, kept secret for 100 years.

GLOSSARY

population trend: the changing size and structure of a population

Identifying trends

Often it is useful to know how a set of figures is moving. The key here is to identify the **trend**. Are the figures clearly moving one way? Is there random movement, or evidence of a cyclical pattern? Are there clear peaks and troughs? When describing a trend you need to keep your answer short.

Another skill in data interpretation is the ability to distinguish between trends and **fluctuations** around that trend. A variable that follows the trend closely is said to behave in a *stable* manner. By contrast, a variable that frequently departs from the trend is said to behave in a *volatile* manner.

GLOSSARY

fluctuation: short-term movement around a trend
trend: the way a variable is moving in the long term

Identifying cause and effect

The last, and in many ways the hardest, task in handling data is to draw conclusions as to *why* variables are moving in the way that they are. Much of economics is, like any science, trying to construct **hypotheses** to test against known data. One simple rule is: just because there is a **direct relationship** or other correlation between two variables, you cannot conclude that one variable is the cause of the other.

Suppose it is observed that, **other things equal**, the sale of fur coats is **inversely related** to average daytime temperature. We might guess any of the following:

- In hot weather, the manufacturers of fur coats find it uncomfortable to work, so stop making them.
- People are more likely to buy a fur coat in cold weather.
- It's a coincidence.

In this case, one might reasonably guess that the second hypothesis is likely to be correct. However, it is not always so easy to identify cause and effect. For example, some economists believe that a small increase in inflation will reduce unemployment, while others believe that an increase in inflation will *increase* unemployment.

GLOSSARY

direct relationship: two variables moving in the same direction
hypothesis: an unproved idea against which to test events
inverse relationship: two variables moving opposite ways
'other things equal': condition attached to theories about cause and effect

Chapter 3
Aims of the firm, legal structures, profit and loss account

UNIT 1

At the end of this unit, you should be able to:

1 Discuss the various aims of firms.

2 Describe the advantages and disadvantages of the various legal structures.

3 Write out and explain a profit and loss account.

4 Deduce a firm's likely size and activities from its profit-and-loss account.

5 Work out profit margins and explain their significance.

6 Explain the difference between profit and cash flow.

7 Work out break-even sales levels and explain their significance.

Aims of the firm

The first of several chapters on the individual company looks first of all at what firms are trying to achieve, at their objectives. In traditional economic theory, the overriding aim is **profit maximisation**. Owners are in business for the money, and the more the better. In the modern **public limited company** (plc), where the owners are made up of thousands of private investors and large financial institutions such as pension funds, this is a fair approximation. The vast majority of private stock market investors are essentially seeking to maximise the return on their investments, although the growth of 'ethical investment funds' suggests there is a minority interest in avoiding companies that operate in ethically dubious ways.

The situation is more complicated where the company has a single owner or a small group of owners, who are often the **entrepreneurs** who set up the company. Here, the personal lives of the owner(s) may be bound up with their firm. The aim may be to provide a comfortable sufficiency for one's family without having to work excessive hours, the so-called **lifestyle company**. The ability to be one's own boss, to achieve **independence** from 'wage slavery' and from working for someone else, may be the target. For a new company, or one experiencing difficulties, the emphasis may be on **survival**. This is likely to be only a short-term objective; once it has been achieved, the true goals of the owners are likely to reassert themselves. Sometimes providing jobs is a high priority.

The motivation theories explored in Chapter 6 are also relevant here. Firms are owned by individuals, so it should not surprise us that the aims of firms are fairly similar to the aims of the average man or woman in the street. For example, a **sole trader** may aim to

achieve company **growth** because of the status attached to owning a large company. Or the **reputation** of the company may increase the owner's self-esteem. Of course, an alternative explanation of the search for growth and fame is that large companies with good reputations will, other things equal, make bigger profits than small ones.

The same observation can be made of altruistic aims too. Is the aim of **providing a service** based on a genuine concern for the customer, or simply a path to increasing profit? One of the great benefits of competitive industry is that even those people who have no real concern for their customers have to act as if they do! Otherwise they are unlikely to stay in business for long.

However, the proliferation of **mission statements** (see Chapter 8) indicates that most people are not interested *only* in money. Work is a search for daily meaning as well as daily bread: 'Where there is no vision, the people perish.'

To conclude, businesses may have a wide variety of aims. While the search for profit may not be the only aim, few companies will last for long if they do not make *enough* profit to meet the essential requirements of survival.

GLOSSARY

entrepreneur: person who sets up a business
growth of a company: aim of company expansion (e.g. of turnover)
independence (e.g. of owner): ability to determine one's own future
lifestyle company: firm whose owner aims for a comfortable life
mission statement: aims, the ultimate goal of a company
profit maximisation: aim of achieving the biggest possible profit
providing a service: aim of satisfying customers
public limited company (plc): firm with shares traded on the stock market
reputation: the way an economic agent is publicly viewed
sole trader (proprietor): one-person business
survival: aim of company, avoiding bankruptcy

CITY OF WESTMINSTER COLLEGE
MAIDA VALE LEARNING CENTRE

DATE ....
BARCODE ....
CLASS NO ....

Legal structures

The relationship of a business to the law of the land is important, and especially so when trouble looms: for example, if the firm fails or is taken to court. But, on the other hand, the *essence* of a business lies in its products and its relationships with its customers. Most of the time its legal identity will not be of great importance. It may, indeed, be changed once or twice in its early years as the balance of advantage switches from one type of identity to another.

The two types of **business organisation** or 'legal structure' in this specification are the sole trader (proprietor) and the **company**, sometimes known as the 'limited company' (plc or Ltd).

The essential difference, from which all others flow, is that sole traders trade in their own right, whereas companies have a legal existence distinct from their owners. The company is incorporated, literally is 'given a body'. From this it follows that a company can be sued, sue, go bankrupt and enter into contracts with customers, workers and suppliers — all without the owners being directly involved. The owners are called **shareholders** and they appoint a **board of directors** to run the company on their behalf — although in many smaller companies the major shareholders are also the directors.

By contrast, sole traders perform all actions in their own name. The law makes no distinction between Ms Bloggs, the individual, and Ms Bloggs, the sole trader. Ms Bloggs is said to have **unlimited liability**. The debts of the firm are her debts: they sink or swim together. Company shareholders, on the other hand, only stand to lose the money they invested in the business, their **share capital**, if the enterprise folds up. The owners are therefore said to enjoy **limited liability**.

Clearly, limited liability is a considerable privilege. Its origins lie in the government's attempts to encourage risk-taking business enterprise without aspiring entrepreneurs fearing ending up in a debtor's prison if the venture failed. In return for the privilege of limited liability extended to its owners, the limited company has to make its accounts available for public inspection. Anyone may receive from Companies House (in return for a nominal fee) a print-out of any limited company's balance sheet (see Chapter 7) and its profit and loss account.

The decision for most small enterprises usually amounts to whether its owners want to gain the protection of limited liability in return for letting their competitors (and nosy friends) read their accounts. If the answer is yes, they will form a company; if no, they will remain a sole trader.

There are minor administrative burdens and expenses entailed in becoming a limited company. A registration fee, currently £20, has to be paid. And annual accounts have to be presented. Owners can perform these tasks themselves, or an accountant can be paid a few hundred pounds a year to do it for them. But governments remain pro-business. Companies House will send anyone free booklets on how to set up a limited company. These can be ordered from www.companieshouse.gov.uk.

The tax treatment of the various types of business organisation is also a relevant consideration. To give just one example, until April 2000, many individuals (particularly in computing) set up limited companies whose only purpose was to hire out the individual to another company. In this way a direct employment relationship with the final buyer of their services was avoided. The personal company then 'paid' the person a small wage and a large profits dividend. Both the individual and the ultimate buyer of services thereby avoided paying national insurance contributions, which are only payable on wages, not profits. As with most tax dodges, the chancellor of the exchequer (in this case, Gordon Brown) eventually caught up with this loophole and changed the law to close it.

Another issue to consider is what might loosely be called 'street credibility'. At one stage, the theory was that people would prefer to deal with a sole trader because the sole trader's personal assets were on the line if they failed to pay up. The alternative point of view is that the more formal arrangement of a limited company (with accounts available for inspection) is more likely to inspire confidence among potential stakeholders: that is, suppliers, employees and customers.

Finally, mention should be made of variants on these basic structures. **Partnerships** are similar to sole traders, except a group of individuals trade under their joint names. They gain **economies of scale** (see Chapter 5) but frequently disintegrate in bitter legal disputes.

Limited companies are themselves split into public limited companies (plc) and **private limited companies** (Ltd). Plcs have to be larger and report their affairs more fully, and they may be eligible to 'float' on the stock market. This enables any member of the public to buy or sell their shares. One traditional route to riches is to develop your own private

limited company until it becomes big enough to float, and then sell off some or all of your shareholding for cash.

GLOSSARY

business organisation: legal status of a firm (e.g. sole trader, plc)
company (incorporated, limited): company with a legal personality, plc or Ltd
directors, board of directors: members of the board that runs a company
economies of scale, synergy: reasons why unit costs fall as a firm grows
limited liability: owners' liability confined to initial investment
partnership: small group ownership of a business
private limited company (Ltd): firm with fixed, named shareholders
share capital, risk capital: money invested in a company by share issue
shareholders: those owning a proportion of a limited company
unlimited liability: owners personally responsible for a firm's debt

The profit and loss account

The key statement of any company's financial affairs is the annual **profit and loss account**. Starting with the enterprise's turnover, successive deductions are made until the final figure records the money left within the company to finance next year's activities. Yet this **retained profit** is not the most significant figure in assessing how well the company is doing. The **pre-tax profit** shows what the company has actually earned. The **profit after tax** shows the money over which the firm has the power of disposal, and which its directors can either retain within the business or distribute to the owners as **dividends** (**distributed profit**) — or, more commonly, a bit of both.

Earlier deductions seek to classify the various costs of the business in some sensible fashion. The immediate costs directly associated with each product line are called the **cost of sales**. For a shop, these would be the cost of buying the goods that are sold on. For a factory, they would be the cost of raw materials and the wages of those working on the factory floor. They are also called **direct costs**, as they can be attributed directly to a specific product line. Another name for them is **variable costs** because they move up and down with the output level of the company. Once the cost of sales has been deducted from turnover, the result is known as **gross profit**.

The second batch of costs to be deducted is the costs that cannot be attributed to a specific product because they are too general in nature. These include the wages of management and office administration, the advertising budget and associated marketing costs. The wear and tear on capital items, known as **depreciation**, is also included. They have a variety of names: **overheads** because they lie over the whole enterprise like a ceiling over a room; **indirect costs** because they cannot be directly associated with particular product lines; **fixed costs** because they do not change with minor changes in the output level; or simply **selling and administrative costs**. Once this set of costs has been deducted, the resulting surplus is known as **operating profit**.

One fixed cost is recorded separately from the rest: **interest payments**. The reasoning behind its separate entry is that once money has been borrowed and spent on company assets, the company has very little control over how much interest it then pays. Deducting this item results in the pre-tax profit mentioned earlier.

You may meet various other features. **Exceptional items**, such as redundancy payments, are often recorded separately so that the long-term trend can be more easily distinguished.

'Discontinued operations' may have their own profit and loss account for the same reason. Sometimes 'non-operating income' is recorded after operating profit — for example, if assets were sold at a profit above their original cost. Here is a standard-format profit and loss account taken from Kwik Save:

	(£m)
Turnover	2,992
(Cost of sales)	(2,552)
Gross profit	440
(Selling/administrative expenses)	(333)
Operating profit	107
Interest payments	(2)
Net profit before tax	105
(Corporation tax)	(25)
Net profit after tax	80
(Distributed profit)	(31)
Retained profit	49

Source: Kwik Save annual report.

For a discount store like Kwik Save, operating in a competitive market, there is not a great deal of difference in proportional terms between what it pays for the goods and what it sells them for. The 'proportional difference' is known as the **gross margin**, and expresses the gross profit as a percentage of the turnover. The same idea can be applied to operating profit as a percentage of the turnover, the **operating margin**, and to the net (true) profit as a percentage of the turnover, the **net margin**. The formulae are:

$$\text{Gross margin} (\%) = \frac{\text{Gross profit} \times 100}{\text{Turnover}}$$

$$\text{Operating margin} (\%) = \frac{\text{Operating profit} \times 100}{\text{Turnover}}$$

One important decision for any company is whether it aims to make its profits from relatively low turnovers with high margins, or (like Kwik Save) to make its profits from relatively high turnovers with low margins. Only a few companies manage to have both high turnovers and high margins. The resulting enormous profits tend to attract competitors, which will drive down the selling price, and hence the size of both the margins and the profits available.

GLOSSARY

cost of sales; direct, variable costs: variable costs of production
depreciation (of assets): loss of value (e.g. due to wear and tear)
direct costs: costs directly attributable to one product line
dividends, distributed profit: payout to shareholders from the profits of a company
exceptional item: one-off item in the accounts, which is unlikely to recur
fixed costs: costs that do not change with small, short-run changes in output
gross margin: gross profit as a percentage of turnover
gross profit: profit on day-to-day trading
indirect costs: costs not attributable to one specific product line
interest payment, interest rate (r): percentage payable on borrowed money
net margin, profit margin: net profit as a percentage of turnover
operating profit: profit before the deduction of interest payments
operating profit margin: operating profit as a percentage of turnover
overheads: costs not changing with output in the short term

> **pre-tax profit:** the true, or net, profit
> **profit after tax:** net (true) profit minus corporation tax
> **profit and loss account:** annual record of a firm's income and expenditure
> **retained profit:** profit kept within a business, the source of internal finance
> **selling and administrative costs:** overheads, not including interest payments
> **variable costs, cost of sales:** costs that change with small changes in output

Cash flow

It should be noted that *profit* is very different from *cash*. A business might be very profitable but short of cash for a variety of reasons. Customers might pay late, or money might have been spent buying a fixed asset that will last for several years. The cost of this asset will be spread out over several annual profit and loss accounts. Each year only the depreciation element of the cost of the fixed asset will be included. But it may still be necessary to pay for the asset up-front in the first year.

Another possible cause of cash shortage is known as **overtrading**. A company may take on more orders than its immediate cash position makes sensible. Bills for raw materials and wages mount up, and if major customers then delay payment, it is quite possible for the firm to go into **receivership**.

With internet start-ups, the relationship between cash and profits is often the opposite of that described above. The company might be cash rich due to a successful stock market flotation, but making significant losses into the foreseeable future. The question then is: will the company run out of cash (and close down) before the profits start flowing? The halving of IT share prices in 2000 reflected a growing realisation that many internet companies were never going to survive into profitability.

A firm's cash position over time is known as its **cash flow**. While a firm's long-term survival depends on its underlying profitability, it should be clear from what has been said that its short-term survival depends on its cash position.

> **cash flow:** evolution of cash held over time
> **overtrading:** expansion too rapid for the financial resources available
> **receiver:** accountant appointed by the court to run a failing firm

Breaking even

The distinction between fixed costs (= overheads) and variable costs (= cost of sales) leads to the idea of a **break-even** sales level. If the fixed costs have to be paid no matter what, then the turnover has to be high enough to generate enough gross profit to pay for these overheads, if the firm is to avoid a loss. So suppose the cost of renting an ice-cream van is £100 per day, and you sell ice creams for £1 each that have cost you 20p to buy. You have to sell enough ice creams for your 80p gross profit on each to pay for the £100 fixed cost. The formula for working out the break-even sales level is:

$$\text{Break-even analysis} = \frac{\text{Overheads}}{\text{Gross profit per item}} = \frac{\text{Overheads}}{\text{Contribution}}$$

In this case, break-even = £100/£0.8 = 125 ice creams per day. On the unlikely assumption that you have no other costs, you need to sell 125 ice creams each day to 'break even': that is, to avoid a loss. Every ice cream sold above this break-even sales level will generate a profit for you of 80p.

When firms have to sink a lot of money into a project before they can start selling, there is clearly the risk of failing to break even. The Channel Tunnel, Euro Disney, the Humber Bridge, Concorde and the Millennium Dome are all examples of projects where millions of pounds were spent on the fixed costs of setting up the enterprise. On each occasion, the sales forecasts failed to materialise, and the projects made significant losses.

GLOSSARY

break-even analysis: calculation of minimum sales required to avoid losses

Chapter 4
Market research and marketing

UNIT 1

At the end of this unit, you should be able to:

1 Explain marketing and the marketing mix.

2 Explain mass and niche markets.

3 Discuss the purposes and limitations of primary and secondary research.

Introduction to marketing

The two defining characteristics of any business are its products and its customers. This chapter examines customers — specifically, how potential customers may be identified (**market research**) and persuaded to buy (**marketing**). Along the way, something will be said about products too, although this is mainly the subject of Chapter 5.

Marketing has been defined as 'the process of identifying and satisfying customer requirements profitably'. A problem with this definition is its wide scope: it could equally well be a definition of business in its entirety. However, this observation highlights an essential fact: marketing is at the heart of any business.

An alternative definition is 'all those business activities involved in assessing and converting customer purchasing power into effective demand for a specific product', or again, 'the all-embracing function that links the company with customer tastes to get the right product to the right place at the right time'. Where firms have separate marketing and sales departments, the marketing department concentrates on the strategy, the market research and the planning, while the sales department runs the actual sales force that is responsible for converting potential customers into hard cash.

Marketing activity can be classified into four components: the product, its price, **promotion** and **place** — that is, the **chain of distribution** used to get the product to the final customer. The blending of these four components is known as the **marketing mix**. Many of the marketing decisions taken will depend on the scale of the market involved. If the product has a wide appeal, the company should be dealing with a **mass market**. The price is likely to be fairly low, and national or indeed global advertising will be the major promotional strategy. If, alternatively, the product is essentially of interest to one particular **social class**, age range or income bracket, the company is dealing with a **niche market**. There will probably be less competition, prices will be higher and promotion will be based around mailing lists, regional advertising and specialist magazines. Finally, a **micro market** describes the target customers of a highly specialised product. Competition may be non-existent, while very high prices are justified on the grounds of the high **unit costs** associated with tiny production runs.

GLOSSARY

> **marketing:** identifying and satisfying customer needs profitably
> **marketing mix (strategy):** product, price, promotion and place
> **market research:** collection and analysis of commercial information
> **mass market:** very large numbers of people
> **micro market:** sub-segment, a very small market
> **niche market:** relatively small, well-defined segment
> **place, chain of distribution:** method of reaching final customer
> **promotion of a good:** attempts to sell a product
> **social class:** population segments related to status in society
> **unit costs, average total cost:** average costs, costs per unit of output

Introduction to market research

Defined as 'the collection and analysis of information relating to a firm's customers and competitors', market research takes place alongside the development of new products (see Chapter 8). It is also undertaken throughout the lifetime of a product, as discussed in the next unit. The relationship between market research and new product research is two-way. It may be that a new idea comes from the production team, whereupon market research is undertaken to see if the idea is commercially viable. Alternatively, market research may reveal a customer need, whereupon the production department is then asked if it can design a product to meet that need.

Market research is essentially concerned with *understanding* consumers. Into what **market segments** can they be arranged? Are there niche markets that are unfilled — a **gap in the market** into which a new product could be inserted? Does the company have the resources to exploit this opportunity? Does it possess some 'competitive advantage' (see Chapter 5) or a unique selling proposition (see Chapter 8): that is, something to differentiate it from the mass of potential providers?

While the popular image of market research is a person with a clipboard asking questions, much of it consists of researching existing published information. Such **secondary** or **desk** research is inevitably a cheaper option. A company that has kept an up-to-date database of its customers can use this to its advantage. Newspapers and the decennial

government census also provide enormous quantities of information. But it is the explosive growth of the internet that is transforming the ability of everyone to find out about markets and, indeed, everything else.

The alternative method of research is called **primary** or **field** research. This entails finding things out for the first time, normally through a survey conducted in person, over the telephone or through the post. Primary research is the only option when gauging responses to a new product: the information will simply not be available from existing sources. Much commercially sensitive information must also be obtained in this way because competitors will naturally want to keep it to themselves. For example, the turnover of any limited company can be obtained from its annual accounts, but the breakdown of this turnover by region or by product is likely to be a closely guarded secret.

The key to primary research is an understanding of the **population** and the **sample**. The population is everyone in whom the company is interested. This might be everyone in the UK over 18 for a chain of estate agents, everyone who goes fishing for a supplier of fishing tackle, or girls between the ages of 11 and 15 for a magazine called *Sweet Sixteen*. It is too expensive to interview the *entire* population: instead, a representative selection known as the sample is approached. The accuracy of the research depends on the sample being truly representative of the population that is being examined.

For this reason, a minimum of 500 people are questioned and care is taken to avoid **bias**. The sample must be selected in truly random fashion; obviously just asking the people you know personally will produce a skewed result. *Perfect* accuracy can never be achieved, if only because the people who refuse to be interviewed, or who are out at the time, may not be typical of the population.

Most market research is **quantitative research**. Large numbers of people are asked relatively straightforward questions and the results are analysed mathematically. The alternative is **qualitative research**, which attempts to uncover the inner motivations and feelings of the sample. A small group of people, known as a 'focus group', are invited to a free-ranging discussion without any formal questionnaire. The group chair then guides the conversation as appropriate. The Labour Party is frequently criticised for its alleged dependence on focus groups to guide its policies, rather than referring to its principles. In a business context, a focus group might be used to discover which of two alternative advertising strategies was more likely to appeal to the target population. The term 'qualitative research' may also be used to describe the informal process whereby the businessperson simply keeps their eyes and ears open, and develops a 'feel' for what their customers want.

GLOSSARY

bias: failure of a sample to represent the population
gap in the market: sales opportunity not yet being met
market segments: sections of an industry's consumers
population: group from which a firm interviews a sample
primary (field) research: market research collected for the first time
qualitative research: in-depth interviewing of a small sample of people
quantitative research: use of large samples of people, with simple questions
sample: representative selection from a population
secondary (desk) research: research from publicly available sources

At the end of this unit, you should be able to:

1 Explain why gaining market share is a zero-sum game.

2 Give examples of market segments.

3 Discuss the following aspects of promotion: advertising, branding, PR and direct marketing.

4 Describe some chains of distribution and comment on the internet in this context.

5 Describe the product life cycle, and comment on its significance for business.

Introduction: marketing and competition

Much of business activity is co-operative in nature. For example, any company wants to remain on good terms with its suppliers and its customers. Nonetheless, even friendly relations with suppliers or customers will be tested when it comes to discussing prices. Other things equal, an increase in price is good for the seller and bad for the buyer. Such negotiations are an example of what is called a **zero-sum game**, a situation where any gain for one side is exactly matched by a loss for the other. Another example of a zero-sum game is when a company attempts to win a greater proportion of the available potential customers in its industry: that is, to win a greater **market share**. It *must* follow that if one company's share goes up from 10% to 15%, then other companies must, between them, have lost 5%.

Hence **rivalry** lies at the heart of every industry that is not a monopoly — and that means about 99% of all industries. Much selling activity can therefore be described as **rivalrous marketing**. The aim is not only to increase sales, but often to increase sales at someone else's expense.

Despite the inevitability of competition in much business activity, there is a general desire not to compete *too* fiercely on price, if this can be avoided. The reasoning is simple: in a 'price war' all businesses end up losing, although consumers have a great deal to gain. There is therefore considerable emphasis on **non-price competition**. 'Promotion' and 'place' will be considered later in this unit, while the product is looked at in Chapter 5. 'Price' is dealt with in Chapter 19 of the A2 course.

market share: proportion of the total market that a firm has
non-price competition: rivalry through the product, its promotion or place
rivalry: competitive attitudes
rivalrous marketing: marketing aimed at increasing market share
zero-sum game: situation where one person's gain is another's loss

Market research: identifying market segments

Any large company will want to know the **purchasing patterns** of its actual and potential customers. The basic ways of segmenting a market are by age and gender, as shown by **population pyramids**. An example of a typical population pyramid for a developed region is shown in Figure 4.1. In the case of a poor country with a rapidly growing population, the population pyramid would show a much higher proportion of young people.

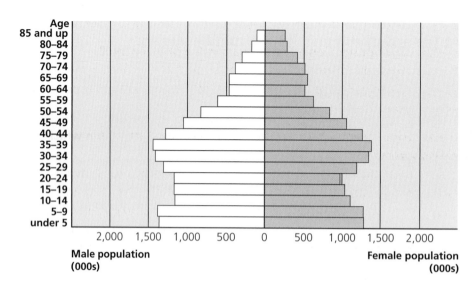

*Figure 4.1 Population pyramid for California in 1997,
showing a bulge representing the postwar baby-boomers*

Markets may also be segmented by social class, by income or by region. So, for example, a company that relies heavily on the **regional market** in the northeast of England should be aware that, as the region's population declines, sales are also likely to decline unless there are compensating factors.

Market research is now so widespread that the names for many market segments have entered everyday language. 'Baby-boomers' describes those born in the population bulge after the Second World War, who are now in their 40s and 50s. Epitomised by Bill Clinton, they are on average reasonably well-off and have liberal social attitudes. 'Yuppies' — young urban professionals — have relatively modest incomes but good future prospects as they climb their career ladders. 'Dinkies' — dual income, no kids yet — describes married or cohabiting couples whose single home saves on expenses, leaving them with lots of spare income for discretionary spending. 'The pink pound' describes the money to be made catering for the gay and lesbian community, the majority of whom do not spend money on children.

GLOSSARY

population pyramid: diagram of a population's age and gender make-up
purchasing patterns: which market segments buy which goods
regional markets, regional demand: distinctive areas of a country (e.g. the northeast of England)

The marketing mix: promotion

Advertising is commonly described as being either 'informative' or 'persuasive' in general outlook. Thus a notice announcing a sale, opening hours, telephone numbers or other means of contact is essentially informative, while the awareness-building mood-creating TV ads for new car models are essentially persuasive in nature.

Not every company has to advertise. It is a cost to the business and, like any cost, has to justify itself in terms of increased sales. Where the industry constantly brings out new products, advertising is important — think of the release of a new film. But local businesses with a stable customer base may simply get by on word of mouth.

Some of the issues raised by advertising and other forms of promotion are as follows.

What effect does promotion have on the firm's demand curve?

If effective, it will shift the demand curve outwards, thereby enabling the firm to sell more goods, and at a higher price. So advertising was included in our list of non-price determinants of demand in Chapter 1.

What effect does promotion have on the market structure within which the firm operates?

Promotion both creates and enhances *product differentiation*. So much of advertising stresses the uniqueness, the special quality, of the product advertised. In terms of market structure (see Chapter 9), successful promotion moves the product in consumers' minds to a position where it faces less competition. **Branding** and **sponsorship** are both about creating a unique identity, about firms creating their **own label** with some element of monopoly power.

Branding is an enormously powerful influence on our society. The best-known phrase worldwide is said to be 'Coca-Cola'. This has been achieved by the expenditure of vast sums of money over several decades by some of the best brains on the planet. The payoff is the premium price that the name commands over its rivals in millions of outlets all over the world. Demand is both increased and made less price elastic.

Does promotion benefit society as a whole?

The question arises because promotion *adds* to costs, whereas technical efficiency suggests that companies should aim to *reduce* costs. In effect, tens of thousands of people are employed worldwide in public relations, advertising, **sales promotion** and **direct marketing** when they could be employed actually producing a good or service. Could promotional activity just be a vast zero-sum game which all companies feel compelled to play lest they get left behind — but whose *net* effect on everyone's sales figures is actually zero?

To use another metaphor, is advertising like a scrum of people pushing to get on a bus — where the net effect of everyone's actions is actually to delay the departure of the bus, to the loss of all concerned?

Faced with these issues, economists have responded by contrasting informative and persuasive advertising. Informative advertising (so the argument goes) serves a useful purpose. By making consumers more aware of the options, it actually increases their choices and so makes market structures more, not less, competitive. By contrast, persuasive advertising tells consumers nothing that they did not already know, so there is no benefit to society in return for its expense. Even if this analysis is true, there is little that can be done about it. It would be impossibly cumbersome and expensive to try to differentiate between informative and persuasive advertisements, when so many of them have elements of both. There is, therefore, no chance of banning the one and retaining the other.

Another issue is whether advertising generates 'external costs' (see Chapter 10). Some billboards are unsightly: there is a good case for restricting their number and locations. And some advertisements offend public taste, or are simply untrue. The **Advertising Standards Authority** regulates this aspect of the industry by performing a 'watchdog' role to try to ensure that all advertisements are *legal, decent, honest* and *truthful*.

A further aspect of promotional activity is **public relations** (PR). Regional newspapers and television are always looking for stories, and are happy to provide what is in effect free advertising for a company with a newsworthy event to publicise.

GLOSSARY

Advertising Standards Authority: regulates the advertising industry
advertising: paid-for messages to influence recipients
branding: establishing a unique identity for a product
direct marketing: targeting individuals (e.g. by mail shot)
own label, own brand: brand using the retailer's (not the producer's) name
public relations (PR): the management of a firm's publicity
sales promotion: consumer competitions and point-of-sale displays
sponsorship: a firm buying association with a public event

The marketing mix: place

The 'place' element of the marketing mix describes the method by which the customer finally gets hold of the good or service at the end of the chain of distribution. Traditionally, goods go through the **wholesaler** to the **retailer** before being sold to the final customer. Mail order, telesales, door-to-door and house parties provide alternatives. And although the 'new economy' share price crash in the year 2000 shows that the internet was oversold, there is no doubt that **e-commerce** will be of increasing importance. E-commerce is currently strongest in the **B2B (business to business)** sector, but **e-tailers** are slowly but surely making inroads into the **B2C (business to consumer)** sector as well.

The key point about 'place' is that it is just as significant a part of the total package offered to the customer as the technical specifications of the product or its brand image. School enterprise clubs tend to produce low-tech products at not particularly cheap prices. What differentiates them from the competition is their *location* within school premises — a location that is normally barred to their competitors.

GLOSSARY

B2B, business to business: one business trades with another
B2C, business to consumer: business trades with a consumer, the end of the chain
e-commerce, e-business: all selling activity over the internet
e-tailer: retailer selling over the internet
retailer, distributor: firm whose main business is to sell to the consumer
wholesaler: bulk purchaser from manufacturers

The marketing mix: price

The profit made on any item is the difference between the unit cost and the price charged. If the unit cost of producing a pub meal is £2 and it sells for £3, then the profit must be £1. The pub's total profit on its meals will then be £1 multiplied by the number of meals sold. The simplest way to choose a price is simply to add a percentage on to the unit cost. In the example, this is a 50% mark-up, which yields a 33% profit margin on the turnover. This approach is known as **cost-plus pricing**. Of course, the pub could just as well charge £4 and achieve a 50% profit margin. The former would be called a 'low-price strategy' and the latter a 'high-price strategy'.

Which strategy proves most successful depends crucially on the price elasticity of demand faced by the enterprise. Suppose the pub faces a price elasticity of demand of −1. A 33%

increase in price from £3 to £4 will result in a 33% drop in sales. But since the profit on each meal will have doubled from £1 to £2, the pub will still end up making a larger profit. This example indicates the problem with a low-price strategy. The company has to sell very much larger quantities for the approach to have any chance of success. In many industries, there is only room for one or two companies whose sales pitch is based around low prices. The majority will try to differentiate themselves from each other using the other elements of the marketing mix, and accept lower sales levels in return for higher profit margins.

The other problem with a low-price strategy is that it may lead to a **price war**. If competitors respond to your lower prices by lowering their prices too, then you are unlikely to gain that many extra customers. However, one set of circumstances in which a low-price strategy may pay off is if the largest company goes for a very low price with the intention of driving competitors out of the market before raising prices once again. Known as **predatory pricing**, this practice is illegal, although it is very difficult to prove. Pricing strategies are considered in more detail in Chapter 19.

> **GLOSSARY**
>
> **cost-based (cost-plus) pricing:** pricing method, adding a fixed percentage to unit cost
> **predatory pricing:** below-cost pricing intended to kill a competitor
> **price war:** tit-for-tat price reductions

Marketing and the product life cycle

Products, like people, tend to have a *birth*, a *growth*, a *maturity* and then a *decline*, leading to death. This **product life cycle** can be applied to a generic product (e.g. mustard) or to a branded product (e.g. Coleman's mustard). The actual length of the life cycle could be anything from thousands of years for something like bread, to a few weeks for a pop song.

Many products never make it to the launch, the birth date. Market research may indicate that the concept is unlikely to be profitable, or a rival may get to market first with a higher-quality (or cheaper) product. But for those that do make it, different marketing techniques will be used at different stages in the cycle. The launch itself will be the most expensive time in marketing terms, with heavy advertising aimed at achieving name recognition, leading to as many people as possible trying the product at least once. A company may launch in just one region to begin with, which will minimise the costs of failure. The expense will be some delay to the national launch if the product proves to be a success.

If the product becomes successful, the marketing budget will be reduced over the growth and maturity phases. This is the time to cash in, recoup the development and launch costs, and fund the next new product (there is more on this in Chapter 5). When the brand shows signs of flagging, a **product extension strategy** may be used to delay the eventual decline. A repackaging, redesign or modification may be used to relaunch the basic product. Many branded products can in this way have their lives extended over a century or more. For example *The Times* is over 200 years old, although the first editions bear very little resemblance to the current newspaper.

But with most products there comes a time when the marketing costs of keeping the brand flourishing can no longer be justified. At this stage, marketing support is much reduced, or eliminated altogether. There may, however, still be several years of profits to extract out of the brand, selling it to loyal customers without the need for marketing costs.

GLOSSARY

product extension strategy: plan to prolong a product's life cycle
product life cycle: sales pattern of a good over time

Chapter 5
Production: efficiency and quality

UNIT 1

At the end of this unit, you should be able to:

Describe efficiency and quality, and comment on the connection between the two.

Introduction

Production is dominated by two main ideas: **efficiency**, also known as **technical** or **productive** efficiency; and **quality**. The fundamental idea behind efficiency is getting a lot out of a production process relative to what is put in. The more efficient person is one whose productivity is greater. A more efficient company is one whose costs are lower, given the amount (and quality) of what is produced. The principle of **cost minimisation** simply states that any company will want to be as efficient as possible. After all, if a company can reduce its costs without sacrificing either the quantity or quality of output, then profits must go up.

Quality is the second key idea. With very few exceptions, firms in any industry produce goods that are widely different from each other. They are **differentiated** in terms of materials used, how carefully they are constructed, where they are sold, what their image is – indeed, in every element of the marketing mix. Goods of a higher quality may well cost the company more to make — and the consumer more to buy. The firm is *not necessarily* inefficient just because its costs are higher than those of a company producing a lower-quality substitute.

Of course, producing high-quality goods often entails **product innovation**. Money must be spent in developing new, improved products. The money spent is, again, *not necessarily* an inefficient use of resources. Development costs are all part of the process of creating the cheap, high-quality goods and services that are the mark of a company that is both efficient and profitable.

GLOSSARY

cost minimisation: one aim of any firm, a description of efficiency
differentiation: the act of making different (e.g. making a product different from its rivals)
efficiency (technical, productive): producing quality goods at minimum cost
product innovation: the development of new or improved products
quality: producing something of high value to the consumer

At the end of this unit, you should be able to:

1 Give examples to illustrate the difference between unit costs and total costs.

2 Illustrate and explain economies and diseconomies of scale using an average cost curve.

3 Comment on the significance of the concept of a minimum efficient scale.

4 Explain the circumstances in which a labour- or capital-intensive production technique might be more efficient.

5 Explain and comment on the ideas of just-in-time, kanban and lean production.

6 Comment on the relative merits of short-term and long-term supplier relationships.

7 Assess the following methods of improving quality: cell production, benchmarking, quality circles, total quality management and quality standards.

The scale of production: is big or small better?

Primary schools typically have between 50 and 500 students, secondary between 250 and 2,500, and universities between 2,500 and 25,000. Hairdressers employ between 1 and 10 staff; car manufacturers between 1,000 and 100,000 staff. A different scale of output appears to suit different markets. Put another way, while there is a *range* of output levels over which firms can comfortably operate, it is possible for a firm to be too small or too large. The precise definition of what 'too small' or 'too large' might mean appears to vary widely from industry to industry.

An understanding of these facts depends on the concept of an *efficient scale of production*: that is, a scale (or size) at which unit costs are as small as they can be. The unit cost is the average cost of producing just one unit of output.

$$\text{Unit cost} = \frac{\text{Total cost}}{\text{No. of units}}$$

A firm that is 'too small' is therefore one whose unit costs could be lowered if only it were bigger. For example, the independent haulier with a 5-ton lorry is more expensive to hire *per ton* than the haulier with a 20-ton lorry. The lorry that is four times the size will not need four times as many drivers or four times the fuel. Nor will it take four times the time to load up. Of course, a 5-ton lorry will still transport 5 tons more cheaply than a 20-ton lorry would, so 5-ton lorries and their owners still have a future. But their customers will still be disadvantaged compared with larger customers who have 20-ton loads to transport at a time.

The reasons why unit costs fall as output expands are known as *economies of scale*. These can be thought of as the savings resulting from being large. Economies arising from the greater efficiency of large pieces of equipment, such as lorries, are known as **technical economies of scale**. Large firms can also spread their risk by producing many different goods and selling them in many countries — a **risk-bearing economy of scale**. Since they are then less likely to close down, banks will lend them money at a more favourable rate of interest, a **financial economy of scale**. Their 'buying power' enables them to buy in supplies at a lower cost — a **marketing economy of scale**. Also they can spread the cost of a top executive over much larger output levels — a **managerial economy of scale**.

On the other hand, it is possible for a firm to be 'too large'. The primary school is an obvious example. Small children need the security of knowing the adult faces around them, something that would not be possible in a school of 2,000. Additionally, their parents want the school to be close by, since they will have to transport the children every day. This will only be possible if there are a large number of small schools rather than a few big ones.

The reasons why unit costs sometimes rise as companies expand are known as **diseconomies of scale**. The example of the primary school illustrates the **managerial diseconomy of scale** — the fact that large firms find it harder to maintain close personal relationships among their staff, both with each other and with their customers. This explains why GP practices, hairdressers and childcare services all tend to be dominated by small companies. The primary school example also illustrates **transport diseconomies of scale**, and explains why corner shops manage to survive in the face of cheaper prices in supermarkets. Additionally, small companies often pay less tax. For example, the smallest companies with a turnover of less than around £60,000 are exempt from VAT: a considerable saving for the one-person business. This may be termed a 'government diseconomy of scale'.

One way of illustrating these concepts is to plot the unit costs of production against the output level. The result is called an **average** (or **unit**) **cost curve**. The size range over which unit costs are at a minimum represents the most efficient size range. Any other size is too small or too large. Firms outside the optimal size range will find it difficult to survive. This is illustrated in Figure 5.1.

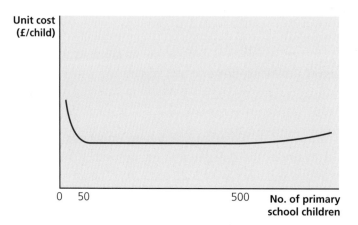

Figure 5.1 A unit cost curve, illustrating why most primary schools have between 50 and 500 children

The size at which unit costs are first minimised — in this case, 50 pupils — is known as the **minimum efficient scale** (MES). Any business needs to get to this size as soon as possible if it is to stand any chance of long-term viability. The principle is vividly illustrated by internet start-ups. They need to attain a minimum number of customers before they turn in a profit: the question is whether they can reach this size before their start-up capital runs out and they are forced to close.

All these economies (and diseconomies) of scale apply to the individual company. They are sometimes referred to as *internal* economies of scale. There is a separate series of cost savings to be made if the *industry as a whole* gets bigger. For example, the concentration of software companies in 'Silicon Glen' in central Scotland enables every company

located there to find new staff relatively easily. Such savings are known as **external economies of scale**.

average (unit) cost curve: curve measuring average cost against output
diseconomies of scale: reasons why unit costs rise as a firm grows
external economies of scale: reasons why unit costs fall for growing industries
financial economies of scale: cheaper finance for large companies
managerial diseconomies of scale: larger firms find communications harder
managerial economies of scale: the spreading of top management costs in large firms
marketing economies of scale: trading large amounts cheaply, 'buying power'
minimum efficient scale (MES): the output level at which unit costs are first minimised
risk-bearing economies of scale: large firms spread risk over many products and markets
technical economies of scale: the lower unit costs available from larger machines
transport diseconomies of scale: customers are nearer to a small firm

Production methods: labour- or capital-intensive? At home or overseas?

The never-ending search for cost reductions is a feature of any competitive business. Sometimes this will involve spending large sums on the latest **technology**. In the USA, 40% of all investment goes on IT. Or it may involve relocating to low-wage economies in eastern Europe or the Far East. The technology may not be as good, but this may be more than compensated for by a compliant, hard-working and — above all — *cheap* labour force. If the product is simple enough to be made in this way and if it can then be easily transported, this **labour-intensive** solution may be the most efficient option. The **capital-intensive** alternative will be used in those industries where the type of product cannot be produced efficiently without large amounts of equipment.

Where it is possible to break down a firm's activities into different functions, different production locations may be used at different stages. So Nike's product innovation, marketing and administration are based in the USA, but actual manufacturing takes place in the Far East. Indeed, the relatively cheap wages of the Far East have led to more and more manufacturing taking place in that region, rather than in the high-wage economies of western Europe, Japan and North America. This is a long-term trend that shows no sign of ending.

capital intensive: production method using a high percentage of capital
labour intensive: production method using a high percentage of labour
technology, technology revolution: the application of inventions to business

Stock control: how can unnecessary expense be avoided?

One key aspect of manufacturing goods is the management of supplies of **raw materials** at one end of the factory, **work-in-progress** on the factory floor and finished goods at the other end. This management is called **stock control**. The basic issue is: how can the firm save on the storage and finance costs of large stocks, yet ensure that it never runs out of something it needs? In household terms, how do you ensure there is always some of what you need in the fridge without having to buy a bigger fridge? Retailers face the same problem with regard to their goods; they always want to have something of everything in stock without having to build an enormous warehouse on the back of every store.

The two basic answers are:

- *Don't order raw materials until you are about to run out*. Householders who buy more milk while they still have plenty in the fridge will soon run out of space. The ideal is to buy more milk **just in time**: that is, just before it runs out. Most manufacturers have adopted the same idea. It normally works fine, until an unexpected event like the fuel blockades of September 2000 interrupt the normal flow of supplies. Then the just-in-time manufacturers suffer from not having a 'buffer stock' of spare raw materials.

- *Don't order raw materials until you have a buyer for the product*. In many fridges and freezers, half the space is taken up with goods that somebody bought some time ago, and no one has ever got round to using. In the end, there isn't room for something that *is* important, such as next week's milk. The parallel for a factory is not to assemble goods until a firm order has been received. Most mail-order computers are manufactured this way. The saving on stock levels is one reason why mail-order computers are cheaper than those bought off the shelf from a shop. The technical name for this approach is **kanban**. Rather than *pushing* goods through the factory, they are *pulled* out of the factory by customers' orders.

More generally, an aggressive approach to saving on waste, taking care to ensure that nothing is bought that is not immediately necessary, is known as **lean production**.

GLOSSARY

just-in-time: principle of a low stock level
kanban: production system driven by customer orders
lean production: production to order, with minimum waste
raw materials: primary products from the start of the supply chain
stock control: organisation of stock levels
work-in-progress (W-I-P): products being manufactured, part of a firm's stock

Supplier relations

Even in a service industry such as a school, where **supplier relations** are comparatively unimportant, there can still be friction with the outside companies that provide cleaners, meals, books and stationery. But for a manufacturer or retailer, supplier relations are a core feature of the business. The emergence of just-in-time stock control means that these businesses would cease to function within a very few days if supplies dried up.

Some companies go down the path of nurturing long-term relationships with suppliers, and indeed with their staff. The company best known for this was Marks and Spencer. Its 75% decline in profits in 1996–2001 is a warning that these relationships can get *too* cosy. It may be difficult to switch suppliers (or sack staff) if existing suppliers cease to be competitive. The alternative **procurement policy** is to chase the cheapest bargain of the day, switching from supplier to supplier depending on who is offering the best price. This is the strategy of Matalan, a low-cost rival to Marks and Spencer, and one that has been enormously successful.

Suppliers will naturally respond to the degree of loyalty shown to them. When they face **supplier constraints** of their own, and are perhaps unable to fulfil all their orders, their long-term, loyal customers are the ones who will get first preference. For this reason, it is normally the discount end of any market that opts for easy-come, easy-go supplier relations, while the quality end is prepared to pay a bit extra for most-favoured-customer status.

GLOSSARY

procurement policy: purchasing guidelines, especially for large companies
supplier costs and constraints: limitations on a firm due to supplier limitations
supplier relations: level of trust built up with input providers

Quality issues

The above discussion of supplier relations indicates that the search for efficiency extends beyond the mechanistic calculation of the effect of different scales of production, different levels of technology and optimum stock levels. Personal relationships (or the lack of them) feed into 'the bottom line' too, as will be discussed in Chapter 6.

For example, small groups feel a greater responsibility to each other than large ones. This observation has led to the development of **cell production**. The technique was pioneered by Volvo, whose cars were constructed by a team of a dozen people rather than by hundreds working on an assembly line. Even though this increased unit costs slightly, the work was so much more enjoyable that quality improved significantly. For a company positioning itself at the top end of the market, this represented an efficiency gain.

Cell production is just one example of the general point that the resources for quality improvement most often lie within the company itself. Another example is **benchmarking**: setting standards with reference to the best department or individual within an organisation. Who is the best doctor at your GP practice or the best checkout operative at your supermarket? Why are the rest not as good? Should the best be teaching the others? Does management even know who 'the best' is? As with any **quality control** method, simply setting standards is not enough. Management needs to monitor the progress towards agreed objectives and ensure that they are met.

A variant on this idea is the **quality circle**, a worker-led meeting normally held outside working hours devoted to improving quality and efficiency. Japanese in origin, it needs a high degree of worker motivation to have any chance of long-term success.

There is a school of thought that says in competitive, high-income markets the *only* thing that will give your product a competitive advantage is superior quality. Known as **total quality management** (TQM), the idea is to exhibit a total commitment to quality, both in the product itself and in the management structures of the organisation. Not only are customers treated like kings, but **internal customers**, those who rely on you within the organisation, are also served with slave-like devotion. As so often, TQM ultimately boils down to motivation: can an organisation persuade its employees to 'buy into' this type of culture?

Finally, can external agencies improve quality? A multitude of products from smoke detectors to double glazing have their own **quality standards**, normally BS or IS (British or International Standard) followed by a four-figure number. These are essentially examination certificates awarded after an inspection of the relevant products and the processes used to make them.

Investors In People (IIP) is another examination certificate for which organisations can apply. They have to show that they have training and communication policies for all their staff, and that these policies are adhered to. As with any exam where the examiners are paid by those being examined, there is always the suspicion that, to please the paying customer, standards will drop as the years go by, and the certificate become devalued.

GLOSSARY

benchmarking: using best practice to set standards
cell production: small group, working together very closely
internal customer: work colleague who relies on the firm, part of TQM
Investors In People (IIP): organisation certifying training standards in firms
quality circle: worker-led continuous improvement, 'kaizen' (from Japan)
quality control: supervision of the quality of a product
quality standards, assurance: external certification of a firm's products or processes
total quality management (TQM): commitment by a firm to total customer satisfaction

Chapter 6
Human resource (personnel) management

UNIT 1

At the end of this unit, you should be able to:

1 Explain what personnel managers do.

2 Comment on the relative merits of short-term and long-term relationships between firms and their workers.

3 Describe Maslow's hierarchy of needs and comment on its significance for personnel managers.

What is human resource management?

Human resource management (HRM) is the supervision ('management') of a company's workforce ('human resources'). The term is American in origin, the British equivalent being *personnel management*. The dominance of the American term reflects the dominance of the idea behind it: people become a 'human resource' to the firm — an input similar to cash (financial resources) or raw materials (natural resources). By contrast, the British personnel manager was historically more paternalistic in outlook. Alongside the financial imperatives of the company, there was a genuine concern for employee welfare — a concern that has been largely overlooked in many large organisations.

How do human resource managers fit into the general management structure?

Management tasks such as **recruitment**, the drawing up of **contracts of employment**, disciplinary procedures possibly leading to **dismissal**, and the general well-being of employees all come under the category of HRM. From this description it should be obvious that, in small to medium-sized firms, HRM will be undertaken by general managers. The sole trader, for example, will be in charge of every management function — marketing, production, accounts and long-term planning as well as human resources.

By contrast, large companies will have their own specialist human resource managers, who do nothing else. However, they remain part of the management team. On interview panels, for example, they will sit together with general, 'line' managers; and they remain committed to management objectives. If they care about employee welfare (and they should), this is *primarily* because a happy employee is likely to be a productive employee. There is an obvious parallel with customers here: look after your customers and you look after your profits. The same could be said of your employees.

One way of looking at the task of human resource management is to consider the three targets that any company should be seeking to achieve from its employees. These are:

- **direction** — how well employees are co-ordinated to achieve company objectives
- **technical proficiency** — how efficient employees are at performing their core tasks
- **motivation** — employees' level of commitment to the company and its objectives

Of these targets, direction will be the task of line management, while human resource managers will have some input into technical proficiency and motivation. Their interest in training should increase technical proficiency, while their general concern for employee welfare should increase motivation.

GLOSSARY

contract of employment: written employer/employee agreement
direction: co-ordination of employees' efforts
dismissal: termination of an employment contract by a firm
motivation: commitment to continuous effort
recruitment (internal, external): finding and appointing staff
technical proficiency: ability to do the work task

What models are available to help human resource managers?

In the USA, the traditional model has been one of short-term commitment between the company and the worker. It is assumed that the worker works for the cash, while the firm employs the worker for the output — and the contract can be easily terminated if either side believes they can get a better deal elsewhere.

By contrast, Japanese HRM has been based around the idea of long-term **relationships** between the two parties, similar to the traditional British approach described above. With large Japanese firms, this extends to lifetime employment. During the 1980s, when the Japanese economy was growing very fast and catching up the USA, their approach was seen by many to be superior.

Interestingly, when the Japanese economy faltered in the 1990s, the American approach gained ground. This short-term, contractual approach has been given enormous impetus by the internet revolution. Many industries are changing so fast that there is no possibility of offering lifetime employment, however flexible the workforce is. But the internet revolution has produced significant benefits for American workers too. The best programmers are in such demand that companies are compelled to offer them an array of perks on top of salary: stock options, crèches and a concierge service for their personal laundry, theatre tickets and so forth. Without these benefits, the best programmers would be lured away by rivals, or seek **self-employment** in their own start-up companies.

In the UK, the role of the human resource manager has become less collective in approach and more individual. The basic reason for this has been the decline of **trade unions** over

the past 20 years. The **labour market** is no longer dominated by powerful unions, using the strike weapon to enforce their will on employers. Their aim was to prevent **layoffs** and protect the **employment** of their members, though paradoxically this often had the effect of increasing national **unemployment** levels. Firms were reluctant to take on unemployed members of the **labour force** for fear of having to employ them indefinitely.

Today, by contrast, **industrial relations** have become 'individualised', with many workers negotiating the best contract of employment they can get on a one-to-one basis with human resource managers or line managers.

The best model for personnel managers is Maslow's *hierarchy of needs*. Writing in the 1970s, **Abraham Maslow** stated that work could provide employees with five basic needs:
- *physiological needs* — the cash to buy food and shelter
- *security needs* — a reasonable level of certainty into the future
- *social needs* — both social contacts in the workplace and the cash to support a social life outside work
- *esteem/status needs* — the approval and respect of the individual's peers
- *creative needs* — the ability of the worker to express and develop himself

Maslow suggested that these needs could be ranked in a hierarchy, with physiological needs at the base of the pyramid. As each successive level is attained, the worker then seeks the next level. This is illustrated in Figure 6.1.

Figure 6.1 Maslow's hierarchy of needs

The implication for personnel managers is that to attract, retain and motivate the best staff, it is not enough simply to offer more money. Jobs have to be designed to meet as many levels of need as possible.

GLOSSARY

employment: the hiring of labour
industrial relations: dealings between employer and employees
labour force, working population: those available and willing to work
labour market: market in which workers are hired
layoff (of employees): dismissal as a firm contracts, often temporary
Maslow, Abraham: author of the *Hierarchy of Needs*, a motivation theory
relationship: state of mutual commitment between agents
self-employment: working as a sole trader or partner
trade union: organisation of workers
unemployment (N): those available and willing to work, who cannot find jobs

UNIT 2

At the end of this unit, you should be able to:

1 Use supply and demand analysis to explain wage differentials.

2 Describe and evaluate the insights of Frederick Taylor, Elton Mayo and Frederick Herzberg.

3 Comment on the need for both formal and informal communication in the workplace.

Supply and demand in the labour market

In Chapter 1 we saw how the price of virtually anything could be explained in terms of supply and demand curves creating an equilibrium price (and equilibrium quantity), towards which the market would move. Non-price determinants of supply and demand then shift those curves, creating new equilibria.

The same theory can be used to explain the price of labour: that is, wages. This is known as the theory of **wage determination**. The equilibrium price becomes the **equilibrium wage** (W^*) for the job in question. The equilibrium quantity becomes the **equilibrium labour force** (L^*) in the industry.

If the supply is low and the demand high (as in the case of top sportspeople and entertainers), the theory predicts a high wage. But where the supply is great and demand low (as in the case of UK farm workers), the theory predicts a low wage. This is illustrated in Figure 6.2.

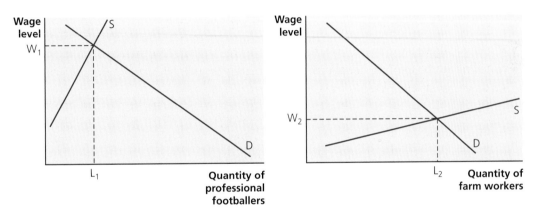

Figure 6.2 The theory of wage determination

The wage itself can be expressed as an hourly rate or an annual salary. This is known as **gross pay**. What is actually taken home after deductions is known as **take-home pay**. Once state benefits are added to this, you get *disposable income*: that is, what the person can actually spend.

> **GLOSSARY**
>
> **equilibrium labour force (L^*):** labour force at which the demand for labour equals its supply
> **equilibrium wage (W^*):** industry wage at which the demand for labour equals its supply
> **gross pay:** pay before any deductions
> **take-home (net) pay:** wage after all deductions by the government
> **wage determination:** methods by which wage levels emerge

Labour as a mechanical input: 'Taylorism' or scientific management

Analysis of the sort used above treats people as a commodity to be bought and sold like any other input or output. The logical consequence of this view is that human resource management should be about technical efficiency. How does the company increase productivity — how does it squeeze the maximum output out of this input at minimum cost? The person associated with this view is **Frederick Taylor** (1856–1915), the US manager of a steel mill in the early twentieth century. He redesigned the task of shovelling raw materials, finding out the optimal load per shovel that would enable the worker to shift a variety of materials at the fastest rate. In his book, *Principles of Scientific*

Management (1911), he advocated time-and-motion studies and tight management control to maximise labour productivity and so company profits. He believed that workers, like managers and owners, were essentially motivated by money. His work remains a cornerstone of much management thinking today.

GLOSSARY

Taylorism: Frederick Taylor's theory of scientific management

The human relations school of management

In the 1930s, **Elton Mayo**, a follower of Frederick Taylor, was conducting experiments on the effect of improved lighting on productivity in a factory at Hawthorne, USA. He found that output went up in the section of the factory where lighting was improved — but so did output in the section where lighting had been left unchanged as a control. He concluded that the personal interest that he and the factory management had shown the workforce was the real cause of improved productivity. From this has developed **human relations management**. Put crudely, the theory is that treating people as human beings is likely to increase company profits. Maslow's hierarchy of needs in Unit 1 is an attempt to define what 'treating people as human beings' entails.

Central to both social needs and esteem needs is the quality of **communication** within the workplace, both **formal** and **informal**. An absence of satisfying communication within the workplace will lead to **alienation** — an emotional withdrawal by the workers from the company. This may not matter too much in times of recession when workers have few alternative places of employment. But in times when jobs are plentiful, the best workers are likely to leave for more congenial surroundings.

Also associated with the human relations school is the US psychologist, Frederick Herzberg (1923–). His basic idea, known as the **Herzberg hypothesis**, is that the factors that make us unhappy at work (which he called **hygiene needs**) are quite different from the factors that make us happy (called **motivators**). Hygiene needs, such as pay, physical conditions and company policy, could cause dissatisfaction — but, if put right, they would not create satisfaction. This could only be achieved if the work itself was interesting and if personal relationships were satisfying. The conclusion was that simply putting right worker complaints would not by itself create a highly motivated workforce.

GLOSSARY

alienation: feeling of separation from the group
communication, interaction: transmission of information
formal communication: communication along the chain of command
Herzberg hypothesis: motivation theory of Frederick Herzberg
human relations management: Mayo's theory, stressing a caring approach to the workforce
hygiene needs: potential causes of dissatisfaction at work
informal communication: person to person, regardless of formal links
Mayo, Elton: founder of human relations management
motivators: elements of working life giving satisfaction

Chapter 7
The balance sheet and investment appraisal

UNIT 1

At the end of this unit, you should be able to:

1 Describe the difference between a stock and a flow.

2 Relate stock and flow to the profit and loss account and the balance sheet.

Introduction to the balance sheet: stocks and flows

The key idea in this unit is the difference between a *stock* and a *flow*. Flows measure the rate at which a particular variable, such as water or cash, travels. Stocks measure a quantity of a particular variable at a given point of time: for example, the volume of water in a reservoir on 1 January 2003 or the amount of money in your bank account at the precise moment you are reading this.

There is a strong *connection* between stocks and flows. When the reservoir is full (stock), we can expect plenty of water in our taps (flow). When the rivers are swollen (flow), we expect an increase in water levels in the reservoir (stock). If Fred is born with lots of money (stock), he will, if prudent, enjoy a healthy annual income (flow). If stockbrokers are well paid (flow), they will, if prudent, build up their savings (i.e. their wealth, a stock).

However, stocks and flows are not necessarily connected. You might inherit enormous wealth in the form of a Norman castle (stock), but be very short of money to maintain it (flow). Equally, a lawyer could earn big money (flow), but never build up any wealth (stock) if all the income were spent on, say, cocaine.

To build up a picture of the water cycle, we need to understand stocks and flows. Similarly, to build up a true picture of an economic agent's financial affairs, we need both concepts. A firm's financial flows are measured by its profit and loss account. So much money comes in over a year in turnover, and so much goes out in running costs. The difference is added to the firm's stock of wealth. This is measured by the firm's **balance sheet**.

GLOSSARY

balance sheet: dated statement of assets and liabilities

UNIT 2

At the end of this unit, you should be able to:

1 Explain each line of the balance sheet, and the information it gives about a company.

2 Work out and comment on the working capital ratio.

3 Work out and explain the significance of a firm's percentage return on capital employed (ROCE).

The balance sheet

The balance sheet of a company measures all the items of worth that it owns on a particular day. These are called its **assets**. Underneath these are recorded its *negative* assets — all the debts of one sort or another that will have to be paid. These are known as its **liabilities**. An example of the very simplest form of balance sheet is shown below.

Kingfisher plc: balance sheet, 31 January 1999 (figures are rough approximations)	
	£ million
What Kingfisher plc *owned* (= its assets)	5,500
Minus what it owed to its **creditors** (= its liabilities)	(3,100)
Equals net assets	2,400
Equals what the company is worth to its owners (= its **shareholders' funds**)	2,400

The figure of £2,400 million for shareholders' funds is a guide to what the company is worth. It does *not* mean that shareholders have this amount in cash. Their investment is tied up in the business of the company. However, if one large shareholder owned, say, 10% of the shares, it should be able to sell them on the stock market for around £240 million. An investment in a public company is a liquid investment, in the sense that someone else can normally be found who is prepared to buy people's shares from them.

The same balance sheet in full detail is shown below.

Kingfisher plc: balance sheet, 31 January 1999 (£ million)	
1. FIXED ASSETS	3,000
2. Stock	1,500
3. Debtors	700
4. Cash	300
5. CURRENT ASSETS	2,500
6. CURRENT LIABILITIES	−2,300
7. WORKING CAPITAL	200
8. LONG-TERM LIABILITIES	−800
9. NET ASSETS	**2,400**
10. SHARE CAPITAL	700
11. RESERVES	1,700
12. SHAREHOLDERS' FUNDS	**2,400**

Notice that both halves of the balance sheet give the same totals as before, namely £2,400 million, while showing in more detail how these figures are made up. Assets are divided into **fixed assets** (line 1) and **current assets** (line 5). Fixed assets are buildings, equipment and vehicles. Kingfisher owns retail outlets, offices, furniture and probably some lorries. Current assets consist of **cash** (line 4) plus assets soon to be converted into cash, namely **stock** (line 2) and people who owe the company money, called **debtors** (line 3).

Rather than list all the liabilities together, it is common practice to subtract debts that have to be met within the year (**current liabilities**, line 6) from current assets. This produces a total known as **working capital** (line 7). Current liabilities are likely to be unpaid bills. In

the case of Kingfisher, the biggest item here is likely to be a few weeks' worth of stock for which **trade credit** has been offered. Any bank **overdraft** is also included here.

The **long-term liabilities** (line 8) are then subtracted to arrive at **net assets** (line 9). This consists of all the company's assets minus all its liabilities — and therefore equals the value of the company to the shareholders: that is, shareholders' funds. The long-term liabilities commonly represent bank loans. If these loans are secured against property, they are known as **mortgages**.

At the bottom of the balance sheet, we see how the net assets have been paid for. In this case, £700 million has come from money put up by the shareholders when shares in the company were first issued. This item is known as 'share capital' (line 10). The remaining £1,700 million comes from the accumulated retained profits of the company (also known as **reserves**, line 11). Again, reserves are *not* cash that the company has. The reserves simply explain where the money originally came from to buy Kingfishers' assets. Together, the money shareholders put in plus the accumulated profits they have left in the company represent their total stake in the business, the shareholders' funds (line 12).

The two sections of the balance sheet must always be equal. The shareholders' funds represent the value of the company to its shareholders. This must be the same as the assets of the company minus the liabilities owed to outsiders.

Often a company is worth far more to its owners than a simple statement of 'fixed assets plus current assets minus loans' might suggest. The reputation of its brand names — the regard in which it is held by its customers — can be worth far more than its physical assets. These **intangible assets** are often recorded in a balance sheet under the heading of **goodwill**.

Companies may also buy shares in other companies. In this case, the asset is recorded under the heading **investments**: that is, financial investments. To keep things simple, goodwill and investments have been omitted from the balance sheet in Figure 7.2.

GLOSSARY

assets: items of monetary value (e.g. recorded in a balance sheet)

cash: notes and coin

creditor: someone to whom money is owed

current assets: cash, and assets easily converted to cash

current liabilities: money to be repaid within a year

debtor: someone owing money

fixed assets: assets that firms intend to hold in the long term

goodwill: intangible value built up through reputation or 'branding'

intangible assets: assets that you cannot touch (e.g. goodwill)

investment (financial): a purchase of future benefit, such as shares or government bonds

liabilities: money owed (e.g. recorded in a balance sheet)

long-term liabilities: money owed, payable in a year's time or more

mortgage: loan secured on property

net assets: total assets less all loan capital

overdraft: standing credit agreement with a bank

reserves: accumulated retained profits of a company

shareholders' funds: the value of a company to its shareholders

stock: levels of raw materials, work-in-progress and finished goods

trade credit: loans from suppliers to buy stock

working capital, net current assets: current assets less current liabilities

The balance sheet: an alternative layout

Balance sheets can also be displayed by shifting the long-term liabilities to the bottom half of the sheet. The simplest form of balance sheet would then be as shown below.

Kingfisher plc: balance sheet, 31 January 1999 (£ million, figures are rough approximations)	
Total assets less current liabilities (= what Kingfisher plc *owned* (= its assets), less its short-term debt)	**3,200**
Long-term liabilities (= what it owed in long-term debt, probably to banks)	800
Plus shareholders' funds (= what the company is worth to its owners)	2,400
Equals **capital employed** (= investment in the company by long-term lenders and shareholders)	**3,200**

The first method of presentation focused on the shareholders' funds. This second method focuses on the capital employed — the money that has been invested in the company both by lenders and by shareholders. With this method, the top half of the table shows 'uses of funds' (i.e. what the company has spent its money on), while the bottom half shows **sources of funds** (i.e. where the money came from). The three main sources of funds are:

- **External finance**, **loan capital** — the £800 million borrowed from outsiders in the long term.
- **External finance**, **risk capital** — the £700 million put into the company by shareholders.
- **Internal finance** — the £1,700 million reserves accumulated over the years in retained profits.

These last two items together add up to the shareholders' funds.

GLOSSARY

capital employed: money invested in a company by lenders and shareholders
external finance: growth paid for from outside the firm
internal finance: growth paid for from retained profits, reserves
loan capital: borrowed money (e.g. a bank loan)
risk capital (equity): money used to buy a share of a company
sources of funds (finance): origin of funds for investment

Liquidity ratios

It is possible to turn up at a supermarket checkout only to discover to your embarrassment that you have forgotten to bring sufficient cash to pay for your purchases. Similar situations arise when people unintentionally go overdrawn because they have forgotten that they have had an unusually expensive month. Both these events *could* be due to poverty, but they are more likely to be due to carelessness on the part of the individual concerned. In technical language, they have failed to attend to their **liquidity**. The problem is poor organisation of assets.

Firms face similar challenges in the organisation of their assets. They need to know what is likely to come into their account in the immediate future, and what is likely to go out. The amount likely to come in is represented by their current assets — their stock, debtors and existing cash. The amount likely to go out is represented by their current liabilities.

It should be obvious that companies would be prudent to keep their current assets at least equal to their current liabilities. Indeed, given that it is not always possible to sell stock quickly, many companies like to keep current assets at double the level of their current liabilities. The ratio of the one to the other is known as the **working capital ratio** or **current ratio**:

$$\text{Working capital ratio} = \frac{\text{Current assets}}{\text{Current liabilities}}$$

In terms of our discussion above, a ratio of 1 would be sensible, while 2 or more would be more secure.

Considerations like these lead some small companies to sell their debtors to a bank in return for immediate cash of perhaps 95 % of the **invoice** (bill). The bank then chases up the debt. This is known as **factoring**. It is one way of improving a company's cash flow, its liquidity. The service is not particularly cheap. Sometimes the adoption of factoring is a warning sign that a company is in financial trouble.

> **GLOSSARY**
>
> **factoring:** exchanging debtors for cash
> **invoice, bill:** written statement of what is owed for a service or good provided
> **liquidity:** speed with which an asset can be cashed
> **working capital (current) ratio:** ratio of current assets to current liabilities

Investment appraisal: percentage return on capital employed

You inherit £1,000. Should you spend it on a series of Easter revision courses, a new saxophone, a summer holiday or clothes? Such decisions are known as *investment appraisal*. You assess ('appraise') the likely return of a series of possible expenditures.

Companies go through the same procedure with their investments. The key measure of success is the annual return on an investment as a percentage of what was put in. So if buying a five-bedroom house to rent to students costs £100,000 and returns £7,000 p.a. after all expenses (other than mortgage payments), then the **percentage return on capital employed** (% ROCE) is 7 %.

In the case of a whole company, the return is its annual operating profit and the capital employed is the long-term loans and shareholders' funds. To work out a % ROCE you need *both* the profit and loss account for the profit *and* the balance sheet for the capital employed.

$$\% \text{ ROCE} = \frac{\text{Operating profit} \times 100}{\text{Capital employed}}$$

% ROCE is a powerful concept. Is a company exploiting a monopoly position? An unusually high % ROCE might suggest that it was. Is BP or Texaco the more profitable company? % ROCE will give a better guide than the headline figure for profits alone. Should you invest in an internet start-up or a conventional retailer? Your guess with regard to *future* % ROCEs will help you decide. Which professional qualification should you aim for? A comparison of all training costs with the likely return in terms of salary gained might be a worthwhile exercise.

> **GLOSSARY**
>
> **return on capital employed (ROCE):** annual (operating) profit as a percentage of the money put into a firm

Chapter 8
Leadership and planning

At the end of this unit, you should be able to:

Explain the role of a firm's leadership with respect to its vision, mission statement, objectives, planning and market orientation.

Introduction

It is hard to overestimate the importance of **leadership**. The organisations led by Napoleon, Hitler, Winston Churchill, Mohammed, Nelson Mandela, Henry Ford and Bill Gates were essentially extensions of the personality of their founder. Exceptional leaders create exceptional organisations; mediocre leaders, mediocre organisations. Of course, very few people can, by definition, be exceptional. Ninety-nine per cent of companies have to make do with the ordinary leaders and managers who are available.

The essential characteristic of any good leader is the ability to communicate a **vision** to the followers, the workforce. George Bush Senior, US president 1988–92, was a competent manager but was felt by many, himself included, to lack 'the vision thing'.

Ideally, a vision can be shared by staff and customers alike. It is often couched in terms of the excellence of the good or service, and the desire to attain substantial market share. Written summaries of the vision are known as *mission statements*, and can be found adorning the walls of most companies.

Leaders may well have another core strength on top of the ability to communicate a vision.

- Some are financially astute, having the skill of reducing costs without crippling the organisation. Carl Ghosn, the French manager brought in by Nissan, Japan, and nicknamed 'le cost cutter', is one such. Brian Souter, of the bus and train company Stagecoach, is another.
- Some are very good at selecting the layer of management underneath them. Richard Branson at Virgin is said to have this skill.
- Some have creative technical ability, such as James Dyson, the inventor of the eponymous vacuum cleaner. Lacking the ability to persuade existing companies to adopt his idea, he eventually built his own highly successful factory. In his case, he has combined **product orientation** with **market orientation**. His technical expertise has not caused him to lose sight of the imperative to create products that people actually want to buy. Sir Clive Sinclair was not always as skilful. He successfully created an early home computer called the ZX 80, but his one-person motorised tricycle, the Sinclair C5, was an engineering triumph but a sales disaster.

While it is fashionable to decry product orientation, it is worth remembering that some of the most outstanding products were created by people with little interest in the market. *The Lord of the Rings*, written over 50 years ago by J. R. R. Tolkien, was created out of a personal interest, even obsession, and made no concession to popular taste. It created

the genre of modern fantasy literature. Mozart and van Gogh both died paupers, while Alexander Fleming discovered penicillin by accident and gave it to the world for free. On a more prosaic level, the need to replace hundreds of kilometres of faulty railway track in 2000–01 could in part be due to a total focus on customer service, to the detriment of the more humdrum requirement of product maintenance.

If vision is essential, so is the ability to implement the vision. The mission statement must be expressed in a series of concrete **objectives**, both long-term and immediate. **Corporate planning** is the process by which these objectives are set, and then one of the key tasks of management is to ensure that the plans are met. It is as easy — and as hard — as that.

GLOSSARY

corporate planning: arranging beforehand how a firm will develop
leadership, management: co-ordination of a group of people
market orientation: focus by the firm on its customers
objectives: targets required for a firm to achieve its aims
product orientation: focus by the firm on its output
vision: mental image of a desired future

UNIT 2

At the end of this unit, you should be able to:

1 Explain different leadership styles and evaluate their effectiveness in different contexts.

2 Sketch an organisation chart and explain the trend towards delayering.

3 Describe a variety of company cultures.

4 Describe the importance of budgeting in the planning process.

5 Comment on the relative merits of organic and inorganic growth.

6 Describe the importance of new product development in the planning process.

Leadership styles

The ways in which managers exercise leadership can be illustrated by a spectrum showing how much input they allow from subordinates. The possible options are:

- *Tells* — the manager issues instructions and expects them to be obeyed without question. This is known as an **autocratic leadership** style.
- *Sells* — the manager issues instructions, explaining why the tasks need to be done.
- *Consults* — the manager asks for suggestions before issuing instructions.
- *Shares* — the manager seeks to establish a consensus among a group of staff before arriving at a decision. This is known as a **democratic leadership** style.
- *Delegates* — within fairly wide boundaries, the manager allows subordinates to make their own decisions. This is known as a **laissez-faire leadership** style.

There is, of course, no such thing as a 'correct' leadership style. Which style will work best depends on a variety of factors:

- *The personality and competence of the leader.* A democratic style needs competent leaders who are prepared to subject their decisions to scrutiny. Sometimes an autocratic style may conceal insecurity on the part of the leader.

- *The competence and expectations of the led.* A laissez-faire style presupposes that subordinates are capable of (and willing to make) reasonably intelligent decisions most of the time.
- *The time needed to make the decision.* Consultation takes time and there may not be time available. For example, air traffic controllers expect (and get) instant obedience from the pilots they direct.
- *The information available to leader and led.* Strategic decisions involving the future direction of the company need to be taken by people with a view of the whole organisation — normally those at the top. Narrow-focus decisions on how exactly to produce an item may be best taken by people much further down the organisation.
- *How the decision will affect the people involved.* For example, no one is going to recommend that they themselves get sacked — or that their department gets a reduced budget.

GLOSSARY

autocratic leadership: non-consultative leadership
democratic leadership: consultative style, seeking a majority view
laissez-faire leadership: hands-off style with minimal input from the leader

Leadership and organisational structure

Every organisation has a **chain of command** — a human chain down which instructions travel, and up which requests (and complaints) may sometimes travel as well. At each level of the chain, instructions become more detailed. So the board might instruct the **managing director** (MD) to 'Aim for a growth rate of 15% p.a.' The MD might then translate this to a European subsidiary as 'Close down product A and aim to double sales of products B and C.' The European director might then instruct the product A manager to 'Present a plan for closing down production within 6 months, while minimising redundancy payoffs.' This process is known as **management by objectives**. Each management layer sets ever more detailed targets for its immediate subordinates.

A chain of command can be constructed only when two related issues have been dealt with. First, how long should the chain be? Second, how many people should each supervisor be responsible for — that is, what should be their **span of control**? The two questions are related because if the company wants to shorten the chain of command (an activity known as **delayering**), it will have to accept that every manager will have more people immediately underneath them. The span of control will widen.

The trend over the past few years has been precisely in this direction. Layers of middle management have been stripped away, to be replaced by computers and increased pressure on the remaining managers and workers, among whom the work of those made redundant is shared out. Provided the company still operates effectively, this results in a considerable cost saving and therefore an increase in technical efficiency.

Following delayering, managers have less time for consultations, so the democratic leadership style becomes less common. In its place, decisions are either taken at the top with little consultation or delegated to those lower down. A clear division of responsibilities may be one of the benefits to emerge from delayering — from moving away from a **narrow organisational structure** towards a **broad** (or **flat**) **structure**.

Managers also need to decide whether the company is organised around broad functions or around products. Young Enterprise clubs are traditionally organised around functions

— there are marketing, sales, finance, production and personnel managers. One possible organisation chart for this type of company is shown in Figure 8.1.

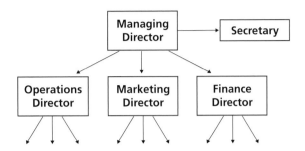

Figure 8.1 A possible organisation chart for a Young Enterprise company

By contrast, secondary schools are traditionally organised around products — the subjects of English, mathematics, science and so on. Even so, finance and secretarial services are normally arranged centrally by a bursar and a school office respectively. In fact, this pattern is also common elsewhere. In many companies, the 'product manager' has a key role. A central management supported by a team of accountants decides which product lines to reward with financial (and other) resources, depending on the performance of their product managers. In this way, the company encourages a degree of competition within itself. The hope is that this will generate the same sort of efficiency gains for the company that competition within an industry generates for the consumer.

This arrangement lends itself to **teamworking** — the creation of small groups within the organisation that collaborate on a particular project, such as the development of a new product. Teams like this are becoming more common, often at the expense of formal **hierarchies** and the chains of command with which they are associated.

GLOSSARY

broad (flat) organisational structure: hierarchy with a wide span of control
chain of command: people through whom instructions travel
delayering: removal of levels of management
hierarchy: management layers, the chain of command
management by objectives: target setting down the chain of command
managing director: full-time employee who leads a company
narrow organisational structure: management hierarchy with a small span of control
span of control: number of workers under someone's direct command
teamworking: group co-operates closely on a project

Leadership and company culture

The culture of any group of people — a nation, a tribe, a group of football supporters — is notoriously difficult to define. A culture includes shared assumptions or beliefs, such as 'Newcastle United are the greatest'. It also includes a shared history: 'the time we beat Manchester United 5-0', and possibly a shared style of dress, as a visit to any football terrace shows. There will be shared patterns of behaviour too: how insiders and outsiders are addressed, what level of violence is acceptable and so on.

Changing a company's culture is normally very difficult. Cultures are built up over many years, and the employees who end up staying long term tend to be those who are comfortable with the existing culture. Where the culture is plainly harming the company,

as when Texaco faced multimillion-dollar law suits in the late 1990s for racial discrimination, the need for change should be obvious to all — yet it may still be difficult to achieve.

Major changes of culture are easiest to achieve when a new managing director takes over. Staff who are not comfortable with the new direction will offer **resistance**. If the MD wins, disgruntled employees may leave. This is often the price that has to be paid to achieve fundamental change.

> **GLOSSARY**
>
> **resistance, inflexibility:** inability or unwillingness to change

Business planning

A famous Nike advertisement reads: 'If you have goals, you'll achieve them.' Similarly, in the army there is a saying, 'Poor preparation produces poor performance.' It is, of course, equally true that if you don't have goals, you won't achieve very much.

In terms of a company, the people who are responsible for setting targets (and ensuring that they are met) are its representatives: that is, its leaders. The task of business planning is one of their most important functions. On a financial level, this entails producing **budgets**. These forecasts of future income and expenditure inevitably contain a fair amount of guesswork, especially on the income side. It is much easier to predict future costs than future sales, because sales depend on customer decisions rather than decisions within the company itself.

On the cost side of the equation, companies divide their expenses by departments. These are known as **cost centres**. Each department head can then be given a mini-budget for the year. If people are not allowed to spend more than their budget, the cost side of the entire company budget will come in on target. Inevitably some cash has to be held back for unforeseen expenditures.

Budgeting needs to cover cash flow as well as the profit and loss account. Any external source of finance — share issues or bank loans — will add to cash. Conversely, capital expenditure on fixed assets, increasing stock levels, debtors delaying payment and the distribution of dividends will subtract from cash.

> **GLOSSARY**
>
> **budgets, budgeting:** the planning of future income and expenditure
> **cost centres:** firm's departments with their own budgets

Planning for growth

Planning is never more important than when a company seeks to grow. The search for new products or new markets involves spending money on what is unknown, and therefore risky. For example, many banks bought estate agents in the late 1980s at prices that soon turned out to be far too high. Laura Ashley, the British fabric and clothing brand, expanded into the USA at the same time, but was unable to repeat its UK success overseas.

Nonetheless, deciding *not* to expand also carries risks. Competitors may expand and reap economies of scale at your expense. As Sir James Goldsmith once said: 'The ultimate risk is not to take the risk.'

The fastest way to grow is to join forces with another company — a process called **inorganic growth**. If one company buys up another, this is described as an **acquisition** or **takeover**. If the two companies combine to form a new one, this is called a **merger**. For example, there was a rush of telecommunications mergers in 2000/01, as companies believed that global players were needed to meet the communication needs of their customers. The AOL/Time Warner merger of 2001 was based on the combination of an entertainment company and a partner that has the means to deliver this entertainment down the internet. This was the biggest of a series of mergers between 'old economy' and 'new economy' firms in 2000/01. The new economy enterprises dominate a revolutionary channel of distribution, while the old economy enterprises have the goods and services that need delivering. Following the dot.com crash of March 2001, it became clear that the internet companies had got very much the better of the deal.

What can go wrong with mergers? Sometimes the two cultures are so different that the partners never successfully establish a single, new identity. Sometimes the industrial logic is faulty: two firms that were both good at one thing become one firm that is not quite as good at either.

The alternative method of growth is simply to increase sales, perhaps by expanding geographical coverage or by diversifying into new products. Known as **organic growth**, this is the slower method, but it normally carries fewer risks.

It is, of course, possible to use both methods. Market leaders such as Tesco and Wal-Mart, Microsoft and Sage, have achieved rapid organic growth. But they are also constantly on the lookout for potential acquisitions.

GLOSSARY

acquisition, takeover: direct purchase of one firm by another
inorganic growth: expansion through mergers or acquisitions
merger: the combining of two companies
organic growth: expansion through increased sales

Planning new products

We saw in Chapter 4 that all products go through a life cycle of launch, growth, maturity, decline and death. This makes it imperative for every company to plan to create new products; otherwise, it too will die. Of course, companies die anyway. The average lifespan of a plc is only 40 years — less than that of a human being. But their owners will seek to delay inevitable death, for their companies as much as for themselves.

The process of creating new products is called **new product development** (NPD). This is part of the wider process known as **research and development** (R&D). Research may not be linked to any specific new product, but just be applied science. Not surprisingly, only the largest companies can afford pure research with no particular end product in view. Much of this research is not undertaken by commercial companies at all, but by government-funded universities. The best universities have 'science parks' nearby where commercial organisations can turn pure research into profitable products.

The proportion of a firm's turnover that is spent on NPD varies widely from industry to industry. A pharmaceutical company will spend a relatively large percentage on NPD. Many new drugs will fail, but one big success — like Viagra — can transform a company's

prospects. NPD also covers **modifications** to existing products. Blue Smarties, stripes in toothpaste, and new flavours and colours all count as NPD.

GLOSSARY

modifications: alterations to an existing product
new product development (NPD): the process by which a firm innovates
research and development (R&D): the background work behind inventing new and improved products

Chapter 9
Market structures

At the end of this unit, you should be able to:

1 Describe the spectrum of market structures that an industry could possess.

2 Explain why producers and consumers stand to gain from opposite ends of the spectrum.

Introduction

Having given a brief introduction to business in Chapters 3–8, we now turn to some economic analysis in Chapters 9–13. The issues raised in these chapters are of direct interest to the individual business as well as to the academic. This is one justification for teaching economics and business studies together. The theory of how economic activity takes place and the practice of what individual companies actually do are closely intertwined.

A sensible place to start on the theory is the differing degrees of competition between firms in various industries: in other words, the **market structure** of each **industry**. This is one of those areas where there is a direct conflict of interest between the business and the customer. For the businessperson seeking a profit, the less competitive the market structure is, the better. But for the consumer the reverse is the case: competition is the consumers' friend, the feature of the market that prevents them being exploited by greedy producers. So whereas the ideal arrangement for the business is a **monopoly**, for the customer it is a very high level of **competition**. The very features that businesses fear, such as being undercut by their competitors, are the very features for which the customer hopes.

But competition does more than just keep prices down. It also forces companies to maintain the quality of their products (relative to the price), and to engage in a ceaseless search for new products and new processes — before similar advances by their competitors put them out of business. Competition keeps companies healthy in the same way that lions keep antelopes healthy: in both cases, the *unhealthy* ones get eaten up.

Faced with a direct conflict of interest between these two groups of economic agents, namely firms and households/consumers, it is of interest whether the government favours one side over the other. In fact, the government favours households over firms, and for a very good reason. The losses to households of high, monopoly prices are greater than the benefits gained by the monopolies themselves. So the *total* benefit to everyone is greater if industries are competitive than if they tend to the monopoly end of the **spectrum**.

GLOSSARY

competition: rivalry in a market with many suppliers
industry: group of products with no close substitutes
market structure: level of competition in an industry
monopoly (in USA: 'trust'): industry with only one firm
spectrum, sliding scale: gradations (e.g. of market structure)

UNIT 2

At the end of this unit, you should be able to:

1 Describe the four main types of market structure.

2 Explain how the size of firms within a market depends on the level of entry barriers, and particularly the minimum efficient scale.

3 Explain how the market structure of an industry depends on the relationship between the size of the industry's market and the size of firms within it.

4 Explain what 'market failure' means, and why monopoly power is one example of market failure.

5 Explain how privatisation may rectify the market failure created by monopoly power.

The spectrum of market structures

Perfect competition

The most competitive markets are those with many companies, each selling an identical product to professional buyers. Identical, or **homogeneous**, products sharpen the competition by removing any possibility of product differentiation, or any claim to a **unique selling proposition** (USP). And selling to professional buyers removes the possibility of exploiting consumer ignorance and charging more than the prevailing equilibrium price. Such markets are said to be **perfectly competitive**. They are not particularly common. Markets in wholesale raw materials (known as **commodity products**), such as wheat, soya, copper and silver, are examples of perfectly competitive markets. The other main ones are the financial markets where currencies, shares and bonds are traded.

The market structure of perfect competition is a perfect illustration of supply and demand theory. At any one point in time, there is an equilibrium price with wholesale, professional dealers normally paying within 1 % of each other. The daily quantity bought and sold is also likely to be known.

Monopolistic competition

The next most competitive markets are those with many companies, but with each company selling a slightly different product. Firms have to be aware of the general level of prices in their industry, but are free to offer higher or lower prices than the average. Perhaps they have a favourable location, excellent after-sales service, unusually knowledgeable salespeople, a famous brand name to exploit — or any one of a hundred factors that can give one company a competitive advantage over another. The firms are said to be **monopolistically competitive**. The industry is essentially competitive, but each firm within it has some degree of monopoly due to its particular USP.

The majority of goods and services that we buy are provided by monopolistically competitive industries. Computers, private schooling in London, holidays to Greece, accountancy services, fitness training, driving instruction, flights from the UK to the USA, taxi rides, clothes and cars are all sold by a host of competing companies. Each company claims to be different, yet cannot afford to ignore the prices charged by the others.

Oligopoly

Further along the spectrum are markets where there are only a few major suppliers. Computer operating software, private schooling in Durham, accountancy software, flights

from Newcastle to London, food from supermarkets, gas supplies and mobile phone services in the UK are all markets where consumers have a choice — but not *that much* of a choice. The markets are said to be **oligopolistic** (from *oligos*, Greek for 'few').

How competitive the industries are in these cases depends on a variety of factors. The suppliers might get together and secretly agree to avoid competing with each other. Sotheby's and Christie's were fined for doing this in 2002. Or one company might so dominate the market, as with the Windows operating system or Sage accounting software, that it does not face particularly fierce competition. On the other hand, there is plenty of evidence that supermarkets and mobile phone companies are competing furiously for our custom. We explore these issues further in Chapter 22 of the A2 course.

Monopoly

Finally we reach the least competitive market structure, monopoly. In most of the world, there is only one company that will provide a house with water and take away its sewage. To send a letter by 'snail-mail' from a UK address, you are compelled by law to use the Post Office. Government-provided services are often monopolies. If you don't find Social Services or the Passport Office particularly efficient, you can't decide to discuss your request to adopt a child or your passport application with someone else.

Figure 9.1 illustrates the spectrum of market structures. Every industry lies somewhere along this spectrum, but may lie between two of the four main types.

| Perfect competition | Monopolistic competition | Oligopoly | Monopoly |

Figure 9.1 The spectrum of market structure

> **GLOSSARY**
>
> **commodity product:** products that are much the same wherever they are produced (e.g. gold, wheat, oil)
> **homogeneous:** property of being the same (e.g. two pound coins)
> **monopolistic competition:** competitive firms with differentiated goods
> **oligopoly:** industry dominated by a few firms; if just two, duopoly
> **perfect competition:** the most competitive market structure
> **unique selling point/proposition (USP):** exclusive characteristic of a product

Explaining the four market structures

Perfectly competitive markets can be explained with reference to the homogeneity of the goods themselves. It is simply a chemical fact that 1 gram of 24-carat gold is very like another. Hence the market for gold is perfectly competitive. By contrast, one pair of earrings is likely to be very different from another. Craftspeople have different design tastes and manufacturing skills. And so the market for jewellery is monopolistically competitive.

But the key determinant of most industries' market structure is the presence or absence of **entry barriers**. If there is **freedom of entry** into an industry, many firms are likely to take advantage of that freedom. The industry will be competitive. If, on the other hand, there are significant obstacles to joining, the industry will be less competitive. It is likely to be oligopolistic — or, if the entry barriers are particularly high, the industry will be a monopoly.

The most common entry barriers are the economies of scale discussed in Chapter 5. If, for example, primary schools need to have between 50 and 500 pupils to operate at minimum unit cost, then a small town with only 80 primary-age children will almost certainly have a single primary school. It will enjoy a local monopoly. Similarly, if car plants need to produce 100,000 cars p.a. to reach their minimum efficient scale, then a small country with an annual demand for 500,000 new cars p.a. is likely to have a car industry with an oligopolistic structure.

There are a few industries whose unit costs fall indefinitely as their output increases. Bigger is always better than smaller. Enormous is better still. The unit cost curves of these industries are illustrated in Figure 9.2.

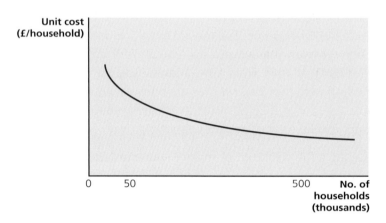

Figure 9.2 The unit cost curve of a water company, an example of a natural monopoly

To operate effectively, a water company needs a comprehensive network of very expensive pipes connecting reservoirs to every town and village in its area. Once the network is established, the marginal cost of hooking up an extra household is comparatively small. If there were rival suppliers, the biggest one would have significantly lower unit costs and could drive the others out of business.

Industries like these are known as **natural monopolies**. As already mentioned, wherever you are in the world, there will probably be only one water company.

GLOSSARY

entry barrier: obstacle to joining (e.g. to a firm joining an industry)
freedom of entry (and exit): firms may join (and leave) an industry easily
natural monopoly: monopoly created by large economies of scale

Evaluating the four market structures

Unit 1 made the obvious point that what constitutes a 'good' market structure depends crucially on who you are. The consumer wants a competitive structure whatever the industry, whereas the businessperson would always like to run a monopoly. It was also seen that governments seek to encourage competition. This section explains why governments (and the electorates they represent) take this view.

Monopolies increase inequality. A free-market system produces enormous disparities of wealth between 'winners' and 'losers' in the economic race. Bill Gates is worth more than the 50 million poorest American households put together. His personal wealth is equal to the annual national income of the state of Israel, or that of several African states combined.

The general feeling in western democracies is that these differences are great enough without increasing them even further by allowing companies to maintain monopoly positions indefinitely. Rather than simply making **normal profit** like any company might expect to make, monopolists make what are known as **supernormal** or **abnormal profit**.

Monopolies are technically inefficient. Most people need competitive pressures if they are to continue to perform effectively. The same is true of any business. Why do people queue 6 months for a passport, but only 6 minutes at the supermarket checkout? Because with the supermarket we have competing enterprises to patronise if the queues get too long.

Monopolies are Pareto inefficient. As explained in Chapter 1, an economy is said to be Pareto (or *allocatively*) efficient, if every industry is the correct size relative to every other, bearing in mind the level of consumer demand. But monopolies raise the prices of their goods way beyond unit costs because there are no competitors to restrain them. Some consumers cannot pay the inflated price and go without. The industry therefore shrinks to beneath its Pareto-efficient size. **Resource allocation** between industries is no longer effective.

Another, more technical, way of looking at Pareto inefficiency is to say that the **net benefit to society** is not as big as it could be. The consumers who opt out because of the high price could have paid a price that would still have left the producer with a profit. Both parties stood to gain — but have been prevented from doing so by the fact that the monopolist can gain even more by ignoring these customers and selling only to those who are prepared to pay over the odds.

In conclusion, monopolies are an example of *market failure* — a set of circumstances where the market produces a less-than-optimal outcome for society.

GLOSSARY

net benefit to society: benefit deriving to society above the cost to society
normal profit: sufficient profit to keep a firm in business
resource allocation: division of inputs between industries
supernormal (abnormal) profit: profit above that needed to keep a firm in an industry

The problem of monopoly power

From this evaluation of the various market structures, it should be clear that monopolies are against the public interest. More precisely, the problem is the ability of some firms to charge prices that bear no relation to their costs. A company that can do this is said to have **market power** or **monopoly power**. This includes all monopolies, but also firms in an oligopoly that raise prices in unison. The **market leader** in an oligopolistic industry may well persuade the others to act in this way.

GLOSSARY

market leader: company in an industry with the biggest market share
market (monopoly) power: control gained in an uncompetitive industry

Government solutions to monopoly power: privatisation

After the Second World War, the Labour government **nationalised** a number of industries, including telecommunications, coal, steel, cars, buses, railways and aeroplanes. It was hoped that the government would run these companies better than their private owners

had done. But nationalisation was not a success. The industries were protected from competition, but nonetheless managed to make a loss. The normal discipline of bankruptcy did not apply: the taxpayer simply ended up paying for the losses. Additionally, the quality of the service declined markedly, and workers managed to secure very good pay through aggressive trade union action.

In 1979, the Conservatives were returned to power under Margaret Thatcher. One of their most successful policies was **privatisation**, a reversal of the nationalisation of 30 years before. In addition to privatising all the above-mentioned industries, the utilities — gas, water and electricity — were also sold off. A genuine 'made in Britain' idea, privatisation has been widely imitated all over the world. In domestic politics, the success of privatisation can be measured by the fact that the Labour Party has extended the privatisation programme since coming to power in 1997 by privatising air traffic control. In the case of the London tube, it is currently proposing a halfway house known as a **public/private partnership**.

Of course, simply selling off a monopoly may just replace a state monopoly with a private monopoly. To get round this problem, some nationalised industries, such as bus transport, were broken up before being sold off. Other industries, such as steel and coal, were opened up to international competition. But where natural monopolies exist, it is impossible to create a competitive structure. The solution here was to create **watchdogs** — small government-funded expert committees whose task was to control the prices and quality standards of the privatised industries in order to prevent exploitation of monopoly power. Examples are OFWAT (Office of Water Supply), OFGEM (Office of Gas and Electricity Markets) and OFTEL (Office of Telecommunications). Over the 15 years or so of their life, the watchdogs have become much better at their task. They have also managed to create competition by forcing the companies running the above industries to hire out their supply networks to competitors.

However, we must be careful not to claim too much for government intervention. If monopoly is an example of market failure, there are also plenty of examples of **government failure**. The railways, for example, were split up before privatisation to create competition. The resulting disastrous structure led to the closure of Railtrack in 2002 and its replacement with a not-for-profit organisation.

Further government responses to monopoly power are considered in Chapter 22 of the A2 course.

GLOSSARY

government failure: inefficiencies created by government intervention
nationalisation: compulsory purchase of an industry by the government
privatisation: sale of government assets to the private sector
public/private partnership: project where both sectors make a major contribution
watchdog: government body to regulate private monopolies

Chapter 10
Externalities

UNIT 1

At the end of this unit, you should be able to:

1 Give examples of negative externalities.

2 Explain why negative externalities are another example of market failure.

Introduction

One of the key questions that exercise economists is whether the activities of business work for or against the common good. It has already been shown that monopolies work against the public interest by providing sloppy, unimaginative services at inflated prices. A further illustration of the failure of business to produce a desirable outcome is the prevalence of **pollution** caused by business activity. The key explanation is that the people who are causing the problem are not the ones who have to pay for it. So the farmer dumps effluent in the river, knowing it is the fisherman downstream who will pick up the bill. The careless pedestrian drops litter on the pavement where the general public suffer, but not in his own home where his family alone would bear the consequences. The sixth former leaves dirty coffee cups around the place to the annoyance of others, but not herself. And many people drive cars that emit harmful fumes and cause traffic jams for other road users. All these harmful consequences are known as negative **externalities** because they are external to the economic agent who creates the problem.

The only way to deal with these problems is for an outside authority to make and enforce rules. Without this, all public spaces would be full of litter, the rivers treated as sewers, common rooms descend into pigsties, and cities disappear beneath enormous traffic jams. In many places in the Third World, where government is inadequate to the task, this is the daily reality.

Externalities are, therefore, another example of 'market failure' — of a situation where the operation of the free market fails to provide society with the best outcome.

GLOSSARY

externalities: costs and benefits paid and received by third parties
pollution: environmental damage – an example of an external cost

UNIT 2

At the end of this unit, you should be able to:

1 Describe the connection between private, social and external costs and benefits.

2 Explain public goods, merit goods and demerit goods in terms of the above categories.

3 Assess the extent to which the market failures created by externalities can be put right by taxes and subsidies, and by legal limits.

What are externalities?

An externality, as Unit 1 showed, is any impact on a **third party** produced as a result of business activity. By a 'third party', we mean anyone other than the producing firm and the consuming household. Sometimes the 'third party' might be someone specific: if A sells B a car, and B runs over C, then C is the third party who has been affected by the initial deal. Or the 'third party' might be more general: if B revs his car loudly, the neighbours in his street are the third party affected. Or the third party might be more general still: B might drive his car impeccably, but the exhaust fumes damage the ozone layer. In this case, all the inhabitants of the earth are the third party. The **business environment** might be satisfactory, but the **geographical environment** has been damaged.

In the above example, all the third parties were affected to their disadvantage. The externalities of death, noise and environmental degradation are called **external costs**. But externalities can also be favourable, in which case they are called **external benefits**. Suppose you have a 'flu injection, as a result of which you don't get 'flu. That is your **private benefit** from the transaction. But equally, you do not pass on 'flu to your classmates. That is the external benefit of your decision to have the injection.

GLOSSARY

> **business environment:** the opportunities and threats around firms
> **external benefits:** benefits enjoyed by society as a whole
> **external costs:** costs not paid for by the producing firm
> **geographical environment:** the surroundings in which people live
> **private benefit:** the gain to a household from its own purchases
> **third party:** person influenced by a deal, other than the buyer and seller

Why are externalities a problem?

Unit 1 touched on this issue: 'the people who are causing the problem are not the ones who have to pay for it'. Builders have to pay for their cement, so they take care not to use more than they have to. But the neighbours pay for the noise and the dust. Unless the builders are unusually considerate, they will mind rather less about these external costs than they do about their private costs.

As with monopolies, externalities lead to Pareto inefficiency. Industries that generate significant external costs tend to be too large because their owners do not take *all* costs (what are known as the **social costs**) into account, only their private ones. A classic example of this is car travel. When people drive to work, they cause traffic jams, parking problems, accidents and exhaust emissions. 'Market failure' occurs because society ends up with more car journeys than would be ideal. Goods such as these, which generate significant external costs, are known as **demerit goods**.

Interestingly enough, external benefits *also* lead to Pareto inefficiency. In this case, industries that generate significant external benefits tend to be too small. Just as firms tend to consider only their private costs, so too consumers tend to consider only their private benefits. Most people who have 'flu injections have them because they don't want to get 'flu — not because they want to avoid passing it on. The external benefits are ignored when deciding whether to have the injection, so *all* the benefits (the **social benefits)** are not taken into account.

Goods that generate significant external benefits are called **merit goods**. Any form of healthcare is a merit good because others always gain from the good health of the individual. The foot-and-mouth epidemic of 2001 gives a clear example: farmers who kept their herds disease-free did their neighbours a favour too.

In a few cases, almost the entire social benefit of a service is external benefit. Such services are known as **public goods** because unless the public sector (i.e. the government) provides them, no one will. For example, people are prepared to pay for external lights on their property because they get most of the benefit. But few people would be prepared to pay for lighting on the street outside their property, which would benefit every passer-by.

The key feature of a service that makes it a public good is **non-excludability**. If others cannot be excluded from enjoying the service, the benefits will almost all be external. Once the street light is erected, it is there for all. Additionally, the light is not 'used up' by individuals, so there is no rivalry in consumption.

GLOSSARY

demerit good: a good generating external costs
merit good: good providing external benefits
non-excludable: cannot be privately enjoyed
public good: good providing *only* external benefits
social benefits: all benefits, both private and external
social costs: all costs, both private and external

What are the solutions?

Internalise the externality

The analysis so far has suggested that the problem with external costs is that the producer, who does not have to pay the costs, has no incentive to minimise them. So why not make the producer pay through additional taxes? The tax system is in part designed to discourage too great a consumption of goods that generate significant external costs. Most of the price of alcohol, tobacco and petrol is, in fact, tax. The process can be finely tuned. If unleaded petrol does less damage, it can be made 2p per litre cheaper. If the new 'environmentally friendly' fuel is low-sulphur petrol, the tax on that can be reduced.

A variant on this approach is for the government to sell **pollution licences**. The government might decide that CFC emissions should be limited to 10,000 tons p.a. It can then auction off the right to generate CFCs, ton by ton, to the highest bidder. This provides firms with the incentive not to generate CFCs. If it is cheaper to change their production processes than to bid for a CFC licence, that is what they will do.

'Internalising the externality' also works for goods generating external benefits: that is, merit goods and public goods. Private schools do not have to pay VAT. It has sometimes been suggested that private health insurance should be tax exempt. Such **subsidies** encourage the consumption of these merit goods.

Legal limits

The government can also influence quantity directly, rather than operating through the price mechanism as described above. Again, this approach works for both merit goods and public goods.

Goods generating external costs can simply be banned. At the time of writing, the possession and use of cannabis is *not allowed*. Restrictions can be placed on who is allowed to buy certain goods: for example, under-16s cannot buy tobacco. Planning regulations are designed to prevent unsightly buildings, or unsuitable occupations, taking place where they generate external costs for others. Or again, chimneys are required for smoky factories, and airports have to adhere to noise limits.

In the case of goods generating external benefits, the government can always provide the good free of charge, whether it is a merit good or a public good. The National Health Service and state schools are examples of merit goods provided free. Of course, these are not merely provided free to ensure that they are consumed in the correct quantities. There is also an 'equality' argument here (see Chapter 14).

In the case of public goods, there is no other option than government provision. Because the *private* benefits of an individual hiring a jet fighter to defend UK airspace are so small, either the government will provide this service or no one will. Note the contrast with merit goods. In the absence of a government, there would still be healthcare. But in the absence of government, there would not be an air force.

GLOSSARY

pollution licence, permit: saleable right to cause specified damage
subsidy, negative indirect tax: payment by the government to producers

Chapter 11
Consumer protection and business ethics

UNIT 1

At the end of this unit, you should be able to:

1 Explain why consumers need protection.

2 Explain the importance of social responsibilities and business ethics.

Why consumers need protecting

One of the best ways of describing the business world is to say it consists of a series of transactions freely entered into by independent economic agents. Agent X buys what agent Y sells. The buyer might be a company buying raw materials, hiring a worker or buying a fleet of cars. Or it might be a household buying anything from a house to a penny sweet. Or it could be the government entering a multibillion-pound contract for a missile defence system or a new motorway.

Chapter 1 described the various stakeholders or economic agents, and illustrated buying and selling activity through supply and demand diagrams. The question then arises: why

should any economic agent need protection from any other? After all, if consenting adults freely enter into contracts, why should one side later complain about the terms of the deal?

The answer is that in most deals one side has more access to information than the other. The technical description of this is **information asymmetry**. In the case of a sale, the seller will usually know more about the product than the buyer. For example, the car manufacturer or garage knows more about the cars it is selling than the ordinary member of the buying public. Even the private seller knows more about the second-hand vehicle she is selling than her potential buyers. This means that sellers may be able to conceal faults from buyers, and when buyers subsequently discover this, they may well seek redress from the seller — or through the courts.

At this stage, a second 'asymmetry' comes into play. If the seller is a company of any size, it will either have its own lawyers or be able to hire expensive ones that are beyond the reach of most of its customers. Faced with the threat of legal bills, customers may well withdraw from winnable cases simply because they cannot afford to fight any longer.

Put another way, the deal between buyer and seller is what the Chinese refer to as an 'unequal treaty' (this was the phrase they used to assert their claim to Hong Kong in the 1980s, even though the nineteenth-century Chinese government had signed it over to the British). And this is why every country has a body of consumer law whose main purpose is to give to consumers some **rights** that they would not otherwise have had.

GLOSSARY

information asymmetry: a situation where one party to a transaction knows a lot more than the other

rights: things to which everyone is justly entitled

Why other stakeholders need protecting

The same financial and information asymmetries that handicap consumers in their dealings with large corporations also handicap the other stakeholders who deal with these centres of power. Employees are vulnerable to the dislikes of their employers, whether these are rationally founded or not. Poor countries may find it difficult to resist the demands of multinationals on which their standard of living depends. Small supplier companies may suffer a cash flow crisis if their big company customers fail to pay on time. And local communities may feel at a disadvantage when complaining about the externalities imposed by the major companies in their midst.

There is, therefore, a great deal of pressure for companies to live up to their **social responsibilities**. Do they treat their staff, customers, suppliers, neighbours and, indeed, the whole environment as they should? The extent of this pressure is likely to reflect societal expectations of business behaviour, and particularly the attitude of the government of the day. Traditionally, the Conservatives in the UK and the Republicans in the USA are more pro-business. The UK Labour Party and the US Democrats are more pro-labour and pro-environment. So the Conservatives and Republicans are more likely to stress the benefits of business, while the Labour Party and Democrats are more likely to stress their responsibilities.

On a rather different level are the actual **values** or **business ethics** that companies wish to maintain. These will often be reflected in the company mission statement. Indeed, the

preservation and enhancement of an organisation's ethos or values is one of the key tasks of leadership.

Underlying the various approaches of institutions are essentially two competing ethics. A company may be absolutely committed to profit, and only consider other stakeholders insofar as it pays to do so. Alternatively, there may be an absolute commitment to certain standards of behaviour regardless of whether this results in an immediate cash benefit. In both cases, the company is likely to admit to ethical responsibilities. In the latter case, it is likely to mean it!

GLOSSARY

social responsibilities: performance owed to others

values, business ethics: moral standards of behaviour or principles held to be important (e.g. by a business)

Chapter 12
Economic growth and the business cycle

At the end of this unit, you should be able to:

UNIT 1

1 Identify whether any particular economic question belongs to the field of microeconomics or macroeconomics.

2 Explain what is meant by economic growth and the business cycle.

Introduction

One common way of looking at economics is to split the subject into **macroeconomics** and **microeconomics.** Microeconomics seeks to explain why individual companies and industries are the way they are. So Chapter 1, 'Supply and demand', shows how industry prices are arrived at, while Chapter 9, 'Market structures', shows why some industries are much more competitive than others. And Chapter 10, 'Externalities', explains why, in some industries, business activity does not always work towards the common good.

By contrast, macroeconomics examines the economy as a whole. So discussion of why a particular industry is growing is a microeconomic consideration, while discussion of why the whole national income is growing is a macroeconomic question. From Chapter 12 onwards, this book examines the main macroeconomic issues. This chapter begins by looking at two of the main macroeconomic variables: namely, the **economic growth rate** and the **business (or economic) cycle**.

GLOSSARY

business (economic) cycle: pattern of booms and slumps around a trend
economic growth rate: annual percentage increase in real GDP
macroeconomics: study of the economy as a whole
microeconomics: study of the behaviour of firms and industries

The economic growth rate

The economic growth rate measures the percentage annual increase in a country's output: in other words, in its real national income (or real GDP). This growth rate is vital to a country's welfare because the more goods a country can produce, the higher its standard of living is likely to be. In the UK, the long-term average growth rate is about 2.5% p.a. This may not seem very much, but it means that UK output doubles every 28 years or so. Other things equal, the next generation is likely to be twice as rich as the present one.

There is a useful **rule of 70**, which states that if a variable grows by x% p.a., it will double approximately every [70/x] years. So with a growth rate of 2% p.a., output doubles about

every 35 years, roughly every generation. But if this annual rate increased to only 3% p.a., then living standards would double every 70/3 = 23 years. In the case of Ireland (see Table 12.1), which achieved a 7% p.a. growth rate through the 1990s, its output doubled in a mere 10 years.

GLOSSARY

rule of 70: a variable increasing at x% p.a. doubles every 70/x years

The business (or economic) cycle

Table 12.1 shows that economic growth does not follow a smooth path, but is subject to years when output actually falls. This is known as a *slump* or *recession*. Conversely, there are years when economic growth catches up for lost time, and grows at a rate that cannot be sustained for long. This is known as a *boom*. The whole process is known as the business (economic) cycle. The UK has suffered three recessions in the last 50 years, in 1974–75, 1980–81 and 1990–92. One of the stated aims of the Labour government that has been in power since 1997 is to replace the business cycle with a pattern of steady growth. It will be several years before it is possible to assess whether this aim has been achieved. However, it should be noted that although short-term movements of the business cycle attract a lot of press coverage, the long-term economic growth rate is ultimately far more important in determining a country's standard of living.

Year	Economic growth (% p.a.)				
	EU15	UK	Republic of Ireland	Germany	France
1990	3.0	0.8	8.5	5.7	2.6
1991	3.4	−1.4	1.9	−0.9	1.0
1992	1.3	0.2	3.3	2.2	1.5
1993	−0.4	2.5	2.7	−1.1	−0.9
1994	2.8	4.7	5.8	2.4	2.1
1995	2.4	2.9	10.0	1.7	1.7
1996	1.6	2.6	7.8	0.8	1.1
1997	2.5	3.4	10.8	1.4	1.9
1998	2.9	3.0	8.6	2.0	3.4
1999	2.6	2.1	10.9	1.9	2.9
2000	3.3	2.9	11.5	3.0	3.1
Average	**2.3**	**2.2**	**7.4**	**1.7**	**1.9**

Table 12.1 Annual economic growth rates in selected EU countries, 1990–2000

UNIT 2

At the end of this unit, you should be able to:

1 Construct and explain an AS/AD diagram.

2 Use the AS/AD model to illustrate and explain the business cycle.

3 Explain how monetary and fiscal policy can be used to control AD.

4 Use the AS/AD model to illustrate economic growth.

5 Discuss and evaluate supply-side policies.

6 Understand an alternative to the AS/AD model: the circular flow of income.

A model of the business cycle

The best illustration of the way the economy as a whole behaves is the **aggregate demand/aggregate supply** model. It can be used to explain all of the four main macroeconomic variables with which we are concerned in this chapter.

The word 'aggregate' simply means 'total'. So whereas an ordinary supply curve measures the supply of one particular product against a range of price levels, an aggregate supply curve measures the supply of *everything* in an economy against the general price level. Both an ordinary supply curve and an AS curve reflect firms' costs of production. In the case of an industry supply curve, the relevant firms are those in the industry concerned. In the case of the AS curve, the relevant firms are all those in the UK economy. An AS curve is illustrated in Figure 12.1.

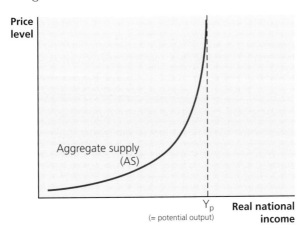

Figure 12.1 An aggregate supply curve

The equivalent of 'price' for an ordinary supply/demand diagram is 'price level' when dealing with the whole economy. This is measured by the *retail price index*, as explained in Chapter 2. And the equivalent of 'output' is 'output of the whole economy', or real national income.

One feature of any economy is that it has a maximum capacity beyond which it cannot at present produce. This is known as its **potential output** (Y_p). The AS curve cannot extend beyond Y_p because, no matter how high the prices offered, UK companies cannot produce more than the current total quantity of inputs enables them to do. Indeed, as Y_p is approached, the AS curve gets more and more inelastic. Big increases in prices are needed at this stage to persuade UK companies to make even a small increase in output.

Similarly, the aggregate demand curve measures the demand not just for one product, but for every single product in the entire economy. This includes all consumer spending (C), government spending (G), company spending on investment goods (I) — and foreigners buying UK goods (X), less imported components of all of the above (M). AD can therefore be summarised by the following equation:

AD = C + I + G + X – M

These five components of AD are, of course, the five main elements of the expenditure approach to national income that was looked at in Chapter 2.

As with an ordinary demand curve, the AD curve has a negative gradient. When the general price level is low, economic agents are likely to buy more goods. By superimposing

the AD curve on the AS curve, the standard AS/AD diagram is obtained, as shown in Figure 12.2.

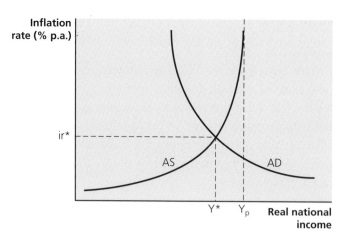

Figure 12.2 The standard AS/AD model

(One significant change from the previous diagram is the replacement on the y-axis of 'price level' with 'inflation rate': that is, the rate of change of the price level. The explanation for this is that whereas a fall in demand for any particular good is likely to result in a fall in its price, a fall in *aggregate* demand results in a fall in the inflation rate rather than a fall in the price level itself. The reasons for this lie beyond the scope of this course.)

We are now in a position to explain both the inflation rate and the output level of an economy with reference to the intersection of AS and AD curves. Figure 12.2 gives us an equilibrium output level (Y*) and an equilibrium inflation rate (ir*).

This basic diagram is incredibly powerful. Take, for example, the 11 September 2001 terrorist atrocity and resultant stock market decline. Households with shareholdings experienced a loss of savings as the value of their shares fell. In an attempt to restore their savings, households cut back on consumption. Since consumption is an element of AD, the AD curve then shifted inwards. This inward shift of AD could trigger a **slump**, as real GDP falls. This is illustrated in Figure 12.3. In the event, the shock following 11 September was not sufficiently great to lead to a recession, although the economic growth rate did slow down.

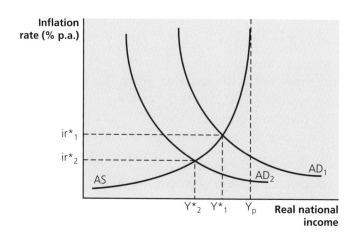

Figure 12.3 Inward shift of the AD curve

GLOSSARY

aggregate demand (AD): demand in the whole economy
aggregate supply (AS): supply in the whole economy
potential output (Y$_P$): a nation's full capacity, productive potential
slump (recession, depression): period of negative economic growth, downturn

Explanation of the business cycle

A share price collapse is just one example of a **shock** — an unexpected event. It is these shocks that provide the best explanation for the business cycle. A shock pushes the economy into a recession, as shown by output falling below Y_p. Recovery eventually pushes the economy back to Y_p again.

A demand shock shifts the AD curve. A supply shock shifts the AS curve. Both the 1974–75 and 1980–81 recessions were caused by supply shocks. In both cases, the supply shock was caused by a rapid increase in the price of oil, which led to sharp increases in firms' costs.

Governments have been trying since the 1940s to influence the position of the AD curve — a procedure known as **demand management**. In the 1950s and 1960s, the main aim of demand management was to avoid recessions. As Figure 12.3 shows, it is possible to keep an economy at Y_p by pushing the AD curve outwards. This was the policy advocated by **J. M. Keynes** in the 1930s and adopted after the Second World War. It was successful for a time — there were no recessions until 1974. However, the cost of this policy was steadily rising inflation.

When **Margaret Thatcher** came to power in 1979, she declared that inflation (rather than recessions and their accompanying unemployment) was 'public enemy no. 1'. Since then, demand management has been used to control inflation rather than output. Since Labour's election in 1997, the inflation target has been 2.5 % per annum (coincidentally, this is also the UK's long-term economic growth rate, but the two variables are entirely different and should not be confused). As you can see from Figure 12.3, it is possible to shift AD to achieve an inflation target if you are prepared to accept the resulting level of real national income.

GLOSSARY

demand management: control by government of aggregate demand
Keynes, John Maynard: the most influential early-twentieth-century economist
Margaret Thatcher: British prime minister, 1979–90
shock: unexpected event (e.g. one affecting aggregate supply or aggregate demand)

How the government manages AD

The way to control AD advocated by J. M. Keynes was **fiscal policy**. If the government wanted to shift AD outwards (known as **expansionary** fiscal policy), it would increase its own spending (G) and/or cut taxes (T), enabling consumers to spend more. For example, Nigel Lawson, chancellor of the exchequer under Margaret Thatcher, cut taxes in 1987 following that year's stock market crash. He feared that the crash would cause a recession, so he cut taxes to head it off. Unfortunately, he cut them too much, giving rise to the **Lawson boom** of the late 1980s. Conversely, a reduction in G or an increase in T will shift AD inwards and is known as **contractionary** fiscal policy.

The current method used to control AD is known as **monetary policy**. The Bank of England can engineer an increase in interest rates, which discourages firms and households from

borrowing money to spend and is therefore contractionary, shifting AD inwards. Conversely, reducing interest rates is expansionary, encouraging spending. Each month, the Monetary Policy Committee of the Bank of England meets to set the interest rate with the intention of shifting the AD curve inwards or outwards so that the 2.5% p.a. inflation target is constantly achieved. Chapter 13 returns to this issue.

GLOSSARY

contractionary policy: demand management reducing aggregate demand
expansionary policy: demand management increasing aggregate demand
fiscal policy: government control of its spending and tax raising
Lawson boom: unsustainable growth spurt in the late 1980s
monetary policy: official control of interest rates
money supply (MS): quantity of money (not just cash) in circulation

A model of economic growth

As mentioned in Unit 1, the long-term growth rate is ultimately more important to people's standard of living than the more newsworthy short-term movements of the business cycle.

In terms of the AS/AD diagram, economic growth can be illustrated by shifting Y_p outwards. A 2% p.a. economic growth rate, say, is shown in Figure 12.4 by a 2% p.a. outward movement of Y_p.

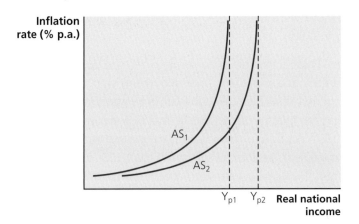

Figure 12.4 Economic growth

How to increase economic growth

The key to understanding economic growth is to appreciate that it can only take place in the long term if there is an increase in Y_p, and therefore in aggregate supply. In the short term, expansionary demand management can increase output up as far as Y_p. You can test this for yourself by shifting AD outwards on the standard AS/AD diagram of Figure 12.2 and seeing how far real national income can expand. It is, of course, also possible for any particular industry to increase output in response to an increase in demand, as in the recent expansion of mobile phones. But a long-term, sustained increase in the production of everything (i.e. in real national income) can take place only if an economy's *capacity* enlarges. The capacity of an economy is its ability to produce (i.e. its ability to *supply*). An enlargement in this capacity is shown by the outward shift in Y_p (and AS) in Figure 12.4. It is for this reason that government action aimed at increasing the long-term economic growth rate is called a **supply-side policy**.

The best framework for explaining supply-side policies is to think of real national income as output that is produced with inputs. The inputs (as described in Chapter 1) are land, labour, physical capital and entrepreneurship. To produce more output, it is necessary either to have more inputs or to use existing inputs more productively. Table 12.2 gives some examples of supply-side policies.

Objective	Policy
Increase the quantity of labour	Tax breaks for childcare for working mothers
	Raising retirement age
Increase the productivity of labour	Individual learning accounts (ILAs) offering subsidised computer training for every working adult
	Encouraging competitive market structures in every industry, for example through privatisation
	Removing restrictions on international trade
Increase physical capital (increasing the capital stock = 'investment')	Tax breaks for companies investing in fixed assets
	Relaxing planning laws
	Lowering the general tax burden
Increase the productivity of physical capital	Tax breaks for R&D expenditure
	Government funding of engineering and science courses

Table 12.2 Some supply-side policies

However, despite the efforts of successive UK governments, the UK's long-term growth rate of 2.5 % p.a. has remained unchanged over the past half-century.

GLOSSARY

supply-side policy: policy aimed at increasing a country's potential output

Economic growth: is there a price?

The annual percentage economic growth rate is a key indicator of any country's commercial success. The rule is: the higher the growth rate, the better. This is for a very good reason. People's standard of living depends upon the output per person: that is, real GDP/head. So economic growth, the increase in real GDP, is the way to increase people's general standard of living.

Nonetheless, economic growth may carry costs of its own. Firstly, the environment may suffer. This is illustrated in Table 12.2 by the observation that 'relaxing planning laws' is one way to achieve economic growth. Second, faster economic growth may lead to a more unequal society. Look at the number of times 'tax breaks' appear in the table. Lower taxes undoubtedly encourage economic growth — but they also leave the state with fewer resources to help the poor. Chapter 14 looks at this again.

An alternative economic model: the circular flow of income

The AS/AD model is the single best way of understanding macroeconomics. An alternative illustration is provided by a picture of the **circular flow** of money in the economy — with

goods and services flowing in the opposite direction to that of the money. It can be used to illustrate the business cycle. As Figure 12.5 shows, the money flowing into UK firms represents aggregate demand (C + I + G + X – M). The money flowing out represents wages and profits, and therefore the income approach to measuring national income (see Chapter 2).

One use of the diagram is to help us understand how AD changes. If we are taxed more, or **save** more, or import more, then money **leaks** out of the economy and AD falls. Both inflation and output go down. Conversely, if governments, foreigners or firms spend more, then money is **injected** into the economy and AD rises. Both inflation and output go up.

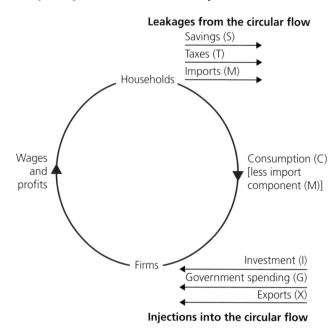

Leakages from the circular flow

Savings (S)
Taxes (T)
Imports (M)

Households

Wages and profits

Consumption (C) [less import component (M)]

Firms

Investment (I)
Government spending (G)
Exports (X)

Injections into the circular flow

Figure 12.5
The circular flow of income

GLOSSARY

circular flow of income: model showing money flows in the economy
injection: demand entering the circular flow of income
leakage, withdrawal: money leaving the circular flow of income
savings: disposable income that is not consumed

Chapter 13
Unemployment and inflation

UNIT 1

At the end of this unit, you should be able to:

Explain what is meant by unemployment and inflation.

Who are the unemployed?

The unemployed are those members of the labour force who do not have jobs. They are available and willing to undertake paid work, but have no work to do. The phenomenon covers a wide array of circumstances, from the mother of young children seeking to re-enter the labour force to the student who signs on during the long vacation. It also includes the person made redundant a few months before he planned to retire, and the coal-miner thrown out of work at 45.

A key aspect of unemployment is that you must be *available* and *willing* to work — or you do not count as unemployed. So, for example, the young mother who thinks she would *like* to work but has no alternative childcare facilities does not count as unemployed. Nor does the taxi driver, who takes Thursday mornings off to sign on for benefit as a way of supplementing his income.

One way of analysing the unemployed is by the length of time they have been out of work. There is a profound difference between being unemployed for 3 weeks, perhaps after your firm has closed down and you are selecting which of many job offers you prefer, and being unemployed for 3 or more years with no prospect of finding a job.

In 2001 unemployment fell below 1 million for the first time since the 1970s. At this level, the number of unemployed is more or less matched by the number of job vacancies advertised by companies.

What does inflation actually measure?

Inflation, as described in Chapter 2, measures the annual increase in the general price level. So an inflation rate of 2.6% p.a. means that prices have, *on average*, risen by 2.6% over the past year. But within this average, the forces of supply and demand will push individual prices both up and down by widely differing amounts. Petrol may have increased by 50%, mortgage payments on housing by 83% and food by 2%. Equally, telephone calls might be 7% cheaper and coffee 32% less. The general pattern in rich countries at the moment is that the prices of goods are coming down. Advances in technology are reducing the number of workers needed to make them, while the long-term shift of manufacturing to low-wage countries means that the workers who are still needed in manufacturing can be paid very much less.

By contrast, the prices of services are rising by more than the 2.6% average. Productivity gains are much harder to achieve in services than in manufacturing, while the option of moving service production to low-wage countries is often not available. So the prices of private education, private health, accountancy, legal services and plumbing are rising briskly in line with the salary increases of the professionals involved.

For a variety of reasons that will be explored in Unit 2, high inflation is harmful to the growth prospects of an economy. Since 1992, successive governments have therefore set **inflation targets**. The current target, set immediately after the May 1997 Labour election victory, is to keep inflation within 1% of a 2.5% p.a. target. As with unemployment, there is good news to report. The UK central bank (Bank of England), which has been entrusted with the task of keeping inflation within the 1.5–3.5% p.a. band, has hit its target every single month since June 1997 until the time of writing in 2003. As Table 13.1 shows, this achievement is unprecedented since the 1960s.

Year	Inflation (% p.a.)			
	UK	EU15	USA	Japan
1961	2.7	3.3	1.0	7.8
1970	7.4	6.6	5.1	6.5
1980	18.8	12.6	9.5	5.4
1990	6.4	5.4	4.3	2.3
2000	0.8	2.1	3.4	–0.7

Source: Eurostat Yearbook, 2002

Table 13.1 Inflation rates in world economies, 1961–2000

GLOSSARY

inflation, inflation rate: average annual change in retail prices
inflation target: government aim to achieve a specified inflation rate

UNIT 2

At the end of this unit, you should be able to:

1 Explain why inflation can be harmful.

2 Use the AS/AD diagram to explain the causes of inflation.

3 Explain and comment on the government's current inflation target.

4 Discuss the consequences of high unemployment.

5 Use the AS/AD model to explain the causes of unemployment.

6 Discuss the solutions to high unemployment.

7 Understand an alternative to the AS/AD model: the Phillips curve.

The consequences of inflation

Over the past 10 years the UK inflation rate has been very low — typically 2 or 3% p.a. As a result, many people have forgotten the damage that high levels of inflation can do. The worst consequences are as follows:

- *Increased inequality.* When prices are rising rapidly, money loses its value. Those with cash savings — often relatively poor pensioners — tend to lose out. Those who have borrowed heavily to buy property — often the affluent young — tend to gain as house values rise with inflation.

- *Menu costs.* At high levels of inflation, prices and wages have to be changed every month – or, in extreme cases, several times a day. If people lose track of what money is worth, they may stop accepting it and resort to barter instead. No modern economy can function like this. In countries with **hyperinflation** (very high inflation), people often conduct their dealings in another currency, frequently the US dollar. Hyperinflation also generates **shoe leather costs** — a description of the time spent rushing to get the best deal and to spend money before it loses its value.

- *Less investment and so slower economic growth.* If inflation is low but rising, companies *fear* that it will accelerate, leading to menu costs. Confidence in government economic

management is crucial to growth, and confidence will be lost if inflation is — or appears to be — out of control.

GLOSSARY

hyperinflation: catastrophic inflation rate, several hundred per cent p.a.
menu costs: cost of changing price lists, due to inflation
shoe leather costs: time wasted spending money during hyperinflation

The causes of inflation

The AS/AD model provides us with an excellent means of understanding inflation. The two curves can be shifted in two directions each, giving four possible shifts. The outcomes are summarised in Table 13.2.

Shift	Effect on real national income	Effect on inflation
AD in	Down	Down
AD out	Up	Up
AS up/in	Down	Up
AS down/out	Up	Down

Table 13.2 Result of shifts in the AS and AD curves

You should be able to sketch all four shifts, so that you can illustrate the effect that these shifts have on short-term output and inflation.

This analysis shows that there are two fundamental causes of inflation. Either AD increases or AS is shifted by cost increases. If AD increases, the result is known as **demand-pull inflation**. This describes a situation where demand is going up across the whole economy, and the economy is already close to Y_p. The additional demand cannot be met with increased output, so firms respond by raising prices instead.

If AS shifts upwards and inwards, the outcome is known as **cost-push inflation**. There may be a situation where costs are rising across the UK. Perhaps, as in the recessions of 1974–75 and 1980–81, this is due to the OPEC countries forming a cartel and pushing up the price of oil. Or perhaps the government has failed to control monopolies, which have taken advantage of the situation to increase prices. Whatever the cause, the AS curve shifts upwards and inwards, both increasing inflation and reducing output. This gives us the worst of both worlds: both rising inflation and falling output. It is known as *stagflation*, i.e. stagnation together with inflation.

GLOSSARY

cost-push inflation: inflation caused by a sudden surge in aggregate supply
demand-pull inflation: inflation caused by a sudden surge in aggregate demand

Solutions to inflation

The key to understanding the economic history of the past 20 years lies in the observation that demand management can control either inflation or output — but not both. Since 1979, governments have used demand management to control inflation, and have accepted that this will sometimes result in recessions. That is why there have been two recessions since then.

The chosen tool of demand management has been monetary policy. Every month the **Monetary Policy Committee** (MPC) of the **Bank of England** meets to discuss what the **base rate** — the basic interest rate — should be. The committee was instructed by the incoming Labour government in 1997 to keep inflation at 2.5% p.a. The *only* job of the MPC is to hit this target. When, as in March 2001, a recession looms on the horizon, many public figures will call on the MPC to reduce the base rate: that is, to adopt expansionary monetary policy to ward off the recession. But if the MPC is true to its brief, it will do this only if it is sure it can still hit the inflation target. Indeed, the whole point of taking away the responsibility for monetary policy from political leaders and giving it to the civil servants in the Bank of England was to insulate decision making from politicians influenced by political considerations.

This arrangement was first adopted by New Zealand, whose **central bank** was given the task of controlling inflation through monetary policy about 10 years before the UK adopted a similar procedure. The German Bundesbank (until the adoption of the euro in 2002) and the US Federal Reserve have similar arrangements in place. Wherever it has been tried, this method of controlling inflation has so far proved successful.

In broad outline, the use of monetary policy to control inflation is known as **monetarism**. While controversial when first introduced in the 1970s because it accepted the necessity of recessions, it is now the conventional wisdom of economic management worldwide.

GLOSSARY

> **Bank of England:** UK central bank, the manager of monetary policy
> **base rate:** interest rate set monthly by the Monetary Policy Committee
> **central bank:** sole government bank in each nation
> **monetarism, theory of M. Friedman:** proposition that inflation is caused by excess money
> **Monetary Policy Committee:** Bank of England group, setting interest rates monthly

The consequences of unemployment

When unemployment is low, as at the time of writing, it is easy to forget the damage that high unemployment can do — just as it is easy to forget the damage of high inflation. Unemployment, especially if long term, has the following severe consequences:
- *It increases inequality* — the unemployed are almost always poor.
- *It reduces real national income* — the unemployed do not contribute to saleable output.
- *It may throw older workers out of the workforce for ever* — in both of the previous two recessions, many people who lost their jobs when aged over 50 never got back into work.
- *It costs the taxpayer large sums in benefits* — money that could otherwise be used to reduce taxation or improve education and health services.

The causes of unemployment

Once again, the powerful AS/AD model provides a useful way of understanding macro-economic issues — in this case, unemployment. Look at Figure 12.3 again. Unemployment will clearly be higher at Y^*_2 than at Y^*_1. At Y^*_2, the economy is further away from full capacity: more workers (and offices and factories) will have nothing to do.

Unemployment that is caused by the economy producing at below full capacity is called **cyclical unemployment** because it is particularly severe in the downturn phase of the

business cycle: that is, in recessions. It is also called **involuntary unemployment** because there is not a great deal that the individuals caught up in it can do.

However, even when an economy is producing at full capacity, there are still large numbers of unemployed. This is called **underlying unemployment**. Whatever the state of the business cycle, there appear to be large numbers out of work. There are a number of reasons for underlying unemployment:

- *Frictional unemployment.* Several hundred thousand people are at any one time between jobs. One job has finished and they are taking their time in choosing the next one.
- *Structural unemployment.* This describes those who have the wrong skills, or who live in the wrong part of the country for the available jobs. This is a more serious problem than frictional unemployment, since it is possible for such people to remain on unemployment benefit indefinitely.
- *Fraudulent unemployment.* An unknown number of those who sign on for benefits are either working already or not really available for work. Strictly speaking, they are not unemployed at all, yet nonetheless show up in the official statistics.

GLOSSARY

cyclical (involuntary) unemployment: unemployment caused by slumps
underlying, natural, voluntary unemployment: unemployment when an economy is not in recession

---

Solutions to unemployment

We have already seen that unemployment carries high costs, both to the families affected and to society at large. However, not *all* unemployment is undesirable. Specifically, some amount of frictional unemployment is beneficial. Just as a company keeps a small stock of goods waiting to be sold, so it is useful to have a small stock of people waiting to take up jobs. It may be good for the workers themselves too: by waiting a few weeks they may well pick up a more suitable job than they would find if they simply grabbed the first one on offer.

Nonetheless, most unemployment *is* costly. The government, the taxpayer and the individuals concerned all have an interest in reducing it. Each type can be considered in turn:

- *Cyclical unemployment.* As discussed, once governments are committed to hitting an inflation target, they have to accept that sometimes economies will suffer a recession — and so suffer cyclical unemployment. The key way to reduce this is to shorten the *length* of the recession. This can be done by encouraging a flexible labour market: that is, one in which wages fall as well as rise. During times of high unemployment there is a surplus of labour, so the price of labour needs to fall. When this happens, the AS curve shifts downwards as firms' costs are reduced. Try drawing this using Figure 12.2 as your starting point, and you will see that eventually equilibrium is restored at Y_p. Encouraging a flexible labour market can be achieved by reducing trade union power (to enable managers to cut wages) and giving tax breaks to the self-employed, whose rates of pay can easily be renegotiated.
- *Frictional unemployment.* Workers can be encouraged to speed up their job search by reducing the level of benefits available. Practical help with applications, such as free advice and free photocopying facilities, may also help.
- *Structural unemployment.* Free computer courses and other subsidised training help people

to switch out of declining industries into expanding ones: in other words, they help to increase **occupational mobility**. Council house sales, the ability to rent a room in your house tax free and paying interview expenses all help workers to move around the country, thereby increasing their **geographical mobility**.

- *Fraudulent unemployment*. Tackling benefit fraud of all kinds is a constant battle. One recent innovation is a free, confidential telephone number where people can report their suspicions about their neighbours.

GLOSSARY

> **geographical mobility:** ability of workers to move regions
> **occupational mobility:** ability of labour to switch industries

An alternative economic model: the Phillips curve

We have already shown that shifting the AD curve moves both inflation and output in the same direction. If AD is shifted inwards, they both fall. If outwards, they both rise.

Put another way, shifting the AD curve moves inflation and unemployment in *opposite* directions. If AD shifts inwards, unemployment rises while inflation falls. If AD shifts out, unemployment falls while inflation rises.

This leads to the attractive idea that there is a trade-off between these two evils. We can have a bit less of one if we are prepared to put up with a bit more of the other. The first economist to draw attention to this trade-off was A. W. Phillips, a New Zealand-born economist writing in 1958. Drawing on UK data between 1861 and 1948, he drew the curve shown in Figure 13.1 (known as the **Phillips curve**) to illustrate the supposed relationship.

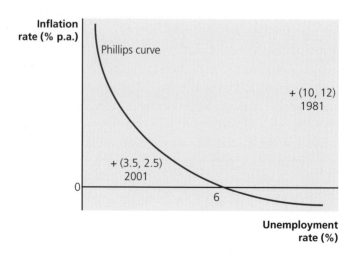

Figure 13.1 The Phillips curve

The Phillips curve is a perfectly good *short-term* explanation of what happens if the AD curve shifts, as a result of either a demand shock or government demand management. But as a guide to the long-term options facing a country it is quite misleading. A country that chooses low inflation may suffer high unemployment for a time. But recessions blow over, while low inflation can be maintained indefinitely. You only have to look at the UK position in March 2001 to see that the Phillips curve is misleading. *Both* inflation *and* unemployment were then at record lows. This is illustrated by the lower cross on the

above diagram — way off the Phillips curve. The upper cross illustrates the unemployment and inflation rates in 1981 — again way off the Phillips curve, but this time in the other direction.

GLOSSARY

Phillips curve: graph showing a short-run unemployment/inflation trade-off

Chapter 14
The government budget and economic welfare

UNIT 1

At the end of this unit, you should be able to:

Explain both the similarities and the differences between the government's budget and that of any other economic agent.

Introduction to the budget

The government is easily the largest economic agent, with an annual **budget** of roughly 40 % of GDP. Quite apart from its ability to make laws, this gives the government enormous power. For example, if the government decided that all firms employing more than 100 people should have at least 2 % of its workforce selected from among the registered disabled, it could pass a law to that effect. But an easier way of achieving very nearly the same result would be for it to instruct all its various departments only to buy from companies that had achieved this target. Few large companies would be able to resist the commercial pressure that this would cause.

Because the government is so large, the discussion and analysis of its budget counts as part of macroeconomics, unlike that of all other economic agents whose budgets are part of microeconomics. This fact is reflected in the national income accounts described in Chapter 2 and in the analysis of aggregate demand in Chapter 12, where government spending (G) is one of the four main areas of expenditure alongside consumption, investment and exports.

That said, the government's budget is not in principle very different from anyone else's. There is the income, which in this case comes from **taxation** (T). There is the expenditure, in this case 'Government spending' or simply 'G'. And there is the difference between the two. In the case of a company, this would be called profit — or 'loss', if negative. In the case of a household, it is saving — or dissaving if negative.

In the case of the government, the difference normally *is* negative: that is, in a typical year the government spends more than it recoups in taxes. The difference is called the **public**

sector borrowing requirement, or PSBR for short. The reason for this name is simple: the government borrows the difference from members of the public. It does this by selling either Post Office savings accounts or IOUs. When issued by a company, such IOUs are called *bonds* or *securities*. When issued by the government they are called *Treasury bonds* or *gilt-edged securities* (*gilts*) because they are reckoned to be as safe as gold.

In financial years such as 2000/01, where the government taxes more than it spends, the difference is known as the **public sector debt repayment** (PSDR). In such a year, rather than borrowing money, the government repays some of the **national debt**. This is the accumulated total of all past government borrowings, going back to the Napoleonic Wars over 200 years ago.

GLOSSARY

budget, the budget: government forecast of annual income and expenditure
national debt: debt owed by the government
public sector borrowing requirement (PSBR): government's budget shortfall met by borrowing
public sector debt repayment: government budget surplus, used to repay the national debt
taxation (T): compulsory levies by government

UNIT 2

At the end of this unit, you should be able to:

1 Describe the objectives of the government's budget.

2 Comment on policy issues raised by the welfare state.

Past objectives of the budget

In the past, the budget had the following objectives:

- *To act as a tool of demand management* (as explained in Chapters 12 and 13). Fiscal policy alone has not been used in this way since the 1970s, as monetary policy is now the preferred method of controlling the level of AD.
- *To pay off the national debt.* During the boom of the late 1980s, it was commonly believed that Mrs Thatcher wanted to use the budget surpluses of the time to pay off the national debt in its entirety. Such an objective has not been met in Britain since at least the eighteenth century.

Present objectives of the budget

The budget currently has the following objectives.

To achieve a balance between government income and expenditure

Subsequently, both Labour and Conservative governments have settled for the much more modest aim of 'balancing the budget over the economic cycle'. By this it is meant that the surpluses achieved in booms should more or less balance the deficits incurred in slumps. At the time of writing (2003) there has been much press comment to the effect that Gordon Brown's last two budgets have committed the government to too much spending over the next 5 years, and that therefore the target of a balanced budget will not be achieved.

To make the economy more Pareto efficient

Apart from social security, the biggest components of the forecast £400 billion government spend in 2002–03 are the NHS (15% of G), education (13%), defence (6%), interest on the national debt (6%), law and order (6%), housing and the environment (5%) and transport (3%). All these items of expenditure can be justified on the grounds that such services generate external benefits. (You should be able to classify them as 'public' or 'merit' goods, as explained in Chapter 10.) The same reasoning also justifies the high taxes on alcohol, tobacco and petrol. These are 'demerit' goods: that is, ones that generate external costs. Punitive taxation reduces their consumption just as free provision encourages the consumption of goods generating external benefits. Both policies are designed to achieve allocative efficiency — to make every industry the right size relative to every other one, bearing in mind all the costs and benefits that they generate.

To increase equality

Free-market economies such as those of the USA and Japan throw up enormous disparities of income between rich and poor. The electorates of Europe have voted for significant reductions in this level of inequality, although in current government pronouncements the emphasis is on **equity** or 'fairness' and the relief of **poverty**. These aims are achieved in four main ways:

- *By generous* **social security** *provision*. Twenty-eight per cent of the 2002–03 UK budget was dedicated to **welfare benefits**. It includes state pensions and housing benefit, child benefit and single-parent benefit, **unemployment and sickness benefits**, working families tax credit and income support.
- *By the provision of free health and education*. Any service that is provided free to rich and poor alike will reduce the proportional difference between them. On top of this, the rich may well elect to pay twice by paying for private services as well.
- *By a* **progressive** *tax system*. The rich not only pay more tax, but a higher *percentage* of their income in tax. This is most clearly seen in **direct taxes** such as income tax, where marginal rates rise from 0% to 10%, then 22% and finally 40%. By contrast, some **indirect taxes**, such as **value added tax** (VAT) and tobacco duty, are **regressive**. They fall most heavily on the poor (a **proportional tax** would take exactly the same percentage of income from rich and poor alike).
- *By* **regional policy**. Regional policy that gives **regional aid** — both from central government and from the EU — to poorer areas increases equality. Scotland and Wales have been the clearest beneficiaries of this approach, but smaller **development areas** such as the Team Valley and the banks of the Tyne and Wear have also attracted funds.

These four features of government intervention have a profound effect on UK national life. There is significant **redistribution** in favour of the less well off. The outcome is known as the **welfare state** or a **mixed economy** — one that possesses a large public sector alongside a large private sector. Of course, it is not only budget legislation that increases equality. The **minimum wage**, set at £4.20 per hour in 2003 for those over 21, is also an attempt to raise the living standards of some of the poorest in society relative to the average.

One way of illustrating the **income distribution** in a society is with a **Lorenz curve**. This plots the percentage of the population in order of income on the x-axis, and the percentage of total national income that they earn on the y-axis. This is shown in Figure 14.1, where line A represents a more equal distribution of income than line B.

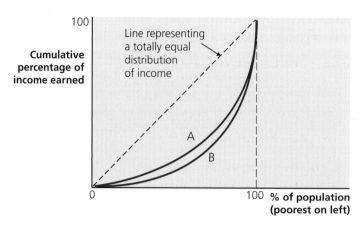

Figure 14.1 The Lorenz curve

GLOSSARY

development (assisted) area: area giving tax benefits to new firms

direct taxation (Td): all taxes on income

equality (inequality): the condition of (not) being equal

equity: fairness

free-market economy: economy in which government plays a minimal role

income distribution: the degree of income equality/inequality in a population

indirect taxation (Ti): all taxes on expenditure

Lorenz curve: illustration of a country's income distribution

minimum wage: statutory minimum, £4.20 per hour in 2002/03

mixed economy: free-market economy with a large government sector

poverty: being too poor to participate fully in society

progressive tax: tax taking a higher percentage of income as income rises

proportional tax: tax that increases at the same rate as income

redistribution: reducing inequality (e.g. taxing the rich to give to the poor)

regional aid (from EU): EU transfer payments to poorer EU areas

regional policy: government attitude to, and support for, poorer areas

regressive tax: tax taking a lower percentage of income as income rises

social security: safety net of benefits provided by the government

unemployment benefit, sickness benefit: transfer payments available to those seeking work or too ill to work

value added tax (VAT): sales tax payable on most items, currently 17.5%

welfare benefit: transfer (gift) provided by the welfare state

welfare state, state provision: system of government-provided benefits

Policy issues raised by the welfare state

To what extent is there an equity/efficiency trade-off?

One of the beauties of the free market is the powerful incentives it provides for working hard. If your standard of living really does depend on your own efforts, then poor and rich alike are motivated to work harder. One of the current objectives of **welfare reform** is to try to ensure that benefits do not discourage people from trying to provide for themselves. To take one example, working families tax credit is designed to ensure that those with children are better off working than relying on benefits. It is only available to families where at least one person is working.

Nonetheless, benefits of any sort will mitigate the hardship of low incomes — and so provide a disincentive to effort. This is seen most clearly in unemployment policy. The

countries of continental Europe that have generous provision for the unemployed also have among the highest rates of unemployment in the developed world.

How much equality do we actually want?

First, do we want equality of opportunity? Is this possible when we are born with different abilities? The political consensus in the UK is that there should be equality of opportunity between genders and between ethnic groups. There is also a consensus to improve state education so that poor children are not further disadvantaged in educational terms.

Or alternatively, do we want equality of outcome? Must all professions have equal numbers of men and women at every level? The original vision of socialism, 'from each according to his ability, to each according to his needs', envisages equal pay for everyone. In **centrally planned** economies where this was tried, equality turned out to mean equal misery for all — all except the governing communist parties, whose members were spared the poverty that their policies inflicted on everyone else. Since the collapse of communism in eastern Europe in 1989, the central planning model has been comprehensively discredited. China is the only country of any size that is still communist in political terms, and even China has been forced to run its economy along the lines of the free-market model.

This issue lies at the heart of the politico-economic debate in the UK, and indeed in most countries. Both the Labour and Conservative parties believe in balanced budgets. However, where the Conservatives have historically wanted lower taxes (and by implication lower levels of government spending), the Labour Party has wanted more government spending (and by implication higher taxes).

GLOSSARY

centrally planned economy: economy dominated by government planning, socialism

equity/efficiency trade-off: proposition that equality and productive efficiency are mutually incompatible

welfare reform: currently, the removal of disincentives to work

Chapter 15
International trade

UNIT 1

At the end of this unit, you should be able to:

Explain the key features of international trade.

Introduction

In most countries, the majority of buying and selling takes place within the national boundary. Both buyer and seller live in the same country, speak the same language, share the same currency and operate under the same set of laws.

However, **international trade** is becoming increasingly significant. World exports (and so imports) are growing faster than world GDP. Put another way, exports and imports account for an increasing *proportion* of most countries' GDP. This process is known as **globalisation**. It has been one of the fundamental movements of the last 50 years and shows no signs of slowing down. In the USA, the percentage of GDP exported is around 20%, in the UK 30%, and in smaller countries such as Belgium over 80%. Within these overall percentages, manufactured goods are much more likely to be exported than services. This is because most services can only be delivered in the physical presence of the customer, whereas physical goods can be parcelled up and sent overseas.

The key features of international trade are as follows:
- *It normally involves buying and selling currencies as well as buying and selling goods.* If you want to buy an American refrigerator, either you, the final customer, will have to buy US dollars or, as is more likely, the store from which you buy the product will have had to buy dollars in order to pay the manufacturer. The need to buy currencies makes international trade slightly more cumbersome than domestic trade, especially for small companies.
- *Consumers stand to benefit very considerably.* International trade increases choice and competition. Businesses have to be *globally* competitive rather than simply nationally competitive. Increasing use of the internet can only enhance customer power. People can now buy almost any manufactured good at the cheapest world price, rather than the cheapest national price.
- *The effect on business is to widen the gulf between the winners and the losers.* Winners win more — they can sell successful products to 6 billion people instead of only their domestic population. But losers lose more heavily — they will find it difficult to export in the absence of a **competitive advantage**, and are in danger of losing their home market to overseas competitors. Twenty-first-century life has been described as a 'winner-takes-all society'.
- *International trade has always been controversial.* In the absence of a world government, each national government tries to make international trade work to the particular

advantage of its own nationals. The resulting disputes and arrangements are considered in Chapter 16.

GLOSSARY

competitive advantage, competitiveness: superiority of a firm compared to its rivals
globalisation: development of worldwide markets
international trade: trade between two countries

UNIT 2

At the end of this unit, you should be able to:

1 Comment on the reasons for international trade.

2 Explain the changing pattern of UK trade.

3 Explain the causes and consequences of floating exchange rates.

4 Discuss the advantages and disadvantages of fixed exchange rates.

5 Understand the balance of payments.

Reasons for international trade

At the beginning of the course it was explained that specialisation enables productivity to rise, and with it the standard of living. Trading internationally is essentially no different: it is simply another opportunity to specialise to everyone's advantage. These **gains from trade** arising from specialisation are formally analysed in the theory of comparative advantage, in Option 1 of the A2 course.

From the point of view of the business, exporting is one route to expansion — a means of repeating successes in the domestic market on a much wider canvas. On the other side of the coin, importing provides the business with more potential suppliers, and the opportunity of selling products that may not be available at home.

From the point of view of the consumer, imports provide greater choice and greater competition. In terms of market structure, any industry that is opened up to international competition is likely to move towards the competitive end of the spectrum, and therefore generate better and cheaper goods for its customers. If a whole *country* opens itself up to international trade, the total gains in terms of increased output, and therefore in standard of living, can be very significant.

GLOSSARY

gains from trade: increase in the standard of living due to international trade

The changing pattern of UK trade

- *A growing proportion of UK trade is in services.* As mentioned in Unit 1, the UK exports over 30% of its GDP, and this percentage is growing. Physical goods (also known as visibles) have traditionally dominated exports and imports. This reflects the fact that many services (or **invisibles**) can only be sold if buyer and seller can meet: health and educational services are obvious examples. However, trade in services is growing rapidly.

The chain of distribution for insurance and banking services is moving to the telephone and the internet. The internet is also increasingly used to sell commercial information, music and video images, and tertiary education.

- *A growing proportion of UK trade takes place with the EU.* While Euro-enthusiasts see this as proof that withdrawal from the EU is a practical impossibility, a less political analysis is possible. The EU is a customs union, so it is natural that, having joined in 1973, the UK should experience some shifting of its trade patterns away from countries outside the tariff wall erected by the EU and towards fellow members. If the UK left the EU, this trend would reverse.

GLOSSARY

invisibles: services that can be traded internationally
visibles: physical goods that are traded internationally

What factors set exchange rates?

One distinct difference between international and domestic trade is that it is only with international trade that the need to change currencies arises. The various currencies become commodities to be bought and sold, just like the goods and services that can be bought with them.

In fact, the major currency markets are a classic example of perfect competition. Each day many thousands of agents buy and sell each of the world's major currencies. The goods they are buying are homogeneous: one US dollar is worth exactly the same as every other. This is a characteristic of any currency. Consequently, the price of a currency in terms of another (known as its **exchange rate** or **exchange rate index**) can be easily explained with reference to a supply and demand diagram, as shown in Figure 15.1.

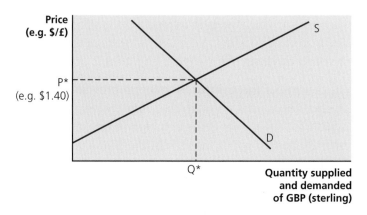

Figure 15.1 Demand and supply of sterling (in US$)

The international supply of sterling comes from UK importers. They sell ('supply') sterling in order to buy the foreign currency with which their overseas suppliers wish to be paid. Similarly, the international demand for sterling comes from UK export activity. Our overseas customers buy ('demand') sterling in order to pay their UK suppliers.

Notice, too, that the exchange rate ensures that the international supply of and demand for sterling are equal. The exchange rate is the price mechanism in operation, ensuring that UK exports and UK imports will in the long run balance each other out. If the exchange rate rises, this is called **appreciation**; if it falls, **depreciation**.

We are now in a position to explain changes in the exchange rate. Suppose UK goods improve in quality relative to other countries. More will be exported and the demand for sterling will rise, pushing the demand curve outwards as illustrated in Figure 15.2. The sterling exchange rate will rise until the extra quality is matched by the extra cost of buying sterling, at which point UK exports will once again be balanced by UK imports.

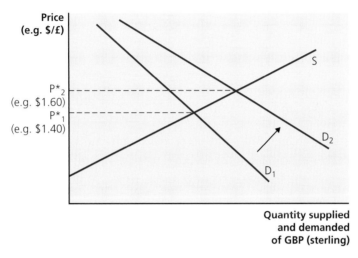

Figure 15.2 An increase in the sterling exchange rate

Exchange rates will change if any factor affects the relative attractiveness of the currencies involved and of the goods behind them. So if UK inflation were higher than that elsewhere, we would expect the sterling exchange rate to fall. Since sterling is now worth less than it was inside the UK, it is not surprising that its **external value** should have fallen too. Conversely, if UK interest rates rose relative to those elsewhere, sterling would give a relatively high rate of return and so its external value would rise.

GLOSSARY

appreciation (of a currency): external value of a currency floats up
depreciation (of a currency): external value of a currency drifts down
exchange rate: price of one currency in terms of another
exchange rate index: measure of change in the value of a currency against others
external value of a currency: what a currency will buy overseas, its exchange rate

What is the impact of a rising exchange rate?

Like the inflation rate and the interest rate, the exchange rate is a key macroeconomic variable over which the individual economic agent has no control. This section will look at the effect of an increase in the sterling exchange rate. The effects can, of course, be reversed for a falling exchange rate.

- *UK exporters lose out.* With the exchange rate changes of Figure 15.2, if they want to sell something in the USA for £1, they now have to charge their customers $1.60 instead of $1.40. If, alternatively, they feel they cannot increase the US price beyond $1.40, they will have to accept a reduction in the sterling price to £0.875 (i.e. 1.40/1.60).
- *UK importers gain.* If they wished to import a US good for $1.40, they previously had to pay £1. Now they only have to pay £0.875 (1.40/1.60).
- *In the short term, the economy contracts.* You will recall that AD = C + I + G + X − M.

With UK exporters losing out (so X falls) and UK importers gaining (so M rises), both effects lead to lower aggregate demand.

● *In the long term, the UK standard of living increases.* Because UK imports are now cheaper, British residents get more of them in exchange for a given number of exports.

The key point here is that UK exporters will complain if sterling rises, even though the country as a whole stands to gain. Given that a high proportion of manufactured goods are exported and that UK manufacturing is in long-term decline, 'the strong pound' will be periodically blamed for this decline. In reality, the decline of manufacturing has little to do with fluctuations in sterling. Instead it is caused by the UK specialising increasingly in those services in which it has a global competitive advantage.

Fixed exchange rates

This analysis of exchange rates has so far assumed that they are set by the forces of supply and demand in a free market. Governments are often perfectly happy with this system of free-moving, **floating exchange rates**. However, governments may also choose another type of **exchange rate regime**, namely **fixed exchange rates**. The UK government last adopted this system between 1990 and 1992, when it was known as the **exchange rate mechanism** (ERM). Under fixed exchange rates, governments simply agree with each other what their exchange rate should be. If the government feels unable to maintain the fixed rate and announces a lower one, this is called **devaluation**. An upward movement in the fixed rate is called **revaluation**.

Enforcing a fixed exchange rate is not easy. If the value of its currency looks like falling, the government can always use its **foreign currency reserves** to buy the currency and so increase its value. But if its reserves are running low, the only other way to maintain the agreed exchange rate is to increase interest rates. This increases demand for the currency and so prevents its price from falling. But this approach has its own problems. If interest rates are being used to hit an exchange rate target, they cannot also be used to hit an inflation target. Put simply, a government can decide either to target an inflation rate (and accept that the exchange rate will fluctuate) or to target an exchange rate (and accept that the inflation rate will fluctuate). Since the early 1990s, the UK government has adopted an inflation target and allowed the exchange rate to 'float': that is, fluctuate.

Why should any country want to fix its exchange rate? The traditional justification is that a fixed exchange rate makes international trade easier, since it removes a major source of uncertainty. The company that agrees to buy or sell overseas at a price expressed in a foreign currency stands to lose if its own currency falls in value. Although this exchange rate risk can be insured against by buying foreign currency in the **forward market**, as with any form of insurance there is an insurance premium to pay. On the other hand, supporters of floating exchange rates point out that the price mechanism is an essential means of balancing supply with demand — and that it is more important to have a fixed, low inflation rate than a fixed exchange rate.

These issues are of direct relevance to the UK at the time of writing. If the UK joins the **euro**, it will in effect have a permanently fixed exchange rate with the other 11 members of **euroland**. The subject of **European monetary union** (EMU) will be considered in more detail in Chapter 24 of the A2 course.

GLOSSARY

devaluation: exchange rate depreciation by act of government

euro (€), single currency: EU currency adopted in 2002 by 11 out of 15 members

euroland, eurozone: 11 out of 15 EU members using the euro in 2002

European monetary union (EMU): move by the EU towards a single currency, the euro

exchange rate mechanism (ERM): former EU fixed exchange rates; UK a member 1990–92

exchange rate regime: government policy towards the exchange rate

fixed exchange rate: government-enforced exchange rate

floating exchange rate: free market determines the exchange rate

foreign currency reserves: store of foreign currency held (in the UK) by the Bank of England

forward market (futures): future delivery of an asset at a price fixed today

revaluation: exchange rate appreciation by act of government

Measuring international trade

The flow of trade across a country's borders is measured by a subsection of its national income accounts. This subsection is known as its **balance of payments**. What is measured is not the goods and services themselves, but the money flowing in the opposite direction. So if a UK company imports £1,000 of refrigerators from New York, the UK balance of payments will record –£1,000 — because £1,000 will have flowed out of the UK in return for the consumer durables. Meanwhile, the US balance of payments will have recorded +£1,000 (or rather the equivalent in US dollars) because this will have flowed into the USA in return for the items.

	Credit: money into the UK		Debit: money out of the UK		Balance of:	
Visibles = physical goods	Exports	187	Imports	(219)	**Visible trade**	(32)
Invisibles						
Services	Sold overseas	80	Bought from overseas	(67)		13
Income from investments	From UK-owned assets	123	From foreign assets in the UK	(109)		14
Transfers = gifts	From overseas to the UK	13	From the UK to overseas	(22)		(9)
TOTAL INVISIBLES		216		(198)	**Invisible trade**	18
BALANCE OF PAYMENTS ON CURRENT ACCOUNT						(14)

Figure 15.3 UK balance of payments on current account, Oct. 2001–Sept. 2002 (£ billion)

The complete balance of payments also includes a **capital account**, which records money flows generated by the purchase of investment goods, such as fixed assets and shares.

GLOSSARY

balance of payments: record of financial dealings with the rest of the world

balance of payments on current account (BOCA): consumption section of the balance of payments

capital account of the balance of payments: investment flows in the balance of payments

Chapter 16
The European Union and the world economic order

At the end of this unit, you should be able to:

Explain the work of the European Union.

UNIT 1

Introduction to the European Union

Within the continent of Europe, the **European Union** (EU) dominates international trade. The EU is both a **free trade area** and a **customs union**. A free trade area is a group of countries that agree to allow trade between members without restriction. For example, the countries of North America have formed such an area, known as the **North American Free Trade Association** (NAFTA). In the case of the EU, totally free trade was supposed to have arrived with the **Single Market Act** of 1993. However, the frequent trade disputes within the EU show that totally free trade is still a future hope, rather than a present reality.

A customs union is a 'free trade area plus'. The 'plus' is a common level of taxation on goods coming into the union from outside. So any goods coming into the EU have to pay the same level of tax. In the case of foodstuffs, this is known as the **common external tariff** (CET). Once inside the EU, goods may be moved around freely.

Every customs union is also a free trade area, but not every free trade area is a customs union. Although Mexico, the USA and Canada have formed the free trade area called NAFTA, they have no intention of proceeding to a customs union.

But the EU is much more than simply a customs union. Founded by the Treaty of Rome in 1957, its original aim was to proceed to 'ever closer union' between member states. This ambiguous phrase is capable of a wide variety of interpretations, but certainly leaves room for the claim that the ultimate objective of the EU is political union with a single government.

From this it should be clear that the EU's attitude to free trade is at best ambiguous. While keen to promote free trade between members — and the adoption of the euro is an enormous step towards this target — it has no particular interest in promoting free trade between the EU and the rest of the world. Hence the EU is frequently criticised by the **World Trade Organisation** (WTO), particularly for its **common agricultural policy** (CAP), which places non-EU farmers at a severe disadvantage. By taxing their exports to the EU, it also significantly increases the prices that EU consumers have to pay for their food.

The political and institutional aspects of the EU are of less immediate concern to this course, but their continued evolution will have a profound impact on the way that EU business develops. The principal institutions of the EU are as follows:

- The equivalent of the British cabinet is the **Council of Ministers**. This is the real authority in the EU. It has a variable membership: if, for example, member governments wished to discuss agriculture, then the council would consist of member states' agriculture ministers.
- The **European Commission** puts the decisions of the Council of Ministers into effect. This is an administrative body, the equivalent of the UK civil service.
- While there is a **European Parliament**, with elected members from every EU region, its ability to make law is considerably weaker than that of national parliaments.

The European Union is an expanding organisation. Its original six members have grown to 15. These are Ireland, the United Kingdom and France; Sweden, Finland and Denmark; the Netherlands, Belgium and Luxembourg; Germany and Austria; Portugal, Spain, Italy and Greece. Notable by their absence are Switzerland and Norway, both of which have voted against membership in referenda. A further 10 mainly East European nations have had their applications for membership accepted with effect from 2004. Turkey would also like to join, but has to overcome opposition from Greece — an existing member and Turkey's historic enemy. Romania and Bulgaria also hope to join at some stage. Existing and potential members are shown in Figure 16.1.

Figure 16.1 Members of the EU in 2003 and likely new members

GLOSSARY

common agricultural policy (CAP): protectionist EU policy helping farmers in member countries
common external tariff (CET): fixed import duties into all EU member states
Council of Ministers (of EU): EU executive, comprising ministers from member states
customs union: group of countries with internal free trade and a common external tariff

GLOSSARY

European Commission: the administration of the EU
European Parliament: the legislative body, still relatively weak
European Union (EU): customs union with political aspirations
free trade area: group of states adopting mutual free trade
North American Free Trade Association (NAFTA): free trade bloc of the USA, Canada and Mexico
Single Market Act (1993): gave EU-wide free movement of inputs and outputs
World Trade Organisation (WTO): international body promoting free trade

UNIT 2

At the end of this unit, you should be able to:

1 Comment on economic and political integration between members of the EU.

2 Briefly describe the World Trade Organisation.

Economic and political integration within the EU

The **integration** of any two or more economic agents describes their drawing together, an overshadowing of the differences between them, and the creation of a new unity. In any free trade area or customs union, some measure of integration is part of the original deal. There would be no point in the members signing up to the **trade bloc** unless they actually desired closer integration. As we saw in Unit 1, an 'ever closer union' was envisaged at the original founding of the Common Market, as the EU was then called.

Part of the integration that occurs in any trade bloc is **trade diversion**. Some of the trade that used to take place, say, between the UK and the USA will be diverted to the EU instead. Given that UK/USA import tariffs stay in place, trade with tariff-free Germany will now appear more attractive to UK companies. The most significant example of trade diversion has been in agriculture. As explained in Unit 1, the CAP places non-EU farmers at a severe disadvantage when selling to the EU. Not only are non-EU farmers hampered by the common external tariff, but the EU guarantees its own farmers generous prices for their goods. In fact, about half the **EU budget** is spent buying up EU farm produce. Reform of this system has proved very difficult.

On top of trade diversion, **trade creation** will also take place. Now that trade with Europe is tax-free, some *additional* trade should be generated that simply did not take place before.

The next level of integration is **harmonisation**. For example, the UK is 'harmonising' its weights and measures with the EU by phasing out the use of Imperial measurements. In April 2001, Mr Steve Thoburn, a market trader in Sunderland, was successfully prosecuted for using scales calibrated only in pounds and ounces, and has at the time of writing lost his appeals. Other areas of harmonisation include the use of commercial language: for example, ensuring that goods labelled 'chocolate' or 'champagne' meet common standards in every EU country.

The argument in favour of harmonisation is that it will be less confusing to consumers if everyone uses the same measures and means the same thing by the same business terms. However, Eurosceptics see a loss of sovereignty in the way harmonisation is developing. They argue that harmonisation could eventually be extended to member countries' legal systems, currencies, defence policy — perhaps even their languages — and that the EU would effectively be a single country.

Following harmonisation, the next level of integration is economic **convergence**. This means that the macroeconomic variables in every EU country are roughly the same. Specifically, government borrowing levels, inflation rates, interest rates, economic growth rates, exchange rate movements and unemployment rates are similar. This is an exceptionally ambitious target: after all, growth and unemployment rates are frequently very different in the different regions of the UK. It also happens that over the past decade the UK has shown greater convergence with the USA than with mainland Europe.

The concept of convergence has assumed particular significance for the UK at the present time. The present Labour government has said that it will only recommend that the UK joins the euro if the so-called **convergence criteria** are met: that is, if the UK's economy is performing in similar ways to the rest of the EU. The subject of the euro is addressed further in Chapter 24 of the A2 course.

Finally, there is an alternative vision of the EU that does not envisage a single European state as the ultimate goal. The alternative vision is 'an association of independent sovereign states' — a customs union with little else added on. This is what the Conservatives fought for in the June 2001 general election, with conspicuous lack of success. A key part of this vision is the concept of **subsidiarity** — the idea that decisions should be taken as closely as possible to the people whom they affect. So, for example, parking restrictions in your local street should be decided by your city council, while the status of the Welsh language in Wales should be decided by the Welsh Assembly. The appointment of a British diplomat to Washington should be decided at national level, while the CAP should be decided at European level. Targets for reducing the hole in the ozone layer above Antarctica would have to be decided at United Nations level.

Conservatives complain that there is no practical mechanism by which the principle of subsidiarity can be put into effect. On the contrary, the principle of **acquis communautaire** states that, once any aspect of policy passes to the EU, it should never be delegated back to the nation states.

GLOSSARY

acquis communautaire: function of government acquired by the EU
convergence: drawing closer (e.g. two economies)
convergence criteria: tests to be met before the Labour government will join the euro
EU budget: EU's forecast for annual income and expenditure
harmonisation: alignment of regulations of all EU states
integration (of economies): several countries becoming well knit together
subsidiarity within EU: principle of delegating decisions to lowest appropriate level
trade bloc, trading group: free trade area or customs union
trade creation: an increase in international trade
trade diversion: switching of international trade to another area

The world economic order

International trade is policed by the World Trade Organisation (WTO). Since China joined the WTO in 2001, every major country in the world is now included among its 140 members. Its mission is to promote free trade and to adjudicate in trade disputes between members, although its powers of enforcement are limited. Chapter 24 of the A2 course returns to this subject.

Chapter 17
AS papers (Units 1 and 2)

The AS scheme of assessment

Unit	Method of assessment	Comment	AS weighting
1	Examination	1 hour 15 minutes	30%
2	Examination	1 hour 45 minutes	40%
3	Coursework (see Chapter 18)	Two pieces: 1 from Unit 1 content; 1 from Unit 2 content	30%

Marking schemes

The four criteria examiners are looking for are:

- *Knowledge* — can you show that you have learnt and understand the meaning of the technical terms?
- *Application* — can you use technical terms in a new context, showing a degree of understanding?
- *Analysis* — can you comment in an informed and logical way on the question, relating it to the data given?
- *Evaluation* — can you produce a balanced response to the question, bringing together your own knowledge and the data provided into a convincing conclusion?

Short questions for 2 marks concentrate on knowledge. In a long question for 12 marks, the balance is likely to be 2 marks for knowledge and application, and 10 marks for analysis and evaluation.

Approaching a question

- *Have you understood it?* See if you can rephrase a difficult question in your own words. Try saying the question out loud — in an actual examination, you will have to whisper it under your breath! Look out for the 'command' word. Are you asked to 'explain' or 'discuss' or 'assess' or 'evaluate'? Make sure that you do whatever you have been asked to.
- *Is there a clue to the answer in the data provided?* You need to read through any text given before you attempt the questions. Sometimes the answer will simply be there in the text. More often, there will be a clue to help you. Highlight any phrase that you will need to refer to in your answer.
- *Which part of the specification will the answer come from?* It should be easy to spot whether the question is about supply and demand (Chapter 1); or an individual business (Chapters 3–8); or an industry-wide issue (Chapters 9–11); or a national issue (Chapters 12–14); or an international issue (Chapters 15 and 16). It is sensible to *learn by heart* your 16 chapter headings. If you are stuck for an answer, it can be helpful to run through the chapters in your head to see which ones might provide relevant information.

The layout of questions

The question layout will not necessarily stay the same year by year, but in 2002–03 AS questions fall into two broad categories:

- data–response questions
- two-part essays for 20 or 30 marks each

At present there is a modest degree of choice, although some Unit 2 data–response questions are compulsory.

This chapter will look at one example of each type of question: a relatively easy data–response question from a Unit 1 paper, and a rather harder 30-mark essay from a Unit 2 paper. The questions are followed by suggested answers and comments.

Unit 1 past paper extract (May 2002 exam)

Evidence A
Jaguar makes its mark on Merseyside

There are an awful lot of neat gardens on Merseyside these days — roving gangs of car workers   1
have helped to improve churchyards and community centres around the Halewood car plant.
This was not out of pure charity, it was all part of a 'bonding exercise' by Jaguar's owners, Ford.
It was aimed at ending almost 40 years of mistrust and suspicion between management and
workforce at the Merseyside factory. Only then did the managers feel that the workers could   5
be let loose on building Jaguar's new range of luxury saloons.

Halewood employees have been given one million hours of training, with 700,000 hours on
the job. Each employee has had 350 hours of training. Halewood was once dubbed the worst
car factory in Britain for its industrial relations. A climate of hostility — between workers and
management, but also between workers — had steadily worsened. Now workers are proud of   10
their refurbished factory — and they have started a love affair with Jaguar, not just building
cars but building something the customer is prepared to pay a high 'premium' price for.

(Source: adapted from *The Times*, 21 April 2001)

Evidence B
Survey calls for changes

'Low inflation has put paid to regular wage rises and bonuses and the switch to   1
 fewer management posts means there is less incentive to get on,' says an Income Data Services
research group survey. Employers must now look to alternative means of motivation. They must
learn from 'younger' firms how to create a stimulating workplace without relying just on pay
to motivate staff. Helping workers with their careers, giving them some influence   5
over their jobs and closely linking bonuses to results are among the lessons a growing number
of companies will have to heed. 'Flexitime', allowing workers to choose their own hours within
minimum limitations, is particularly useful for working parents. 'Duvet days', allowing some
days off simply because employees want a break, are advocated by stress expert Cary Cooper.

The well-established department store, John Lewis, could probably teach younger   10
companies a thing or two. Staff, or 'partners' as they are known, have the use of three ocean-
going yachts, subsidised holidays, half-price theatre tickets, three golf courses, a campsite and
annual profit bonuses. The government has taken the profit sharing motive to heart with the
announcement of a new incentive scheme aimed at helping companies to recruit, motivate

and retain staff. The incentives will enable employers to give shares in the company to   15
key employees.

(Source: *BBC online*, September 2001)

(a) **What is meant by:**
- **'low inflation' (Evidence B, line 1)**   (2 marks)
- **'motivation' (Evidence B, line 3)**   (2 marks)
- **'incentives' (Evidence B, line 15)?**   (2 marks)

(b) **Identify reasons why customers might be prepared to pay a high 'premium' price for Jaguars.**   (4 marks)

(c) **Why might 'flexitime' and 'duvet days' be more appropriate for some employers than others?**   (6 marks)

(d) **Assess the likely impact of Ford's Halewood training programme on both cash flow and profits.**   (6 marks)

(e) **Assess the relevance of the ideas of Maslow to the treatment of workers by Jaguar and by John Lewis.**   (8 marks)

Suggested answer

(a) ● Inflation measures the annual increase in average retail prices. So 'low inflation' means that prices are on average hardly rising at all, perhaps by only 2% per annum.

    ● 'Motivation' refers to a person's commitment to a task. So in this case, if pay rises no longer encourage workers, companies must look for other ways to get all workers trying as hard as they can.

    ● 'Incentives' are the benefits that help to motivate people. In this case, giving key employees shares acts as an incentive because if they work hard then the value of their shares will rise.

> Each part of question (a) needs a very brief explanation and the shortest of illustrations to get 2 marks.

(b) Customers might be prepared to pay more for a Jaguar than for other cars because the other three elements in the marketing mix are sufficiently good for the customer to believe the car was worth more. So the 'product' might be of unusually high quality — the acceleration could be exceptional, or the leather and walnut trim attractive to the eye.

Equally, the car's 'promotion' might successfully communicate the concept of a luxury car. Perhaps celebrity characters on film and TV use it, or perhaps a Jaguar car wins a grand prix event.

Either way, the car becomes more valuable in the eyes of potential customers and this justifies the higher, 'premium' price.

> To 'identify' could just mean to 'list', but since there are 4 marks going, a little bit of explanation and commentary is required. (A simple list of 4 points would probably not get more than 2 marks out of the possible 4.) Two different reasons are needed with a brief comment on each. Marketing and production are the obvious areas to consider.

(c) Flexitime and duvet days only work if the production process of the employer involved can accommodate it. So an advertising agency might be able to tell its creative team:

'Come up with a proposal this time next week.' The team members might agree tasks and then decide to meet for an initial discussion at 4 p.m. the following day. Until then, how they organise their time is up to them — provided they have their bit ready for the meeting.

On the other hand, switchboards have to be manned at set hours; fire, police and ambulance crews have to provide 24-hour cover; and teachers have to be in front of their classes at the advertised times. There is very little scope for 'duvet days' in any of these jobs. Of course, any employee can call in sick and those with a cold might decide they were not well enough to work. A sympathetic employer might turn a blind eye if this happened rather more often than was strictly necessary — this might amount to an unofficial 'duvet day' policy.

Equally, police officers on duty might be compelled to turn up when they are needed to patrol the streets, but be allowed to do their paperwork either at the end of the shift or before the next one started. This would amount to flexitime: the core time being the shift.

In conclusion, employers have to consider the needs of their customers before allowing any kind of flexibility over hours — but they also need to consider how easy it is to recruit the people they want, and ask themselves whether a little bit of flexibility would enable them to attract better qualified staff.

> This question needs careful reading. It refers to employers, not employees. The basic idea lying behind the question is: which employers need their workers turning up at exact, specific times, and which employers only need the work done by a certain time but do not mind precisely when it is done?
>
> With 6 marks available, you must get into some kind of analysis, and offer a conclusion.

(d) 'Training' describes instruction aimed at equipping people to do specific jobs — in this case, build Jaguar cars. Training is a type of investment: you spend now and hope to get a return in the future.

Like any investment, training must at first have a negative impact on cash flow. Trainers have to be paid — and the workers also have to be paid even though they are not producing any cars. However, if the training is successful, the cars then produced will be of better quality and therefore sell for higher prices. If the training has been properly thought through, all the money lost will be recovered and more gained. Cash flow will improve beyond its original position.

Likewise profits could eventually go up, if not in the year when most training takes place then in the following years as the benefits of the training come on stream.

In conclusion, we cannot predict the 'likely impact' on cash flow and profits. The outcome will depend on the strategic planning and implementation skills of Ford's management. The only thing we can be sure about is that cash flow will at first worsen.

> Here you are asked to 'assess', so some kind of analysis and judgement is needed. At the same time, you are given two questions rolled into one — make sure both angles are covered.

(e) Maslow's main point was that people work not only for the cash that meets their daily, physiological needs, but for a variety of other needs as well. Between Jaguar and John Lewis, all the other needs are illustrated.

First, people's need for security is provided by Jaguar's training programme. The fact that Ford is prepared to pay for 'one million hours of training' demonstrates a long-term commitment to the Halewood plant. Additionally, the training will make Jaguar workers more employable if they decide to leave. Either way, their 'security needs' have been met.

Second, the 'social' or 'affiliation' needs of the John Lewis staff are very generously catered for with an impressive array of leisure activities available to them at prices subsidised by the company. While this looks very expensive, given the size of the John Lewis chain, the unit cost per employee could actually be quite low.

Third, the 'status' or 'esteem' needs have been met in small, but important, ways. Calling staff 'partners' speaks of a desire to treat staff on a basis of equality. And paying for your workers to clean up the neighbourhood can only increase the esteem in which Halewood workers are held by the local community — and also increase the esteem in which Ford is held.

Finally, the 'self-actualisation' or 'creative' needs of Halewood workers may be met by their higher levels of skill following training — and the higher quality of car they are now equipped to build.

In conclusion, Maslow's ideas seem very relevant to both companies — and, I suggest, to all employers. Nothing is free and the company's efforts to meet fully the needs of their staff will undoubtedly cost money. But the expenditures may well pay for themselves in terms of reduced staff turnover, lower levels of absenteeism and a better-quality final product.

Both companies' humane employment policies may well be tested in a recession when cash is short and savings have to be made. However, John Lewis' survival over many decades and through many recessions suggests that it is on to a winner with its personnel management approach.

> This question illustrates the importance of a secure factual grasp of the specification content. If you don't know Maslow, you will probably get zero. However, if you only repeat Maslow you will be lucky to get 2 out of the 8 marks. You are asked to apply the theory to two groups of workers, and 'assess the relevance' of Maslow's ideas.
>
> You would be well advised not to begin with a blow-by-blow account of Maslow. This would take up too much time. Instead, your knowledge of Maslow should come out as you deal directly with the question. You must also make explicit reference to the two companies mentioned.

Unit 2 past paper extract (May 2002 exam)

Section B

> **(a) Examine the likely consequences of 'a strong pound' for British firms.**
>
> (10 marks)
>
> (Note: the quotation 'a strong pound' refers back to the previous data–response question, which is not included here. It began with the following brief reference to the exchange rate: 'Britain's motor industry has been so badly affected by falling sales and the strong pound, that concern about the environment may not be expected to be high on their agenda...'.)

(b) Critically examine the measures a government might introduce to help British firms to sell their goods abroad, and the impact that such measures may have upon economic growth. (20 marks)

Suggested answer

(a) A 'strong pound' means that the value of sterling is higher in relation to other currencies than it normally is. So if, for example, the normal exchange rate was £1 = €1.5, then a strong pound would be £1 = €2.0. The pound would be worth 33% more than the usual amount of euros. Put another way, 1 euro would have fallen in value from 67 pence to 50 pence.

When the external value of sterling rises, all UK exporters stand to lose out. Suppose Rover wanted to export cars to Europe for £5,000. At the old exchange rate, those in euroland would have to pay €7,500 for Rover to get its sterling price. At the new exchange rate, they will be charged €10,000. Clearly sales will fall very steeply. The *extent* of the fall will depend on the price elasticity of demand for Rover cars. Since they have many close substitutes in the form of other cars, demand is likely to be elastic and the fall in demand very great. Only products with no close substitutes and very low PED are likely to maintain sales levels.

Of course, Rover could decide to stick to the old euro price of €7,500, but in this case it will have to accept a mere £3,750 per car against the £5,000 it used to receive. Whatever it does, Rover's profits from euroland sales will fall. Fortunately for British exporters, a 33% increase in the external exchange rate for sterling is unusual. But even a 10% rise means they have to charge about 10% more to their overseas customers, if they are to receive the same in sterling for each unit sold.

For British importers, on the other hand, a rise in the external value of sterling is very good news. Bottles of champagne that used to cost £10 (€15) to import now only cost £7.50 (still €15). The UK distributor can either cut the sterling price and enjoy increased sales, or alternatively go on charging the old sterling price and make an extra £2.50 profit on each bottle.

For many British firms, the consequences will be much less than this. The majority of small to medium-size service companies will neither export nor import, so the exchange rate will have little effect on them. And other companies might import raw materials and then export some of their output, so the two effects will cancel each other out. Again, companies that know they are exposed to exchange rate risk can insure themselves against adverse swings by trading currency in forward markets.

In conclusion, the effect on British firms of a 'strong pound' depends entirely upon the nature and extent of their overseas trading. Some will gain, others will lose, and for many there will be no change. But we may be sure that the losers will complain loudly and blame the strong pound (and probably the government) for their misfortune. They might do better to reflect on why they were so vulnerable to an adverse shock in the first place.

> A good answer will include a brief numerical example, which will help candidates to clarify their thoughts. Crucially, it will consider the consequences for exporters and importers. You may wish to refer to Chapter 15, Unit 2, where this issue has been discussed. With 10 marks going, strong analysis and evaluation are needed for a top mark.

(b) Governments, like other economic agents, function best when they try to do a few things well rather than a bit of everything. It may therefore be asked whether it is really the job of government to help UK firms export their goods. Government is already heavily involved in providing public and merit goods, reducing inequality, ensuring that market structures are competitive and controlling the macro economy, especially inflation. Where government became heavily involved in running companies through the nationalisation programme of the 1960s and 1970s the result was mismanagement and waste. It is also important to remember that most forms of help to exporters are going to cost money and ultimately lead to higher taxes. Perhaps the best form of 'help' is simply to control government expenditure and keep taxes low.

Part (a) of this question showed that a 'strong pound' makes it difficult for UK firms to export. One way of helping exporters would therefore be to operate a fixed exchange rate — presumably a *low* fixed exchange rate. This was last tried in 1990–92, when the UK joined what was known as the exchange rate mechanism. As it turned out, the exchange rate was too high and was one of the causes of the 1990–92 recession. The recession did not end until the UK was forced out of the exchange rate mechanism. It could therefore be argued that fixed exchange rates slow down economic growth — to address the second half of this question.

If the UK joined the euro, this would lead to a permanently fixed exchange rate with our European partners. The removal of exchange rate uncertainty would help exports to Europe — but the cost would be more uncertainty about inflation. At the moment, inflation is controlled by the Bank of England manipulating interest rates to achieve the 2.5% p.a. inflation target. If the UK joined the euro, the European Central Bank would set interest rates with the whole of the EU in mind. We would have to expect the UK inflation rate to be more volatile — and that would *slow down* economic growth.

An economy is rather like a balloon. If you stop it bulging in one place, it is more likely to bulge somewhere else. That is, if you fix the exchange rate, you are more likely to have a volatile inflation rate. At the moment, the UK has opted for a fixed inflation target and accepted a volatile exchange rate as a result.

A more thoughtful approach to helping exporters is for the UK government to campaign for the reduction of trade barriers. This will also help importers, and by encouraging international competition will make every industry more competitive. This will not only help exporters but also encourage economic growth as each country specialises in what it does best. Of course, free trade always results in some losers. In every country, some firms will be unable to cope with the new competition — but overall each country stands to gain.

The government should, therefore, support the work of the WTO. The recent accession of China to the WTO should certainly make it easier for every country to trade with China, which is the most populous nation and has a rapid economic growth rate. Furthermore, the UK government should support the WTO in its attempts to reform the common agricultural policy (CAP). By taxing food from the rest of the world, the CAP makes it easier for UK farmers to export. But it also invites retaliation in other areas. For example, UK steel exports are currently suffering because of the USA's measures to protect its domestic steel industry.

There are a few specific measures that can be sensibly targeted at UK exporters. Given that the UK maintains diplomatic missions around the world, it is relatively cheap to add

trade advisers to UK embassies, who can then organise fact-finding trips for groups of UK businesspeople. The local UK representative on the ground will have the local knowledge that is so important when conducting business overseas, and may be able to provide introductions to potential local business partners.

The competitiveness of exporters is influenced by the quality of their goods and the skills of their workers. If government support for education and training can lead to improving the skills and productivity of workers, this could eventually help UK firms to compete, assuming the support offered is cost effective.

In conclusion, there is little merit in the UK government using a great deal of taxpayers' money to 'help exporters'. There may be some relatively cheap activities, like trade missions, where the government can use its existing expertise effectively. But in general, the government would do well to consider the bigger picture. Low taxes, low inflation, free trade and low levels of regulation will all encourage economic growth. Exporters will benefit along with everyone else. There is no specific market failure tied up with exporting which would justify a greater level of government intervention.

> This is a challenging question, particularly in view of the large number of marks available. There is normally a connection between parts (a) and (b) of an essay question. In this case, the effect of a strong pound on British exporters provides a useful paragraph.
>
> Thorough knowledge of the specification is needed, and some imagination to link what you have learnt to the title. In addition, a lot of analysis and evaluation are required to score highly, and care must be taken to answer both halves of the question.

Note: Edexcel accepts no responsibility whatsoever for the accuracy or method of working in the answers given.

Chapter 18
AS coursework (Unit 3)

Introduction

Towards the end of the AS year, your teacher has to submit *two* pieces of coursework from each candidate. Strictly speaking, one should be based around Unit 1 and the other around Unit 2. However, most topics are covered in both units, so you may find that you have considerable freedom of subject choice. Your two pieces combined count for 30% of your total AS mark.

Many teachers will expect you to do more than two pieces of coursework, and will select the best two for the examination board. Teachers are allowed to give you a great deal of help with coursework, so be sure to use them to the full. If you have the opportunity for your teachers to look over your coursework before you hand it in, take it. Their advice may help you to push your coursework marks up by several grades.

Of course, your teachers can only run an eye over your coursework if it is completed well in advance of the final deadline set by your centre. And that is the key to a good project.

Start *early* and aim to finish *early*. This gives you plenty of time to make improvements as you go along, and to explore new avenues that you might not have thought of at the beginning.

What you need to include

- The suggested maximum word count is 1,250 words, excluding appendices.
- A typical format might be title page, contents page, introduction, between three and six main sections, a conclusion, a list of sources and appendices.
- Make the presentation interesting. Photographs, diagrams, charts and cartoons all enliven your project and help you to communicate your ideas.

The marking scheme

Each project is marked out of 100, under four criteria worth 25 marks each. Below is an extract from the specification showing what you need to do to get within each mark band on each of the four criteria. You should bear in mind that the extent of your 'knowledge and application' is not expected to be as great for your first project as for your second.

Knowledge

0–6	Has shown some elements of knowledge
7–12	Has shown knowledge of concepts and ideas in a generalised way
13–18	Has shown a good knowledge of concepts and ideas
19–25	Has shown a wide-ranging knowledge of relevant concepts and ideas

Application

0–6	Has attempted to use some concepts and ideas
7–12	Has used some concepts and ideas
13–18	Has used a relevant selection of concepts and ideas
19–25	Has used a wide range of relevant concepts and ideas

Analysis

0–6	Has made a limited attempt to use analysis
7–12	Has used some relevant analysis
13–18	Has used good analysis of economic and business problems
19–25	Has used wide-ranging analysis of economic and business problems

Evaluation

0–6	Has attempted to evaluate
7–12	Has evaluated partially and reached some simple conclusions
13–18	Has evaluated well and reached organised conclusions
19–25	Has evaluated effectively, reaching conclusions that are original

Knowledge and application go together. You are being marked on how well you have shown that you know and understand the course content. The key to whether you really understand an idea is whether you can apply it in a new context. A good piece of coursework will show that you can do exactly that. A typical project should use, in an appropriate context, a dozen or more of the terms appearing in bold type in this revision guide. Some markers find it helpful if you underline your technical terms so that they can pick them up as they read through the project.

Analysis and evaluation also go together. You have to put something of *yourself* into the project. Analysis means that you have commented in a logical and informed way on the data you have uncovered. Evaluation means that you have *related* what you have discovered to your project title, ideally in an original and perceptive judgement.

These are more advanced skills than knowledge and application — but they still carry half the marks. Some students prefer to have a brief conclusion at the end of each chapter. Others have a longer final conclusion. Whatever you do, make sure it is obvious to the reader where your analytical and evaluative sections are. Tired teachers with a stack of projects to mark will appreciate your clarity. And you do not want them to miss anything that will give you some marks.

Remember, any piece of coursework is an exercise in *communication*. What are you trying to say exactly? If you do not know yourself, no one else will be able to work it out either. And do not be too ambitious. It is always obvious to markers when students are using words that they do not understand. Say it clearly, say it well, keep it simple.

How to choose a title

Teachers may suggest titles to you, but are normally more than happy if you come up with your own. The key point about any title is that it should enable you to get 100 % of the marks. Here are some guidelines.

- Consider how easy your title will be to *research*, ideally using both primary and secondary sources. The internet has transformed people's ability to find out about an enormous range of topics, but you still need to be careful. If you are looking at one or two companies, either choose a large company (or companies) about which there will be a lot of published information, and which you might be able to visit as a customer; or choose a small company (or companies) where you have some personal contact. For example, a family member or family friend might work there and give you an introduction to people whom you could interview. Be imaginative in your choice. Students have written excellent projects based on a business they visited on holiday, whether at home or abroad.
- Reflect your *personal interests*. If you are a keen basketball player, violinist, filmgoer or user of make-up, why not base a project around your enthusiasm? Are you taking part in Young Enterprise? There is almost certainly a project title there. Or link in with another school subject. How about 'Creating a global brand: how effective are the marketing strategies of Salvador Dali?' Or 'The economics of satellite launches: what has changed the cost per kilo of payload sent into geosynchronous orbit?' The point is that it is *your* project. You are much more likely to write a good one on a subject that interests you.
- Give yourself room both for using *business and economics terms*, and also for *analysis and evaluation*. The title 'What is the marketing mix of Tesco?' does not leave you much scope for comment. Better would be 'Why is Tesco the market leader in food retailing? An evaluation of its marketing mix.' Equally, 'Is Damien Hirst a good artist?' is probably straying too far from the subject area. But 'Damien Hirst — production genius or marketing genius?' would enable you to discuss his art in a business context.
- Consider a *topical title*. In 2001–02, the foot-and-mouth outbreak and the 11 September atrocity provided obvious events with a clear business and economics angle. Examples of titles based on these subjects are given below. When you write your projects, there will be other recent events that will lend themselves to analysis.

- If you are short of time, consider a title based on just *one aspect of one company*. Projects do not have to be broad. Provided you apply a wide variety of specialist terms within your particular area, and include full analysis and evaluation from a reasonable range of sources, that is enough to score well. Many of the best investigations have a specific and limited focus.

Some ideas for titles

It would be possible to get 100% with any of the titles below. However, titles that reflect your *own* interests would be even better. The numbers in brackets after each project indicate which chapter numbers in this revision guide are most helpful in answering that title.

For a *first or second project* (information from Unit 1 would be sufficient):

- What HRM techniques might enable firm X to get away with paying relatively low wages? (6)
- How might the government's more relaxed attitude to cannabis affect the Rizla Company (providers of rolling paper)? (1)
- How can the library at X attract more teenagers? (4, 5, 8)
- What were the most important reasons behind the closure of firm X in year Y? (any)
- What factors affect demand for the products at the X pub? (1, 3–8)
- What competitive advantage does newsagent X have over its rivals? (3–8)
- Evaluate how Boots is responding to the threat of supermarket chemists' departments. (3–8)
- To what extent are X bakery and Y sandwich shop in competition with each other? (1, 3–8)
- How does X use IT to create a competitive advantage? (1, 3–8)
- Does profit motivate the owners of small shops? A comparison of X and Y. (3, 8)
- To what extent has John Lewis achieved its mission statement? (3, 8)
- How could the England cricket board improve its efficiency? (5)

For a *second project* (information from Units 1 and 2):

- How and why did Microsoft alter the launch of Windows XP following the atrocity of 11 September 2001? (4)
- Evaluate the action taken by the US government after 11 September 2001 to avoid a recession. (12)
- How competitive is the market for video hire in the town of X? (9)
- Will UK call centres survive in the face of overseas competition? (4–5, 8, 15)
- How can Bible House extend and improve its marketing strategies? (4)
- What factors have influenced the Manchester United share price in the last year? (any)
- Evaluate the effect of the foot-and-mouth outbreak of 2000 on the tourist business of X. (1, 3–8)
- How fast is the UK economy likely to grow in the next year, and why? (12)
- Assess the impact on pub X in Kent of the illegal sale of alcohol brought across the Channel, allegedly for personal use. (1, 15–16)

The A2 specification
Units 4–6

Chapter 19
Increasing business competitiveness: marketing and production

The key idea in Unit 4, the core section of the A2 course, is *competitiveness*. This issue will be approached at the level of the individual firm, the industry and the economy as a whole — and finally from an international perspective. The broad outline of the AS course, which you have already studied, will be followed. The A2 course builds on the AS work, and we shall frequently refer back to it.

The opening two chapters of the A2 course — Chapters 19 and 20 — examine how individual companies can improve their competitive position. The discussion is based on the themes of marketing, production, human resource (personnel) management and planning — themes with which you will already be familiar from the AS course.

At the end of this chapter, you should be able to:

1 Explain how market segmentation, market positioning and exports can be used to increase competitiveness.

2 Comment on attempts to differentiate products in commodity markets.

3 Explain the reasoning behind a firm's decision to adopt either a high- or a low-price strategy.

4 Explain how an efficient cost structure can lead to increased competitiveness.

5 Explain how differentiation through quality can lead to increased competitiveness.

Market segmentation (see also Chapter 4)

One common way to improve a company's competitiveness is to tailor the product to the precise needs of a relatively small group of customers. Such an approach is known as *segmentation* because the market is divided into a number of smaller groups. These groups may be defined in terms of age, income, gender, geographical location, lifestyle or personal tastes.

The company may try to cater for more than one segment. So supermarkets typically offer a 'value' range of own-label products for their poorer customers, and a web-based delivery service for their richer ones. Or again, credit-card companies offer gold or platinum cards with a number of extras, such as free travel insurance, in return for a higher annual fee. Sometimes the cards are only offered to people whose income is above a particular level.

More commonly, companies will focus on one particular market segment. For example, Saga sells holidays exclusively to the over-50s, while Club Med has traditionally focused on those aged 18–30.

Market positioning

This term describes a segment's location within the context of an entire industry, and is usually used with income segments; hence the phrases 'up-market', 'down-market' and 'mid-market' to describe products catering for the rich, the poor and those in the middle. Steadily rising standards of living have led to a drift towards up-market providers and products. Companies may seek to reposition themselves upwards in the hope of avoiding competition — but rarely downwards.

Exporting

One way of looking at exporting is that the market is being segmented along geographical lines. Many poor countries have a relatively small market for the type of consumer and investment goods considered commonplace in the West. As a result, many large companies will simply not bother to sell into these markets, thereby leaving monopoly possibilities to those that make the effort. A company selling modern washing machines to Mozambique, or designer sandals in Senegal, may well find that it is the only company to do so. Knowledge of local ways of doing business and contacts in government departments are the prerequisites for success in exporting to many developing countries.

Tactics for differentiation in commodity markets

So important is it for a company to differentiate its products from those of its competitors that even commodity products like petrol and electricity are heavily promoted. In the case of petrol, the major companies each have a distinctive logo by which motorists can recognise their brand. In an attempt to build customer loyalty, the major petrol retailers offer points that frequent users can exchange for various rewards.

With electricity, the problem of differentiation is even greater, as each firm can only supply precisely the same commodity as every other. Some companies, such as Northern Electric, have tried to brand their products by creating a regional identity. Others, such as United Utilities in the northwest, emphasise their ability to provide both gas and electricity, and offer small discounts to customers who sign up for both.

A tactic that has served the public less well has been to produce ever more complex tariffs, which prevent the customer from making easy price comparisons between rivals. This approach is common with telephone companies and credit-card suppliers as well as gas and electricity businesses. Having failed to differentiate themselves from each other, companies' response has been to conceal the true price that they are charging. Combined with aggressive door-to-door selling, this approach has gained some companies significant market share.

All these tactics are attempts to shift the market structure away from the perfectly competitive end of the spectrum — which is where commodity products tend to be found. This was discussed back in Chapter 9.

High-price strategies

All the above ways of increasing a company's competitiveness will, if successful, enable the company to charge a higher price. The normal method of pricing used by most companies is simply to charge as much as they think they can get away with. This approach is known as **demand-based** or **market-orientated pricing**. Essentially, it asks what is the highest price that potential customers will be prepared to pay before significant numbers are lost due to price resistance. It is particularly common among small businesses, which rely on a unique selling proposition to charge rather more than normal.

When a company is first to the market with a new or radically improved product, the possibility exists of charging very high prices before competitors catch up. In effect, the company has a temporary monopoly until the product is imitated. Unless the product can be defended with a patent, it will only be a matter of months before the firm's rivals create copycat products. In these circumstances, the high-price strategy that the firm is likely to adopt is known as **creaming** or **skimming**. It is commonly used in high-technology industries where there is a constant stream of products incorporating technical advances.

A logical variant of this approach is **price discrimination** — charging different groups of customers different prices for the same product. This only works if two conditions are met. First, the company must be able to identify two groups of people with a different willingness to pay. These might be firms and households, or people of different ages, or people who book different amounts of time in advance, or people who use a service at different times of day. Second, there has to be something to prevent those charged less from buying on behalf of those charged more. Cinemas can offer children half-price tickets because a child cannot watch a film on behalf of an adult, but supermarkets cannot offer children half-price food or their parents would simply take them to do the shopping. Where groups can be separated, those willing to pay more (who will have less price-elastic demand) can be charged higher prices. Extra profit is likely to be the result.

GLOSSARY

creaming, skimming: charging a high price for the latest product
demand-based (market-orientated) pricing: pricing strategy based on customers' willingness to pay
price discrimination: charging different groups of people different prices

Low-price strategies

Within any industry there is normally space for a few companies to sell their products strictly on the basis of the low prices they charge. Aiming at the low-income market segment, they stand on its head the normal argument about product differentiation. Rather than seeking to justify a higher price, they make a virtue of the fact that they charge a low price. For this strategy to work, the company needs to charge *consistently* low prices over a long period of time. It needs to establish a reputation as a low-price provider. The Esso 'Pricewatch' campaign and the ASDA slogan 'Permanently Low Prices For Ever' are both attempts to establish a low-price reputation.

However, as economic growth takes place and standards of living rise, the number of consumers who are attracted by this approach inevitably falls. The low-price niche market shrinks and some companies seek to reposition themselves within a higher price band. Argos is an example of a company currently undergoing this process.

There are circumstances when companies use low prices either for just a few products or for a short space of time. In the former case this is known as a **loss leader** pricing strategy. For example, a pub might sell food at or near cost price while making its real profits on drinks. In this context the food is the 'loss leader'. Loss leaders should be heavily advertised or there is little point in having them; hence the country pubs that display signs such as 'Three-course Sunday lunch for only £4.99'.

Firms using a low price for a short space of time while they get established in their market are adopting **penetration pricing**. The special offers used on the opening day of a new shop, and the low prices charged by an individual seeking to set up as a plumber or car mechanic, are illustrations of this principle.

An illegal low-price strategy is **predatory pricing**, which involves charging a low price with the intention of driving out smaller rivals. The large company is more able to bear the temporary losses of pricing low, perhaps subsidising the loss-making venture from other product lines. When the small company withdraws, the survivor then raises the price. Microsoft's offer of free internet software, designed to drive out Netscape, is a notorious example. The tactic has also been used by airlines trying to drive smaller competitors off particular routes.

While predatory pricing is illegal, it is very difficult to prove. It is normally in the interests of consumers for companies to charge low prices. The accused firm can always say that it is simply competing effectively, and cannot be blamed if its rivals are less successful and have to close down.

GLOSSARY

loss leader: selected good sold at a loss to attract buyers
penetration pricing: low-price strategy by a new firm to gain market share
predatory pricing: low-price strategy aimed at driving out competition

Production techniques (see also Chapter 5)

One useful way to look at how a company achieves competitive advantage is to ask whether its products sell primarily on the basis of a low price, or on the quality of the product.

- A very competitive price is possible only if a firm's costs are also very competitive, otherwise the firm would make a loss. Such a firm is known as a *cost leader*: that is, a company that sets and achieves a high target in cost reduction.
- By contrast, a firm that sells primarily on quality is known as a *product differentiator* — because a higher quality makes it different from its rivals.

These two approaches are briefly outlined below. Chapter 20 returns to the subject when discussing Porter's 'four general strategies'.

Using cost structure to improve competitiveness

The key idea here is **competitive costing** — the ability to produce a good at a lower unit cost than rivals. For companies competing at the cheap end of any market, this is an essential skill. It may involve scouring the world for the best deals: for example, Matalan has built its success partly on finding the cheapest source at any one time, rather than cultivating long-term relationships with suppliers as Marks and Spencer does. Or it may

involve a solicitor working part-time from home to avoid office expenses. In terms of employing staff, it entails paying low wages, and therefore requiring managers to work harder to cope with a high staff turnover.

Another aspect of cost minimisation is the opportunity open to firms with a wide **product mix** to exercise some discretion in allocating their overhead expenses, also known as *indirect costs* (see Chapter 3). For example, a few years ago BT had an effective monopoly on local calls, but faced growing competition for national and international calls. It responded by offering competitive rates for the national/international calls, while charging high prices for line rental and local calls. Effectively, it had decided to charge its overheads to (and make its profits from) the local network, while pricing other calls at only a little over **marginal cost**. This approach is also known as **contribution costing**. As long as the national/international calls cover their marginal or direct costs, even a little extra revenue will make a contribution towards the fixed costs. Such a tactic hovers on the edge of illegality. When BT offered its physical telephone equipment at or below cost in order to compete with cheap imports, it was instructed by the courts to raise its prices.

Chapter 5 showed how economies of scale and low stock levels can also be used to achieve a competitive cost structure.

GLOSSARY

competitive costing: production at a lower unit cost than rivals
contribution costing: assigning costs to specific product lines
marginal cost: cost of producing one extra unit of output
product mix (portfolio): range of products sold by a company

Using quality to improve competitiveness

Any attempt by a company to improve the quality of its products will, of course, help it to differentiate itself from its competitors and to achieve a competitive advantage. So the quality control techniques of benchmarking, cell production, quality circles, total quality management and quality standards discussed in Chapter 5 may all be used to improve competitiveness.

Only one further point needs to be made here: continuous improvement is a requirement in every competitive industry. Whatever standards a company achieved yesterday will not be good enough for tomorrow. In particular, the impact of globalisation and of the internet is exposing most companies to more competition than they have ever had before.

The Japanese word for 'continuous improvement' is **kaizen**, which describes the practice of making continuous, incremental improvements based on ideas generated by worker participation. It is argued that this is a more cost-effective way of improving quality than the traditional Western approach based on expensive investment in new technology every few years — with little improvement in the intervening time.

GLOSSARY

kaizen, continuous improvement: principle of incremental, worker-led quality gains

Chapter 20
Increasing business competitiveness: human resources and planning

At the end of this chapter, you should be able to:

1 Explain the terms 'education', 'training', 'empowerment', 'delegation' and 'decentralisation' in the context of 'letting go'.

2 Comment on the extent to which personnel management can improve a firm's competitiveness.

3 Explain the following elements of strategic planning and comment on their usefulness to a company in the never-ending search for competitive advantage: identification of core competences; research and development; SWOT analysis; product portfolios and the Boston Matrix; Porter's four general strategies and cost leadership; mergers and demergers.

Letting go (see also Chapter 6)

Following on from the work of Mayo, Maslow and Herzberg discussed in Chapter 6, personnel managers have developed a strong belief in the natural ability of the human race. The emphasis is on trusting people, on giving them the space to do jobs in their own way within fairly wide boundaries, and therefore on leaving behind autocratic management styles. This trend has been described as 'letting go'. It is most noticeable in professional-level employment, where the investment in **human capital** is greatest — but it is also indicative of a long-term trend in every occupation.

Against this background, **training** becomes an essential complement to school and university **education**. From the initial **induction programme** onwards, staff training is becoming an ongoing commitment for every company. The recent growth in Investors In People certification reflects a growing understanding of the importance of providing (and being seen to provide) staff training.

One of the best stimulants for training is **delegation** — the passing down of decision taking and responsibility to staff lower in the hierarchy. If delegation is done intelligently, it may **empower** staff to achieve targets that they did not know they were capable of achieving. Delegation may also result in **multiskilling** — the ability of workers to do more than one task. The benefits of multiskilling are significant. Not only can staff fill in for each other, but also the general level of self-confidence is likely to rise. And this is a crucial determinant of anyone's success.

Training also leads to **job enlargement**. This increases the interest that people have in their work, and maintaining a high level of interest in any job is vital if it is to be done effectively. Even at an unskilled level, **job rotation** will add interest and motivation to routine tasks.

The delegation of work is often accompanied in large firms by **decentralisation** — the shifting of decisions away from a headquarters building and towards the staff who are closest to customers. But the principle of delegation can work equally well in small companies. Provided senior management is prepared to 'let go' and allow more junior staff to make a few mistakes, there is no reason why a small firm should not delegate too. Indeed, if the company is to grow, delegation may well be the first step. Only then can management get off the treadmill of daily tasks and take the time to plan strategically.

GLOSSARY

decentralisation: dispersal of decisions out of HQ
delegation: the passing down of decisions to juniors
education: the development of one's general capabilities
empowerment: job enlargement (e.g. achieved by delegation)
human capital: marketable skills tied up in human beings
induction programme: introduction to a firm for new employees
job enlargement: increasing the responsibility of a job
job rotation: taking turns to do the most boring tasks
multiskilling: training of workers in many tasks
training (on-job or off-job): instruction directed at a specific job

To what extent does human resource management increase competitiveness?

It is clear that training a workforce to perform daily tasks better, and ensuring that employees have sufficient space within their work to develop, has the potential to improve the competitiveness of the business. However, not all training turns out to be valuable after it has taken place — and any change within an organisation carries a cost in terms of time taken to learn new ways of doing things. Nor is there any guarantee that the change will always be for the better. Like every other aspect of business, the personnel function has to be wisely managed to ensure that the company gets value for money.

Improving competitiveness through strategic planning (see also Chapter 8)

In this and the following sections, we consider common ideas in **strategic planning**. A strategic plan, objective or decision is a long-term one, in contrast to **operational** or tactical plans, which are essentially short-term. The tactical decisions are important too. When will you get up tomorrow morning? What will you do during the day? But these short-term decisions only make sense in the context of a long-term plan. What do you get up *for*? Where do you want to be in 5 years' time — and in 25?

In the context of a business, strategic plans will always be the responsibility of the highest level of management, the board of directors. In highly **centralised** companies, many of the tactical decisions will take place there too. But while these can be decentralised away from headquarters, responsibility for strategic planning always lies with top management.

GLOSSARY

centralisation: gathering of decisions into headquarters
operational planning: the setting of tactical, short-term objectives
strategic planning: the setting of longer-term strategic objectives

Identification of core competences

The **core competence** of any economic agent is what it has specialised in and what it has a proven track record at. It is also known as a **core capability**. The usual advice is for companies not to stray too far from their core competence. Are you a scientist? Then don't try to make a living as a jazz musician. Does your company run a chain of super-markets? Then don't try to make own-brand goods yourself. BP specialises in the oil business: it would probably be a poor use of its resources to run wilderness holidays to the areas in which it drills.

This principle explains why so many firms seek to contract out non-core areas of their business. Why *should* a school employ caterers, or an old people's home accountants, when there are many specialist companies providing precisely these services? There is a clear competitive advantage in being able to tell potential customers that the company does only one thing, and does it very well.

GLOSSARY

core competence (capability): company focus on what it is good at

Research and development (R&D)/new product development (NPD)

Chapter 8 showed that R&D is a necessary expense for any company in a competitive environment. Other companies will improve their products, so it is important to do the same. The main stages of R&D are shown below. At each stage, many potential products will fail to make the grade — and will be abandoned before they cost the company any more money.

1 *Ideas generation.* Ideas are gathered from the R&D personnel, or indeed any employee within the company. Customers and competitors may also be a source of ideas.
2 *Screening.* Potential new products are gauged for whether customers will like them, and whether the firm can make them.
3 *Business analysis.* Investment appraisal is carried out to determine whether the idea is likely to generate an adequate return.
4 *Product development.* Prototypes are produced and tested.
5 *Test marketing.* The product is marketed among a representative sample of consumers to see if demand is high enough.
6 *Product launch.* The product is launched on to the market.

The amount of money spent on R&D varies widely between industries, with high-technology companies spending the most. Since R&D is a fixed cost, those companies that need to spend a lot on it tend to be large.

In the search for competitive advantage, some companies rely on a constant stream of innovative products to give them a lead. Others spend much less on R&D, and focus on adapting other companies' ideas to the extent that they can manage this without breaching patent laws.

SWOT analysis

This is one of the better-known pieces of business jargon among the wider public. The acronym **SWOT** stands for strengths, weaknesses, opportunities and threats. The idea

is that the company (or other economic agent) looks at its *current internal* position: its strengths and its **internal constraints** or weaknesses. Strengths include the assets represented on the balance sheet, the key employees and intangible assets such as goodwill and customer relationships. Weaknesses could be financial, perhaps excessive debt or unusually high costs eating into profits. Or they could be organisational: an unwieldy management structure or a poor employee in a key position.

The company then looks to its *future*, and particularly the opportunities and **external constraints**, or threats, that changes in its environment are sure to bring about. Opportunities might include rising incomes, an advantageous change in fashions, the elimination of a competitor or technological discoveries such as the internet. Threats include the development of a better product by rivals, a recession and falling incomes, theft (including electronic theft), war or civil disturbance, and so on. Strategies to deal with possible threats are known as **contingency plans**.

The firm may, of course, be able to address its strengths and weaknesses directly, but it may also be able to *match* present strengths to future opportunities, and present weaknesses to future threats. So, a strong brand identity (e.g. Coca-Cola) could be matched to a future opportunity (e.g. rising incomes in China) to launch an export drive. Alternatively, a weakness (e.g. high debt) could be matched to a threat (e.g. rising interest rates) and a decision taken to sell off a subsidiary in order to reduce company debt.

SWOT analysis can lead to increased competitiveness by increasing management's understanding of the firm itself, of the outside environment and of likely future developments. However, as with any piece of formal analysis (and two more models are considered below), the firm's competitiveness will be increased only if the analysis is acted upon. There must be a *bias for action*.

GLOSSARY

contingency plans: scenario plans for future damaging events
external constraints: limits imposed on a firm by its environment
internal constraints: limits imposed on a firm by its history
SWOT analysis: analysis of a firm's options, looking at its strengths, weaknesses, opportunities and threats

The product portfolio

A vital part of any firm's strategy is to plan the development of the range of products, or *product portfolio*, that it has to offer. The main message of the product life cycle is that even the best products do not last for ever. So products that are current success stories must be used to finance the next generation of winners.

The model best suited for this analysis is known as the **Boston Matrix**, named after the Boston Consulting Group in the USA which first devised it. The technique is to classify existing products first by their stage in the product life cycle (introduction/growth or maturity) and secondly by their individual market share (high or low). The resulting diagram is shown in Figure 20.1. The profits from the **cash cows** can be used to finance the **rising stars** — and perhaps to rescue the **problem children**. It is not worth spending money on marketing **dogs**, which should be withdrawn from the market as soon as they cease to make a profit.

Market share / Stage in life cycle	High	Low
Growth	Star	Problem child
Maturity	Cash cow	Dog

Figure 20.1 The Boston Matrix

GLOSSARY

Boston Matrix: method of classifying the product mix
cash cow: high-share, low-growth product
dog: low-share, low-growth product
problem child: low-share, high-growth product
rising star: product with a high market share in a growth area

Porter's four general strategies

Porter's four general strategies are a method of classifying companies associated with Michael Porter. Within an industry, firms are grouped on the basis of two criteria. First, are they aiming at mass or niche markets? Second, does their expertise lie in **cost leadership** (i.e. producing at a low cost) or in producing something with a unique selling proposition (USP) that differentiates it from the competition? These choices classify companies within an industry into four groups. They can be cost leaders aiming at a niche market, cost leaders aiming at a mass market, product differentiators aiming at a niche market, or product differentiators aiming at a mass market. These are illustrated in Figure 20.2.

Size of market / Market position	Niche	Mass
Cost leader	Aldi, Costco	Asda, Kwik Save
Product differentiator	Thornton's chocolates, Fortnum and Mason	Marks and Spencer, Tesco

Figure 20.2 Porter's four general strategies: examples from UK food retailing

The main purpose of this model is to warn against the dangers of being neither one thing nor the other. There are advantages in being different, and there are advantages in being cheap. It is less clear that there are advantages in being moderately different and moderately cheap. The same thing could be said of the size of a company. There are clear advantages in being large, and also in being small, as was seen in the discussion of economies and diseconomies of scale in Chapter 5. It is the intermediate-size companies that may struggle to find a competitive advantage.

GLOSSARY

cost leadership: keeping the firm's unit costs lower than those of competitors
Porter's four general strategies: analysis of a firm's market positioning

Mergers and demergers

Chapter 8 explained how mergers and takeovers (i.e. acquisitions) are one route to achieving rapid growth. Economies of scale may be gained, as in the case of telecommunications companies — many of which merged over 1999–2000 to achieve the global reach that they anticipate their customers will want. Of course, mergers also reduce the number of potential competitors: they make the market structure less competitive. This is another potential benefit for the firm — though not for the consumer.

As with any investment, the acquisition of another company can turn out to be a mistake. Marconi faced a £5 billion loss as a result of its decision to switch out of defence contracting and into telecommunications just before the internet bubble burst in March 2000. Likewise, BT shares lost two-thirds of their value as the company bought up other telecommunications companies just prior to the crash.

But one type of acquisition that has a better chance of succeeding than most is the **management buyout**. Managers often know far more about their company than the other stakeholders — the workers, customers, suppliers and shareholders. If they are aware of methods of improving the profitability of the company, they may well prefer to buy the firm themselves before they put their ideas into practice.

Since the merger frenzy of the 1980s, there has been a shift towards **demergers** and/or selling off parts of enterprises — a process known as **divestment**. The reasoning has been that diseconomies of scale are too often ignored. The bigger, merged firm is unwieldy to manage, may never become truly integrated and lacks the focus of a tightly defined product range. This is particularly true of mergers between two firms in unrelated industries, known as **conglomerate integration**. Mergers between firms in the same business (**horizontal integration**), or between firms at different stages of the same supply chain (**vertical integration**), are more likely to be successful.

One common pattern is that a gifted entrepreneur builds up a business empire whose unifying theme is the energy and character of the man himself (and they are still largely men). Upon the death or retirement of the founder, the empire's lack of internal logic becomes apparent and the various businesses split up. This happened with Hanson plc, built up by Lord Hanson in the 1980s and subsequently dismantled. It will be interesting to see if the same fate awaits the Virgin group once Richard Branson is no longer active.

There are few bigger strategic decisions that management can make than a major acquisition or a major divestment. The long-term competitiveness of the company may well depend on the right decision being taken.

GLOSSARY

conglomerate integration: mergers between firms producing unrelated products
demerger: division of a company into two
divestment: sale of part of a firm (e.g. to focus on the core area)
management buyout: purchase of a firm by its managers
vertical integration: mergers up or down the supply chain

Chapter 21
Measuring the competitiveness of an industry's market structure

At the end of this chapter, you should be able to:

Discuss the relative merits of price elasticity of supply, market share, concentration ratios, contestability and the percentage return on capital as means of measuring market (or 'monopoly') power.

Introduction

This chapter looks at competitiveness from the point of view of the industry as a whole. This is quite different from the perspective of the individual company. When a *company* is said to be 'competitive', it is technically efficient; its costs are low relative to the quantity and quality of its products. This in turn will enable it to flourish in the face of its rivals. When an *industry* is said to be competitive, it contains a sufficient number of directly competing firms to force them to become technically efficient. This is very much to the advantage of consumers, of course. In this happy situation they are said to exercise **consumer sovereignty**.

As Chapter 9 showed, the market structure of any industry lies on a *spectrum* between perfect competition at one end and monopoly at the other. It is often very important for the government to decide just how competitive an industry is. Only then can it assess whether monopoly power is (or might be) abused, and decide what steps to take in defence of consumer interests. Chapter 22 will look at government responses to monopoly power. This chapter considers some of the ways in which monopoly power might be identified.

consumer sovereignty: situation where 'he who pays the piper calls the tune'

Price elasticity of supply (see also Chapter 1)

Price elasticity of supply (PES) is exactly the same as price elasticity of demand (PED), except in this case the responsiveness of *supply* to changes in price is measured, rather than demand. As you might expect, its formula is very similar:

$$\text{PES of good X} = \frac{\%\ \text{change in quantity supplied of X}}{\%\ \text{change in price of X}}$$

Whereas PED always has a negative value, **price elasticity of supply** is always positive. If the price that a company can get for its products goes up, then (other things equal) the company would like to produce more of the product, not less. This is illustrated in

Figure 21.1. The place where the supply curve hits the y-axis indicates the price beneath which the company is not prepared to supply any of the product at all.

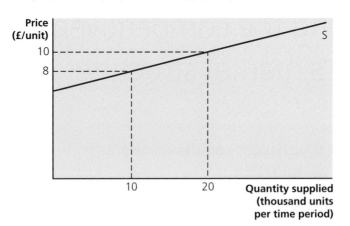

Figure 21.1
A typical firm's
supply curve

The same language of *elastic* and *inelastic* applies to supply just as it did to demand. Table 21.1 is very similar to that for PED in Chapter 1 (Table 1.3).

What happens to supply when prices rise	Value of PES	Description of good
Supply is unchanged	0	Totally inelastic supply
Supply rises less than proportionately	Between 0 and 1	Inelastic supply
Supply rises more than proportionately	Greater than 1	Elastic supply

Table 21.1 Terminology for price elasticity of supply

In the example of Figure 21.1, a 25% increase in price from £8 to £10 leads to a 100% increase in supply from 10,000 to 20,000 units. So in this case, the value of PES at the point (10,000, 8) is +100%/+25% = +4. See if you can work out that the value of PES at the point (20,000, 10) is +2.5.

A key determinant of PES is the time period over which it is measured. In the short term, supply is often totally inelastic. Imagine that interest rates are suddenly cut, making it cheaper to borrow money to buy a house. The demand for new housing shifts outwards, but builders need several months to get planning permission to build more houses, let alone actually build them. Until they can do this, the supply of new housing remains unchanged. This is illustrated in Figure 21.2.

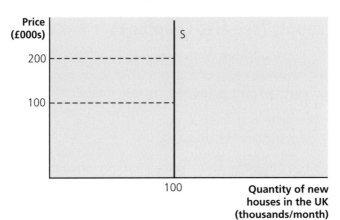

Figure 21.2
A totally inelastic
supply curve

In the long term, supply is generally elastic. Given time, industries can normally increase their output at little or no extra unit cost. The two main exceptions to this rule are:

- Those industries where output depends on an input that has inelastic supply. For example, if the demand for one species of fish rises, it may not be possible to supply more — and the attempt to do so may drive it to extinction.
- *Aggregate* supply becomes inelastic as the economy reaches potential output (Y_p). At this point there is a general shortage of inputs, which makes it impossible to supply more. (This was discussed in more detail in Chapter 12 under Figure 12.1.)

What is the connection between the competitiveness of an industry's market structure and its price elasticity of supply? The general rule is that an *inelastic* supply makes an industry *less* competitive. Should the industry experience an increase in demand, then if supply cannot be increased significantly, the extra demand will be soaked up by rising prices. The inelastic supply is evidence of some sort of entry barrier that, in the short term at least, prevents new firms from joining.

In the extreme case of a monopolist, the supplier has total discretion over the amount it supplies, and therefore has a totally inelastic supply curve. In this instance, the company can adjust the supply to gain whatever price it chooses.

A classic example of this behaviour is the diamond market. Just one company — De Beers — controls most of the world's supply. By carefully adjusting the supply, the company has ensured that the price of diamonds never goes down, only up. This is illustrated in Figure 21.3. In a normal year, the company might sell 1,000 units per time period at $500 per carat. But when demand is low, as illustrated by the right-hand panel, De Beers accepts a much lower level of sales (450 units) to keep the price of diamonds at its previous level ($500), and thereby maintains the image of diamonds as a scarce, luxury commodity.

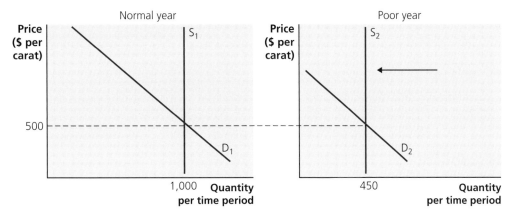

Figure 21.3 Manipulation of supply in the diamond industry

GLOSSARY

price elasticity of supply: responsiveness of supply to changes in price

Market share (see also Chapter 4)

As Chapter 4 explained, a firm's *market share* is the proportion of the total sales in an industry that is accounted for by that firm: the higher its market share, the greater its

degree of monopoly power. So a firm with a 60% market share has much more market power than a firm with a 20% market share. The UK government used to have a simple rule: if any firm would, through merger, acquire a market share greater than 25%, then there were grounds for investigation with a view to prohibiting the merger.

One key difficulty with the concept of market share is defining the 'market' in the first place. Suppose there was only one firm of builders in East Anglia. Does it have a market share of 100% — or would it be more accurate to say that it has a 5% share of the total UK market? Or suppose 20 airlines fly from Manchester airport, each to a single destination. Do we say that each airline has a 5% market share — or that each airline has a 100% market share of its particular route? In practice, governments normally ignore regional monopolies, and monopolies in niche markets. So there are literally thousands of small niche markets up and down the country — like girls' private schooling in Durham or the website for the Jewish community — enjoying monopoly profits, unhindered by government action.

Concentration ratios

Suppose industry A consists of five companies, each with 20% of the market, whereas industry B has one firm with a 20% share, and a further 80 firms with 1% each. Which industry would be more competitive? Clearly Industry B — yet in both industries the biggest firm has the same market share. This illustrates the weakness of simply looking at the market share of the market leader as a means of deciding how competitive an industry is.

One way of expressing the difference in market structures between these two industries is to look at the share of the biggest three (or five or seven) firms in an industry. The resulting figure is known as the three-, five- or seven-firm **concentration ratio**. The higher the resulting percentage, the less competitive the industry is. So in industry A, the three-firm concentration ratio is 60%, whereas in industry B it is a much more competitive 22%.

GLOSSARY

concentration ratio (three-, five- or seven-firm): market share achieved by the largest N firms

Contestability

One defence that a monopoly can offer is that, although it *is* a monopoly, it has no monopoly power. There are no entry barriers, the company claims, and the only reason why other firms have not entered the market is that the existing firm is charging very competitive prices rather than monopoly prices. If at any time the firm tried to exploit its position, its monopoly profits would soon attract new entrants into the market, and the monopoly would vanish. Such an industry is called a **contestable market** on the grounds that it *could* be 'contested' (i.e. competitive) even if, at the moment, it is not. In such an industry, the *fear* of competition performs the same function as actual competition — it compels firms to be efficient and charge low prices.

An obvious problem with using contestability to establish the competitiveness of an industry is how we can decide whether a market *could* be contested when at present it is not.

GLOSSARY

contestable market: a market that is or could be competitive

Percentage return on capital employed (see also Chapter 9)

Chapter 9 showed that companies with monopoly power tend to make excessive, monopoly profits. The best way of measuring what profit might be considered abnormal is to look at the figure for % ROCE (see Chapter 7). The higher the figure, the more likely it is that the company in question enjoys some degree of monopoly power. However, the problem with this approach is that a high % ROCE *could* indicate exceptional efficiency on behalf of an individual company, rather than abuse of monopoly power.

A distinction therefore needs to be made between the *average* % ROCE in an industry, and that of an individual company. If the average is high, this suggests that all the firms are managing to enjoy monopoly profits — perhaps by carving up the market among themselves. However, if only one firm among many enjoys a high return, we may reasonably attribute this to a commendable level of efficiency, rather than the exploitation of a monopoly position.

The most commonly used methods of identifying monopoly power are unusually high profits, as measured by % ROCE, and the market share of the firm in question. In the next chapter, we examine the government's response to monopoly power.

Chapter 22
Government and consumer action to promote competitive market structures

At the end of this chapter, you should be able to:

1 Discuss the entry barriers that lead to monopolistic or oligopolistic market structures.

2 Discuss game theory, a particular feature of oligopoly.

3 Evaluate government action to promote competitive market structures.

4 Discuss the role of pressure groups in protecting the consumer and advancing business ethics.

Introduction

Chapter 9 evaluated the four main types of market structure, and came to the conclusion that monopolies (and often oligopolies) were against the public interest. Monopoly power tends to increase inequality and leads to both technical and allocative (Pareto) inefficiency. If you are not sure why, you should revise Chapter 9 before proceeding further.

Why are some industries monopolies or oligopolies?

In Chapter 9 it was explained that entry barriers were the main determinant of an industry's market structure, of whether it is competitive, oligopolistic or a monopoly. We now look at the main entry barriers in more detail:

- *Technical economies of scale.* Industries with very high R&D costs (pharmaceuticals, aircraft, satellites) tend to be worldwide oligopolies because firms have to be enormous to pay for the research needed to bring out a new product. Likewise, industries with expensive physical networks (water, gas, electricity, transport) tend to form regional or national monopolies because unit costs are minimised if the industry has a monopoly structure — see Figure 9.2 illustrating the *natural monopoly*.

- *Marketing economies of scale.* In consumer goods industries, where brand names are important (detergents, toothpaste, perfumes and luxury products), the structure is often oligopolistic. The maintenance of the brand's power costs hundreds of millions of pounds every year, and this discourages rivals from entering. The ultimate achievement for a company is to get its brand name used as the generic name for a product (Sellotape, Hoover). This generates enormous market power.

- *Industry standards.* If a product takes a long time to learn to use, then one version is likely to become the industry standard — and thereby to acquire significant market power. This has clearly happened with Microsoft Office and Sage accounting software.

- *Vertically integrated supply chains.* It is possible to extend a monopoly (or oligopoly) up or down the supply chain by vertical integration. For example, Microsoft can bundle internet (or any other) software with Office; oil companies can buy up petrol stations; and brewers can buy up pubs. As it happens, rivals who stood to lose out have challenged all these moves in the courts.

- *Small markets.* If the market for any product is particularly small, there may well be room for only one or two firms, creating a monopoly or duopoly structure. These kinds of monopoly are mostly unregulated by government, and offer long-term monopoly profits to their skilful (or lucky) owners. Local monopolies are of this type.

- *Markets in which international trade is restricted.* In such markets, the size of the market is reduced to that of the individual country — and this may eliminate a lot of potential competition. EU farmers used to enjoy monopoly profits for this reason.

- *Patents.* This entry barrier, like the previous one, is unusual in that it is government imposed. The argument for the patent system is that inventors would be discouraged from their valuable work if anyone could copy their idea. The granting of a 20-year monopoly to the inventor acts as a spur to innovation.

Game theory: wheeling and dealing in an oligopolistic structure

Before turning to the question of how governments should restrain monopoly power, it is necessary to examine oligopoly in more detail because this market structure lies on the borders of monopoly and competitive structures. An oligopoly is not a pure monopoly, but neither is it truly competitive. Oligopolies often wield monopoly-like power — or, as it is sometimes called, *market power*.

The key starting point for understanding oligopoly is that firms in an oligopoly are **interdependent**. This means that the best course of action for any oligopolist depends on what the others are doing. This feature is unique to oligopolists. The study of oligopoly behaviour

is known as **game theory** because it entails trying to outwit rivals who are trying to outwit you. Firms in competitive structures have so many competitors that the actions of any single one will not have a significant impact on its rivals, while true monopolists do not have any competitors to worry about.

The basic choice for the companies in an oligopoly is whether to *compete* with each other in a conventional 'price war', or to agree to charge the same, monopoly price. Agreeing to charge the same price is normally illegal. It is a form of **collusion**, and firms that collude in this manner are said to form a **cartel**. The incentive to collude is a powerful one. If all the firms agree to charge the same price, they can all share in monopoly profits. Other forms of collusion that give the same result are: taking it in turns to win contracts, artificially restricting output to push up the price, and carving up the market by geographical or other means, with each firm sticking to its own patch. Whatever the method, the intended result of **collaboration** is the same: the elimination of true competition to the benefit of the firms involved — and at the expense of the consumer.

The fact that collusion is illegal does not, of course, prevent firms from behaving in this way. If they stick to verbal discussion on the golf course, the chances of being found out are relatively small. However, the penalties in the UK are becoming stiffer. Instead of fining the companies involved, at the time of writing it is proposed to adopt the American practice of jailing the directors responsible.

One common response among oligopolists is to confine the arrangement to a **tacit agreement** — one that is unspoken. If three oligopolists dominate an industry, they should be able to copy each other's price increases and not provoke each other to a price war, and all without a word being said. In general, the smaller the number of oligopolists in an industry, the easier it will be for collusion to be maintained.

The potential benefits of collusion have to be weighed up against the potential losses should rivals cheat on the agreement — or should everyone get found out and be punished under the law. Game theory is an important branch of economics at university level.

The best-known example of oligopolistic behaviour is that of the Organisation of Petroleum Exporting Countries (OPEC). Since 1974, OPEC countries have, at intervals, tried to drive up the price of oil by agreeing to reduce their output. At times they have enjoyed spectacular success, in the first instance achieving a fourfold increase in its price. But as time has gone on, the high price has tempted some members to cheat on the deal by producing more than they agreed to. Meanwhile, countries such as Norway that are not members of OPEC have increased their output. The high price has also encouraged research into alternative forms of energy, which in the long term will reduce OPEC's power.

GLOSSARY

cartel: oligopolists behaving as a monopoly
collaboration: working together; if illegal, called collusion
collusion: illegal agreement (e.g. most cartels)
game theory: analysis of interdependent (oligopoly) behaviour
interdependence: two agents, both relying on each other
tacit agreement: silent, unspoken agreement

Government solutions to monopoly power: the Competition Commission

Chapter 9 explained that one possible response by the government to a non-competitive market structure is privatisation of a state monopoly, followed by supervision by a 'watchdog'. A more general solution is provided by the government body known as the **Competition Commission**. Formerly called the **Monopolies and Mergers Commission** (MMC), the Competition Commission was established by the Competition Act of 1998. It has three main tasks:

- *To prohibit oligopolists from making agreements that restrict competition.* This includes agreements to charge the same prices, to restrict output, or to take it in turns to win contracts. It includes tacit agreements, also known as *concerted practices*. The Competition Commission does not have to prove that an agreement has actually been made, only that there has been an adverse effect on competition in a specific market as a result of the actions of the firm or firms in question.
- *To prohibit dominant firms, whether they are monopolists or oligopolists with large market shares, from abusing their position.* This includes limiting output to drive up the price, refusing to sell to discount retailers and changing the design of the product so that other companies find it harder to supply complementary products.
- *To oversee all proposed mergers between large firms to judge whether they are in the public interest.* If competition would be significantly reduced, permission to merge might be refused. Alternatively, permission might be granted on conditions — a typical condition being that one of the firms sells a subsidiary whose product would lack much competition once the merger took place.

Legislation is enforced by the **director-general of fair trading** (DGFT), who heads the **Office of Fair Trading** (OFT). In the case of newly privatised industries, the relevant watchdog is responsible for enforcement. Firms breaching the regulations can be fined, and other companies that have suffered as a result of their behaviour can seek compensation. Finally, a *structural remedy* is possible — the offending company could be forced to sell off some of its operations, or be split up entirely.

As with most areas of public policy, the European Union has its own, parallel **competition policy** and this will be analysed in Chapter 24.

GLOSSARY

Competition Commission: government body to encourage competitive behaviour
competition policy: government principles to encourage or enforce rivalry
director-general of fair trading: manager of the Office of Fair Trading
Monopolies and Mergers Commission (MMC): name of the Competition Commission until 1998
Office of Fair Trading (OFT): body whose purpose is to enforce fair trading

Consumer pressure groups

One of the fundamental freedoms of a democratic society is freedom of association. This means that like-minded people can band together for virtually any reason. Once such a group seeks to persuade corporations or governments to change their ways, it becomes a **pressure group**. It tries to win the battle for public opinion, and thereby alter company policies and the law of the land.

Some pressure groups represent producer interests — e.g. the National Farmers' Union (NFU), the Road Haulage Association, and the Freedom Organisation for the Right to Enjoy Smoking Tobacco (FOREST). Trade unions clearly represent worker interests. This section looks at what may be termed *consumer pressure groups* and *ethical pressure groups*.

Many consumer pressure groups have sprung up in response to clear examples of monopoly power. So there is a Rail Users' Consultative Committee and a Gas Consumers' Council to do battle with the monopoly providers in rail and gas supply respectively. If the industries were competitive, the firms would feel compelled to pay closer attention to the needs of their customers. The consumer pressure groups are, therefore, seeking to act as substitutes for the competition that is lacking.

However, consumer pressure groups do much more than simply respond to monopoly power. The Consumers' Association (best known as publishers of *Which?* magazine) seeks to balance up information asymmetry (see Chapter 11) by providing the general public with objective information on products. And any number of environmental pressure groups, of which Greenpeace is the best known, seek to make companies live up to their responsibility to the environment, since the market fails to provide an incentive for companies to do so.

One further market failure we have touched on is *inequality*. Much of the charitable sector is, of course, devoted to reducing inequality. Many charities get into the area of general campaigning for their causes and may therefore be thought of as pressure groups. Leading this cause in recent years have been the anti-globalisation protests surrounding every international summit. Sometimes referred to as anti-capitalism protests, they have lacked a clear agenda and have therefore achieved very little other than widespread publicity.

Equally controversial are the many groups who promote a particular ethical stance, normally one about which there is at present no consensus. Often rival pressure groups exist on both sides of the ethical debate. So the Countryside Alliance (pro-hunting) faces the League Against Cruel Sports (anti-hunting). Or Stonewall (gay rights) faces the Christian Institute (for Christian sexual ethics). Similar groups exist on both sides of the abortion debate and of the parental smacking issue. Businesses tend to try to avoid giving offence to either side of such issues. It is difficult to act ethically in the eyes of society, if that same society has not made up its mind about what is right and what is wrong.

Pressure groups use a wide variety of methods to achieve their aims. Letter-writing campaigns mobilise supporters to bombard decision-makers with a particular point of view. For example, supporters of Amnesty International write to despotic governments to argue for the release of individual prisoners of conscience. Other groups use paid **lobbyists** to communicate with legislators and other influential persons: at one stage there were seven lobbyists in Washington for every US member of Congress.

Simple advertising may also raise public awareness. If this is linked to a consumer boycott campaign, the effect can be devastating. For example, Shell abandoned its plans to dump an obsolete oil platform (called Brent Spar) in the Atlantic in 1995 because of a boycott of Shell petrol by German motorists. Despite having scientific opinion on their side, Shell felt unable to resist the actual and potential loss of business.

More aggressive techniques include demonstrations, either peaceful or violent. The anti-globalisation protests mentioned earlier have been the most successful in getting large

numbers of people on to the streets and achieving wide coverage in the media. Other forms of direct action include blockading engineering projects, such as new roads or airports; invading private premises, such as military or civilian nuclear facilities; and criminal damage and assault, such as the attacks on the Huntingdon Life Sciences (HLS) animal-testing laboratories in 2000–01.

People's view of pressure groups is likely to depend on their views of both the causes they support, and the methods they are prepared to use. Many people would approve of the pressure placed on Nike to ensure that its Far Eastern suppliers look after their workers properly, but would take a very different view of the sending of letter bombs to scientists engaged in animal testing.

From the business perspective, a pressure group's activities force the company on the receiving end to engage in some serious analysis. Is the complaint justified? Should the company change its ways, or perhaps meet the objection halfway? If the company believes the complaint is *not* justified, how should it respond — ignore the protests, mount a counter-campaign, or give in for the sake of a quiet life? One problem the company will face is that its public position will often prevent it from using the same tactics as its opponents. Advertising can be met with counter-advertising, but letter bombs can hardly be met by sending other bombs back.

The attitude of other stakeholders will also be relevant. HLS, for example, lost both its bankers and its stockbrokers because these stakeholders were successfully intimidated by animal rights campaigners into severing their association with HLS. Its shares are now registered on the New York Stock Exchange, where the names and addresses of share-holders can be kept confidential.

GLOSSARY

lobbying: direct persuasion, especially of politicians
pressure group: people combining to influence government

Chapter 23
Government action to promote national competitiveness

At the end of this chapter, you should be able to:

1 Explain the concept of infrastructure and comment on its contribution to economic growth.

2 Discuss some government enterprise policies.

3 Discuss government policies to deal with unemployment.

4 Evaluate the advantages and disadvantages of low exchange rates.

5 Evaluate the impact of multinationals.

Introduction

This chapter examines various macroeconomic policies that may have the effect of making the UK more competitive than its trading partners. Following on from work in Chapter 12, the chapter looks first at some more supply-side policies that the government can undertake to increase economic growth. It also returns to the issue of government action to reduce unemployment, first raised in Chapter 13.

The chapter then looks at the circumstances in which low exchange rates benefit a country, following on from Chapter 15. Finally, the role of multinationals is discussed — both in creating national competitiveness and in making the entire world a more competitive marketplace.

Infrastructure

Any country can be divided up into its private spaces and its public ones. Firms and households own the private spaces, and access is only possible with the owner's permission. The public spaces normally allow unrestricted access to members of the general public going about their business. Public spaces are therefore a *public good*. They are *non-excludable* and any facilities that they offer must be provided by government out of general taxation (see Chapter 10).

These facilities are known as a country's **infrastructure**. A good infrastructure is one of the determinants of economic growth. Firms are much more likely to locate in areas with a good infrastructure — where roads are in good repair, libraries and parks are well maintained, and active policing discourages vandalism and anti-social behaviour.

Of course, infrastructure like anything else comes at a price. Countries with the best infra-structure are likely to have high tax levels — and high taxes act as a clear disincentive to economic growth. This once more raises the issue of technical (and allocative) efficiency. Companies want the taxes that *are* spent on infrastructure to be spent well, creating the best possible business environment for the amount of money spent. And impossibly wise politicians are needed to work out exactly *how much* of the national income should be spent on infrastructure relative to all the other competing needs. If the politicians get it right, it is possible to talk about the infrastructure being 'competitive'.

Sometimes the concept of infrastructure is widened to include all sorts of support services provided by the private sector. For example, rail and air travel are normally considered part of the infrastructure, whether these services are privately or publicly owned. The price — and availability — of basic utilities such as water, sewage, gas and electricity could also be included. At a rather different level, the concept can be extended to include health care, golf courses for managers, and good schools for their children.

GLOSSARY

infrastructure: government-owned capital (e.g. roads, hospitals)

UK enterprise policies

Much of the analysis of infrastructure also applies to **enterprise policy**. Once again, government policy is to assist companies — and this may lead to faster economic growth. And once again, it must be asked whether the money is being well spent. However, there

is one very significant difference. While some forms of infrastructure spending are inevitable (on roads, for example), it could be argued that *nothing* needs to be spent by government on enterprise policies. Put another way, it may be the case that the best enterprise policy of all for the government is to save money and offer low taxes. This is the classic free-market approach currently being practised by the Australian government.

GLOSSARY

enterprise policy: government action to help new start-ups, and firms to grow

'Enterprise policy' covers an enormous range of government initiatives. Any government action that encourages firms to start up and/or grow counts. So straight cash aid to encourage firms to locate in a particular region (such as Siemens received to build a microchip plant in north Tyneside) is an example. Small business start-up advice, and government advice on exports, training, finance, design, company incorporation and so on, is all included in the enterprise policy. Reducing corporation tax, reducing the minimum wage, providing tax subsidies for child care, offering free training through individual learning accounts, and working families tax credit — all have their 'enterprise' angle.

As is often the case, action to achieve one government objective may well make another harder to achieve. So while the reduction (or elimination) of the minimum wage would undoubtedly be enterprise friendly, it would also increase the level of inequality. This is one example of the equity/efficiency trade-off looked at in Chapter 14.

In a mixed economy such as the UK, the amount of cash and other assistance on offer is so varied that one important entrepreneurial skill is simply to tap into all the grants on offer. The economist needs to consider whether it is money well spent. The individual business is primarily concerned with extracting the most cash out of the situation.

Current employment policies

At the time of writing in 2003, unemployment is at its lowest since the 1960s, so the current political focus is not centred on this particular problem, even in the **assisted areas**. In the current favourable conditions, the emphasis of government **employment policy** is to work on the supply side rather than the demand side. Rather than trying to persuade employers to *offer* jobs, the emphasis is on persuading people to *take* jobs. Particular attention is being paid to:

- *The low-paid.* The national minimum wage rose to £4.20 per hour for those aged 22 and over from October 2002. For those aged 18–21, it rose to £3.60 per hour.
- *Lone parents.* These continue to receive lone-parent benefit and are now expected to return to work once their youngest child has reached the age of 11.
- *Large families.* Working families tax credit (WFTC) now offers up to £200/week for families on low pay with just two children.

Information technology has also been harnessed to speed the matching of jobs and workers. At the website **www.newdeal.gov.uk** anyone can type in the nature and location of work they are looking for, and receive a list of all matching vacancies registered at **job centres**.

Although structural unemployment is currently very low, the government is anxious to improve the national stock of IT skills. A recent innovation with respect to training was

the offer of individual learning accounts (ILAs). Any employee could register and receive up to £200 of training per year, with the government paying 90 % of the cost. However, from October 2001 ILAs were suspended after it was discovered that some training providers had been taking the money, splitting it with the trainee and not providing the training!

This illustrates a general problem: government financial assistance is often the subject of fraud. The problem is particularly acute for high-spending governments that seek to achieve equality and employment objectives by offering cash rewards for people to behave in certain ways. It is questionable how far employment policies are increasing the nation's competitiveness. If it is the case that much of the tax revenue spent is being wasted, it is reasonable to ask whether competitiveness might be better served by offering lower taxes and lower benefits.

GLOSSARY

assisted areas: deprived UK areas eligible for extra government help
employment policy: government action aimed at raising the level of employment
job centre: government-provided employment exchange

A low exchange rate: a competitive advantage?

As discussed in Chapter 15, UK exporters stand to gain if the sterling exchange rate falls. UK goods appear cheaper ('more competitive') overseas. At the same time, importers are likely to charge more for their goods in sterling terms, giving a cost advantage to UK manufacturers. A falling exchange rate is, therefore, often welcomed on the grounds that it 'increases competitiveness'.

However, it also means that the UK has to pay more for imports — for other countries' goods. This reduces the standard of living for UK residents. To welcome a depreciation in the sterling exchange rate is rather like welcoming a cut in your hourly rate of pay on the grounds that it will make you 'more competitive'. No doubt it will — but it also means you can buy fewer of other people's services in return for your own.

The only circumstance in which people welcome a cut in their pay is if the alternative is redundancy. Likewise, the only circumstance in which the UK as a whole should welcome a cut in the sterling exchange rate is if it proves impossible to sell UK goods at the going rate. In practical terms, a cut (*depreciation*) in the sterling exchange rate is welcomed when the UK is in a recession. In 1992, just such a depreciation helped to end the 1990–92 slump. With a lower exchange rate, UK goods became relatively easy to sell once more. As UK exports increased, so the AD curve shifted outwards, ending the recession.

Multinationals: creators of more or less competition?

International trade is always more complex than domestic trade. Most international trade is, therefore, undertaken by large companies with interests in several countries. These are the **multinational corporations**, also known as **transnational corporations** (MNCs/TNCs). With budgets often bigger than those of some of their poorer host countries, their operations are often surrounded by controversy. Do they really benefit the countries in which they operate, or are they self-seeking giants trampling weaker agents underfoot?

The debate is best understood in the context of traditional economic theory. Provided markets are Pareto efficient (i.e. are competitive and have no externalities), the self-interest of companies leads to the benefit of consumers too. The same basic point needs to be made about MNCs. Provided they operate in competitive markets, their activities should benefit all their stakeholders — and not just their shareholders. In this vision of the world, every country stands to gain from **free trade**, from a series of interlocking **open economies** where most domestic markets in most countries are subject to a high degree of **import penetration**. As demand and supply curves shift in every industry, so **trade patterns** will change to reflect the new patterns of consumer demand and the new specialisms of the world's economies. This is the vision of globalisation; of a single, competitive world economy.

MNCs — and international trade in general — play a crucial part in this process. By opening up so many domestic markets to outside competition, they give these markets more competitive structures to the benefit of consumers everywhere.

Nonetheless, the new century has witnessed the rise of a powerful anti-globalisation movement. These protestors call for a higher level of **import controls** and other forms of **protectionism**. MNCs no less than governments are the targets of anti-globalisation protestors. We therefore need to look briefly at the wide range of criticisms aimed at MNCs:

- They take advantage of lower environmental standards in economically less developed countries (ELDCs) to pollute the environment. Notoriously, the cyanide leak at a Union Carbide plant in Bhopal, India, killed hundreds in the 1980s.
- They take advantage of weaker consumer legislation in ELDCs to sell products that are banned or restricted in rich countries (e.g. cigarettes).
- They (or their suppliers) take advantage of weak employment legislation to exploit ELDC workers, particularly child labour.
- MNCs can become so large that they actually *reduce* competition. In small countries, an MNC can easily become a monopoly provider of products that, in its absence, would be delivered by many competing local companies.
- By manufacturing where wages are lowest, they undercut workers' standard of living in OECD countries.
- Benefits for the host country are limited: profits are repatriated to shareholders in the West.
- With international trade comes a form of cultural imperialism: local dishes are replaced by McDonald's fast food, local languages by English and local ethical standards by the immorality of Hollywood. In extreme form, the terrorist acts of 11 September 2001 were in part caused by the perception that the USA was imposing its way of life on the rest of the world.

The economist's traditional response to these complaints is that individual instances of market failure, such as the first four points above, need to be addressed. However, it can be argued that the potential benefits from globalisation are so profound and far-reaching — not least for the poorest members of the world community — that it would be foolish to throw away these benefits simply because the behaviour of MNCs so often falls short of what we have a right to expect. These issues are discussed in greater detail in Option 1.

From the domestic point of view, strong UK multinationals are essential to competitiveness. The UK has always been an open economy, exporting (and importing) over 30% of its national income, and this proportion is rising.

GLOSSARY

free trade: situation where international trade is unhindered
import controls: government-imposed restrictions on imports
import penetration: market share of an industry met from abroad
multinational corporation (MNC): firm with activities in many countries
open economy: nation with a large proportion of exports and imports
protectionism, protected market: use of trade barriers to reduce international competition
trade pattern: who trades with whom, and how much
transnational corporation (TNC): US term for a multinational

Chapter 24
Creating a competitive world? The work of the EU and the WTO

At the end of this chapter, you should be able to:

1 Explain the arguments for and against UK membership of the euro.

2 Evaluate whether European monetary union will create or inhibit competition.

3 Discuss the work of the EU competition commissioner.

4 Explain EU enterprise policies.

5 Explain the work of the WTO, with reference to trade blocs and trade barriers.

6 Comment on the criticisms faced by the WTO in its mission to spread free trade.

The euro

Chapter 16 discussed the moves towards economic and political integration within the European Union (EU). The level of integration most debated at the time of writing is the single currency project, the euro (€). From 1 January 2002, 11 out of the 15 EU members adopted the euro as their joint currency. These 11 countries are collectively known as euroland. The single currency is organised by the **European Central Bank** (ECB). The project is also described as European monetary union (EMU).

GLOSSARY

European Central Bank (ECB): EU bank setting interest rates for the eurozone

The UK chose not to join the euro at the beginning, and both major political parties in the UK have undertaken not to sign up without first holding a referendum on the issue. In 2000, the Dutch voted 'no' in such a referendum, despite the fact that *all* their major political parties recommended a 'yes' vote. This divergence of views between the political elite and the ordinary voter is common over much of Europe with respect to further European integration.

Should the UK join? The key to understanding the issue is twofold. First, joining the euro is like having permanently fixed exchange rates with other EU countries, an issue touched upon in Chapter 15. Second, the decision is as much a political as an economic one. Arguments for and against the UK joining the euro are presented in Table 24.1.

Arguments for the UK joining the euro	Arguments against the UK joining the euro
The political argument: the UK will become much more closely integrated with its EU partners (e.g. a single currency implies a single central bank and a single monetary policy). Europhiles say sovereignty will be 'pooled'.	The political argument: the UK will become much more closely integrated with its EU partners (e.g. a single currency implies a single central bank and a single monetary policy). Eurosceptics say sovereignty will be 'lost'.
Exchange rate risk will be eliminated for trade between the UK and other EU members.	The UK will lose a 'shock absorber' (e.g. it will not be able to get out of a recession by depreciating the currency as it did in 1992).
The UK will have much lower transactions costs with EU partners (e.g. no bank commission would be payable when trading with or visiting Europe, since no other currency would be needed).	There are one-off costs associated with joining: the time and expense of the transition, and one-off inflation as shopkeepers round up prices to their nearest Euro equivalent.
Every industry will have a more competitive market structure to every consumer's advantage. It will be much easier to compare prices across the entire EU.	The UK will lose the ability to set its own inflation target. A single currency can only have a single interest rate, which is set by the new ECB.

Table 24.1 Arguments for and against joining the euro

The Labour government has pronounced itself in favour in principle of joining the euro 'when the economic conditions are right'. As mentioned in Chapter 16, it has announced convergence criteria that have to be met before it will recommend the electorate to vote for membership in a referendum.

The key convergence criterion is whether business cycles and economic structures are compatible, so that the UK and others in Europe could live comfortably with euro interest rates on a permanent basis. In other words, does the UK economy behave in such a similar fashion to the rest of Europe that every country always suffers recessions at the same time, and always requires the same interest rates to hit inflation targets? If this degree of convergence is met (and it will inevitably be a subjective decision), this would remove the main economic arguments against joining that were listed in Table 24.1.

GLOSSARY

Europhile: enthusiast for European integration
Eurosceptic: enthusiast for keeping UK sovereignty
sovereignty: ability to control one's own future

European monetary union: creator or inhibitor of competition?

What would be the effect of joining the euro on the level of competition existing in the UK? On the plus side, it will be much easier to compare prices across euroland if all prices

are expressed in the same currency. This additional knowledge will assist all consumers in making purchasing decisions and so force companies to price more competitively. If one company charges prices way out of line with its euroland competitors, this will be much more transparent. Additionally, there will be much lower transaction costs for EU trade. Bank commission and the normal **exchange rate spread** will no longer be payable within euroland.

The alternative view is that the adoption of the euro by the whole of Europe is essentially anti-competitive, because it will reduce the number of currencies — and so economic policies. A uniform Europe would be one with fewer competing visions to be tested against each other.

GLOSSARY

exchange rate spread: the difference between the buying price and the selling price of a foreign currency

The EU commissioner for competition

The EU's most direct impact on competitiveness is through its own **EU competition policy**. Proposed mergers between two companies from different member states come under the EU's jurisdiction, and there is a set of rules very similar to those of the UK's Competition Commission designed to protect the consumer by preserving competition.

The EU's equivalent to the UK's Competition Commission is headed by a commissioner, currently Mario Monti. He has been successful in enhancing competition in a number of areas. First, he has often prohibited governments from subsidising their own industries when other EU members have complained. For example, the UK government was forced to reclaim a secret subsidy paid to Rover cars in the early 1990s. More recently, the Spanish government has been caught in a similar position with respect to SEAT, a subsidiary of Volkswagen.

Second, he has used the sheer size of the EU market to address competition issues in US-based companies — even though the USA is outside his jurisdiction. To give one instance, in 2000 Monti prevented a merger between the US firms General Electric and Honeywell International, although the merger had already received approval in the USA. This power over the USA supports one of the Europhiles' key arguments. No individual country has anything like the leverage with the USA that the EU has. The opposing point of view is that it is unreasonable for mergers between US firms to be subject to scrutiny twice: once in the USA, then again in the EU.

GLOSSARY

EU competition policy: EU law designed to foster competition

EU enterprise policies

In Chapter 23, we looked briefly at some UK enterprise policies designed to increase UK competitiveness. As in so many areas of government, there is an EU equivalent: the **EU enterprise and industrial policy**. We will look at just one example — so-called **Objective 1 funding**. This is available to areas of the EU where GDP per head is less than

75% of the EU average. These poorer areas tend to lie on the periphery of the EU, such as in Northern England, Greece, Portugal and Spain. Local authorities in these areas can apply for grants to spend on enterprise objectives such as training, marketing assistance and capital investment. For example, the training organisation Investors In People has received some of its financial backing from this source.

GLOSSARY

EU industrial and enterprise policy: EU attitude towards, and support for, business
Objective 1 funding: EU help for areas where GDP is less than 75% of the EU average

The World Trade Organisation: creator of global competition?

The World Trade Organisation (WTO) was founded in 1995 as the successor body to the General Agreement on Tariffs and Trade (GATT). Based in Geneva with a staff of 500, its main task is to chair negotiations with all its 140 member countries to try to get them to agree to reduce **trade barriers**. The main trade barriers are:

- **Import tariffs** (i.e. taxes on imports). The common external tariff (CET) is the name for the tariffs imposed by the EU on goods from outside.
- **Import quotas** (i.e. restrictions on the *quantity* of a product that can be imported). These are sometimes known as **voluntary export restraints** (VERs). A current EU example applies to Japanese-made cars, which are restricted to 17% of the EU market.
- **Domestic subsidies.** An alternative way of putting foreign competition at a disadvantage is for government to subsidise its own industry. Many governments offered subsidies to their airlines following the loss of business in the wake of the terrorist attacks of 11 September 2001.

Negotiations on the reduction of trade barriers take place within the framework of a series of 'rounds', with each round lasting several years. The current round is called the Dohar round, which has taken over from the previous Uruguay round.

The task for the WTO in these rounds is to get governments to see that, in aggregate, they stand to gain from free trade, even if any particular reduction in barriers might work to their disadvantage. Thus the work of the WTO can be summarised in the phrase **trade liberalisation**, which is one example of general **deregulation**.

However, countries may seek to restrict trade for a variety of ostensibly good reasons. The problem for the WTO is then to decide whether these are genuine reasons, or whether they are simply being used as an excuse to keep out competitors. The dilemmas faced are not easy. In which of the following cases would you support unrestricted free trade?

- *Child welfare.* Rich countries seek to ban the import of carpets made with child labour, citing their concern for child welfare. Afghanistan responds by saying it cannot afford to provide universal children's education, and that children's earnings are vital to family budgets in a desperately poor country.
- *Health and safety.* EU countries seek to ban genetically modified (GM) foodstuffs from the USA because they have not been proved safe. The USA responds by saying there is no evidence that they are *not* safe. It claims that the EU is only taking this line to protect its inefficient farmers from US competition.
- *Externalities.* The EU seeks to ban tuna that has been caught with vast drift nets, since these kill everything in their path, including dolphins. Poor countries claim this is an

excuse to freeze out their tuna — and anyway they cannot afford the more sophisticated dolphin-friendly fishing method.

- *Intellectual property.* The rich, populous countries of Europe, North America and Japan belong to the **Organisation of Economic Co-operation and Development** (OECD). They are fed up with poor countries copying books, videos and software wholesale and never paying for it. They want their intellectual property defended, and say they will restrict imports from the guilty countries until they play by the rules. Poor countries reply by saying they are doing their best to catch pirates, but cannot afford to police every factory within their borders.

- *Time to adjust.* Free trade always produces losers — the relatively inefficient companies that cannot compete now that they can no longer shelter behind trade barriers. Much of the WTO's caseload is concerned with desperate pleas from countries that are faced with one or two inefficient industries going under, and which are asking to be allowed to maintain some form of protection for a few more years. For example, Caribbean banana producers were, in 2002, allowed to continue until 2005 the arrangement whereby the former colonial powers, France and Britain, guaranteed to buy 750,000 tonnes of their bananas each year — even though cheaper ones are available from US-owned plantations in South America.

As you can see, it is one thing to proclaim the virtues of free trade. It is another thing to bring it about within a global community where national cultures, views of right and wrong, and financial resources are all very different.

GLOSSARY

deregulation: removal of rules (e.g. to develop competition)
domestic subsidy: cash grant by government to firms in its own country
import quota: fixed annual limit on imports of a product
import tariff: tax imposed on an imported good
Organisation for Economic Co-operation and Development (OECD): an association of wealthy countries, known informally as the 'rich man's club'
trade barrier: obstacle to international trade
trade liberalisation: removal or reduction of trade barriers
voluntary export restraint (VER): quota negotiated between two countries

Trade blocs: creators or inhibitors of competition?

As Chapter 16 showed, free trade areas encourage trade between member countries while putting no additional obstacles in the way of other countries. They are, therefore, a force for greater competitiveness. The best known of these free trade areas is the North American Free Trade Area (NAFTA), comprising Mexico, the USA and Canada.

By contrast, trade blocs are groups of countries that offer each other preferential trading arrangements. They are common throughout the world. West Africa has the Economic Community of West African States (ECOWAS); and southeast Asia has the Association of South East Asian Nations (ASEAN). Trade blocs that are customs unions impose significant trade barriers against non-members. In the case of the EU, this barrier is known as the common external tariff (CET).

Chapter 25
Option 1: what is the global future?

Introduction

This option is based on the theme of globalisation. Globalisation describes the process by which goods and services are increasingly traded on an international scale, rather than simply a national one. The concept was first encountered in Chapter 15. Chapters 15, 16 and 24 form the essential background to Option 1. These chapters should be treated as an integral part of your revision for this option.

Globalisation will be analysed in four sections:
- *How does business manage globalisation?* This looks at how the individual business deals with the opportunities and threats created by globalisation.
- *How can globalisation promote economic growth?* This looks at the macroeconomic impact of globalisation.
- *How and why is globalisation regulated?* This looks at the work of the International Monetary Fund and the World Bank, and some issues faced by the World Trade Organisation.
- *What ethical issues arise from globalisation?* This looks at issues surrounding the global environment, income inequality and corporate responsibility.

How does business manage globalisation?

At the end of this section, you should be able to:

1 Explain practical ways of exporting a product.

2 Comment on strategies for competing in a global market.

3 Comment on production issues of particular relevance for a multinational.

4 Discuss personnel issues arising from globalisation.

How to go about exporting: joint ventures, licensing, franchising

Doing business outside your home country tends to be difficult. You do not know the local customs and culture — and the fact that you are an outsider makes it much easier for you to be cheated. Almost all exporters end up entering into some kind of partnership with local people. One way to do this is simply to employ local managers to run your operation for you. Someone with a foothold in both countries may be particularly valuable. For example, a person who grew up in India, and then came to the UK aged 20, might be an ideal person for a UK company to employ in the UK to begin with and then send back to run its Indian operation 10 years later.

The other approach is to enter into a formal relationship with a local company, which will handle the other end of the operation. The various possibilities are as follows:

Joint ventures. The exporting company from a **developed economy** sets up a new company with a local partner in an **emerging economy** or **developing economy**, perhaps with the share capital split equally. The multinational provides the technology; the local company, the marketing. Manufacturing may take place in either country.

The local partner may offer government contacts without which business might not be possible. At its simplest, the local firm is owned by a person of influence, who promotes the company in return for half the profits. Alternatively, the local firm may be run by a more modest individual, who simply knows how business is conducted — possibly including the knowledge of who has to be bribed and by how much.

Franchising. The parent company, the **franchisor**, provides the formula — the product with its brand name. A local businessperson then buys the right to provide the product within a defined geographical area. The local business (or **franchisee**) is responsible for employing staff and promoting its branch at a local level, while the parent company provides national marketing. The Body Shop, Tie Rack, KFC, Prontaprint and McDonald's are all companies that operate in this way.

Normally the local business has to invest somewhere between £20,000 and £1 million to buy the franchise for a defined time. It also has to buy its products from the parent company, and pay a royalty on sales. In return, it gets a business with a much-reduced risk, and the back-up of an internationally known brand.

From the point of view of the franchisor, franchising provides a rapid method of expansion for a successful idea, with other people providing the finance. It also utilises managerial diseconomies of scale. Small businesses are likely to keep a very sharp eye on costs compared to salaried managers, and to be strongly motivated to market the product energetically.

Licensing. This entails selling the right for someone else to manufacture the product for a specific market. The exporter hires out the technological know-how to a local company, which is then responsible for manufacturing and marketing. Licensing is often used by companies that hold patents as a means of extracting maximum value from intellectual assets in a **global market**.

How does global marketing take place? (see also Chapters 4 and 19)

The key to global marketing is to establish a global brand. You should be able to think of global brands in many industries — for example, in football, soft drinks, cars, computer software, computer hardware, luxury clothes, fast food and children's films. Global brands tend to be dominated by multinationals from the rich OECD countries. Quality expectations are normally higher there, and their brand names therefore enjoy greater esteem.

Global branding enables a company to leverage up the success and reputation it has enjoyed in one country into other countries too. This process is an example of marketing economies of scale: establishing a reputation in ten countries can be done for a lower average cost per country than establishing a reputation in just one. The internet is an excellent example of this principle. The cost of setting up and maintaining a website is a fixed cost. Adding satellite websites in different languages for different countries is far cheaper than setting up the original one.

Having said that, multinationals will prosper only if they respect the differences that exist between the markets that they serve. Different levels of competition (and different income levels) will make price discrimination a natural strategy. For example, most goods are sold for less in the USA than in the EU, due to the greater levels of competition in the USA. The USA is a fully integrated, single market in a way that the EU can at present only aspire to.

Equally, advertising will normally be controlled on a country-by-country basis. Different views of what is acceptable, different senses of humour and a different legal framework mean that promotional activity is best handled by the local partner.

What production issues arise from globalisation? (see also Chapter 5)

The key to production for a global market is the repetition of a successful formula. The principle of cost minimisation suggests that any successful product should be sold to the widest possible market. The gains from product innovation and **process innovation** are then leveraged up. In other words, overheads are spread, enabling companies to enjoy technical economies of scale. Unit costs also fall as materials are **sourced** from the cheapest country and then made available internationally. Take, for example, McDonald's. The basic **format** is the same everywhere: a franchised operation serving cheap food quickly and using a distinctive logo that is recognised worldwide. At the same time, there is some space for local variation — for example, in the precise menu on offer.

Management will seek to centralise everything that can be centralised, leaving to local discretion whatever cannot. So the **standardised** main ingredient in Coca-Cola, the syrup, is exported from the USA, as is the distinctive design of the bottle. But the amount of added sugar (as well as other areas of the business, such as employment practices) can be left to local bottling partners. The same principle works the other way round as well. ELDCs manufacture computer parts, which are then shipped to OECD countries. Here they are **customised** to individual customer specifications within a day or so of an order being received.

One key difficulty in production for a global market is the need to work with longer **lead times**: that is, longer times between an order being received and that order being fulfilled. Physical goods still take a few weeks to ship round the world, while airfreight is relatively expensive. On the other hand, international communication is becoming faster and cheaper all the time, as the airline network expands and the price of both flights and phone calls comes down.

At a time of falling prices, it is particularly important to cut lead times so that stock levels can be kept to a minimum. For example, the current market leader in computer sales is Dell Corporation. It reckons the price of computer parts is falling by 1% each week. So its ability to get by with 1 week's worth of stock rather than its rivals' 3 weeks gives it an immediate cost advantage of 2%. This could make the difference between a 4% and a 6% profit margin — a gain of 50% on its competitors.

What are the personnel management implications of globalisation? (see also Chapters 6 and 20)

Although each country stands to gain in total from international trade, within each country there will be industries that cannot compete against global competition and which

therefore stand to lose out. The consequences for employment are fairly obvious. An open economy will create more opportunities — but will also be subject to more shocks. Both the opportunities and the shocks create a demand for *flexibility* on the part of companies and their workforces.

In some cases, new overseas competition will be so severe that the domestic industry has no option but to contract rapidly. For example, UK clothing manufacturers rapidly contracted over the 1990s in response to a wave of high-quality, cheap imports. Marks and Spencer tried to maintain its 'Buy British' policy — and suffered as a result. The decline in UK-made textiles is still going on. Companies faced with this situation will lobby their governments and the EU to maintain existing trade barriers a little longer. They will institute a freeze on recruitment and then ask for voluntary redundancies. Even if the situation is hopeless, there is still merit in winding up the affairs of the company in an orderly manner. This minimises the pain to employees and shareholders alike.

In less extreme circumstances, the company may simply need to **downsize**, accepting that its market is no longer as big as it was. Often it is the more expensive products for which there is still a market. The surviving workforce may need to be retrained so that their **employment skills** can meet the higher-quality products that are still demanded. It is also possible that workplace relocation will be needed. Often a company will close one of a handful of plants, and be able to offer at least some of its affected workers a job in one of the other centres.

Open and honest communication with the workforce will improve their morale — and may lead to the extra flexibility that the company needs to survive. Traditional **working practices**, such as refusing to cover for absent colleagues, may be changed by agreement. Another type of flexibility that may be necessary is a willingness to work a shift pattern that includes weekends and nights. If an expensive factory can be kept busy all the time, this will reduce the unit cost of its products. In extreme cases, trade union members have even voted for a pay *cut* if they have been convinced that this is the only way their employer can survive.

Equally, globalisation can lead to the opposite set of human resources problems. The opening up of new export markets may create a large increase in demand for the product, requiring the exporting company to recruit more staff, to outsource anything that can be outsourced and to increase labour productivity.

GLOSSARY

customisation: alteration of a product to suit a particular buyer
developed (mature) economy: economy where people enjoy a relatively high standard of living
developing economy: economically less developed country
downsizing: sgnificantly reducing a firm's labour force
emerging economy: fast-growth nation, in the process of catching up economically
employment skills: abilities enabling someone to do a job
format: standard product formula (e.g. for a franchisee)
franchisee: independent person buying a franchise
franchising, franchisor: firm selling rights to its brand
global market: industry with internationally traded output
joint venture: project with two or more participating firms
lead time: time between a decision and its execution
licensing: sale of the right to manufacture a product

GLOSSARY

process innovation: major improvement in a production technique
sourcing: act of a firm finding the suppliers it needs
standardisation: process of making similar goods identical
working practices: traditional work habits in an organisation

How can globalisation promote economic growth?

At the end of this section, you should be able to:

1 Explain how the theory of comparative advantage shows that all countries' output will increase if free trade takes place.

2 Explain the terms of trade.

3 Explain the role of inward investment in increasing economic growth.

Why every country gains from trade: the theory of comparative advantage (see also Chapter 15)

Chapter 15 showed that countries gain from international trade because the increased competition forces participants to become more efficient. We also mentioned that international trade works to every country's advantage because each country can specialise in the products that it is best at producing.

So Saudi Arabia can produce oil very cheaply, while the USA has the world's best armaments industry. Both countries stand to gain if they specialise in their own areas of expertise and then trade. In this example, both countries are said to have the **absolute advantage** in oil and armaments respectively. This means that Saudi Arabia can produce a barrel of oil with far fewer resources than the USA. And the USA can produce an up-to-date tank with far fewer resources than Saudi Arabia.

More interesting is the case where one country is better at producing *both* goods. It can be shown that specialisation can still work to the benefit of both countries if the less efficient country specialises in the good at which it is 'less bad': in other words, the good in which it has a relative or **comparative advantage**. The other country then specialises in the good that it is 'more good' at producing.

The same argument works at the individual level too. We might ask why professional couples often employ childminders to look after young children when a parent is likely to make a better job of it. The economic justification is that the parent might be merely twice as good as the childminder at looking after children, but might be ten times as good as the childminder at being a lawyer (or whatever). So the parents stand to gain financially by both specialising as lawyers and paying the childminder. And childminders stand to gain by specialising at childminding and then paying for a lawyer if required, rather than trying to cope with legal matters themselves.

The beauty of comparative advantage is that every country must have the comparative advantage in something. Even if, say, Albania is not the most efficient producer of

anything, there must be *something* at which it is 'least bad': that is, in which it has a comparative advantage. So the theory provides the intellectual backing for free trade because it shows that every single country stands to benefit from it. This crucial fact is by no means obvious — but it has convinced almost every economist that free trade is worth fighting for. The work of the WTO is the world's attempt to put this theory into practice.

Are there any drawbacks to the theory? There are two issues that have to be considered. First, no allowance has been made for **transport costs**. These can add considerably to the overall cost of a purchase. A *slight* comparative advantage may not be enough to make specialisation and trade worthwhile. However, bulk shipping using containers is now very cheap, adding a relatively small percentage on to the cost of most products traded in bulk. As a result, most internationally traded products cost roughly the same anywhere in the world, as the **law of one price** predicts.

Second, international specialisation creates losers. Although both *countries* gain, within each country there will be industries that must die if the gains from trade are to be achieved. The workers in these industries will lose out, until and unless they retrain in the expanding industries. Geographical and occupational mobility is clearly an issue here (see Chapter 13).

Finally, what determines the possession of comparative advantage? The key idea here is **relative factor** (= input) **endowment**. The goods that require an input with which a country is relatively well supplied are likely to be the goods in which that country has the comparative advantage. So countries with a lot of land (relative to their population and capital stock) tend to end up specialising in agriculture. Countries with a lot of unskilled labour end up specialising in simple manufacturing. Countries with a lot of capital and skilled labour end up specialising in high-technology manufacturing and international services. Australian cattle farms, Chinese assembly plants and American pharmaceutical companies are illustrations of the point.

Who gains most from international trade? The terms of trade

Although the theory of comparative advantage shows that all countries stand to gain from international trade, the extent to which each country gains will vary widely. The actual gains from trade will depend on the price a country can get for its exports relative to what it has to pay for its imports. The price of a country's exports relative to its imports is known as its **terms of trade**. This in turn depends on the global market for the products concerned.

Countries that rely heavily on one or two exports may experience particularly volatile terms of trade as their exported commodities fluctuate in price. This difficulty is mostly faced by those ELDCs that depend on one or two primary products, such as Nigeria's oil, Zambia's copper and Namibia's diamonds. However, producers can always sell in forward markets if they wish to eliminate the risk derived from falling prices.

The most spectacular switches in the terms of trade take place when cartels are formed — or collapse. The famous example is the Organisation of Petroleum Exporting Countries (OPEC), which in 1974 managed to engineer a fourfold increase in the price of crude oil. Over the subsequent decade its members enjoyed unprecedented prosperity — until new oil fields (developed in response to the high price) came on stream and prices returned to more normal levels.

Many charities engaged in helping ELDCs take the view that if the terms of trade of poor countries deteriorate over several years, this is somehow *unfair*. It is perhaps better to view such a development as the impersonal operation of market forces. The appropriate response is for the ELDCs to take account of the signals of the price mechanism — and diversify into new products. In the short term, there is a case for rich countries increasing the amount of aid.

Since most countries export and import thousands of different products, the only way to measure the terms of trade is to construct a price index for both exports and imports. These indices will both be given the value of 100 in their base year, and subsequent movements of average export (and import) prices will then be reflected in these indices.

$$\text{Terms of trade} = \frac{\text{Price of exports} \times 100}{\text{Price of imports}}$$

So if the price of exports rises 20% from the base year, while the price of imports rises only 5%, the new value of the terms of trade is $(120/105) \times 100 = 114$. This is called an *improvement* in the terms of trade because the country can now buy more imports for the same amount of exports.

One very obvious way in which a country's terms of trade can improve is if its exchange rate rises. As already mentioned in Chapter 15 (and again in Chapter 21), a rising exchange rate leads to an increased standard of living as more imports can be bought for the same amount of exports — always provided the exports can still sell at the increased price.

Inward investment: the global route to rapid economic growth (see also Chapter 12)

Chapter 12 showed that economic growth can be achieved only if either the quantity of inputs or their productivity increases. The particular difficulty of increasing the capital stock through investment is that present consumption has to be sacrificed so that savings can be built up and used to invest in expansion. In a poor country, saving is difficult to achieve. Poor people find it difficult to save because the resources that they possess are urgently needed for immediate consumption.

There is a neat way round this difficulty: borrow the money from richer countries, or persuade the multinationals to invest directly. But it is not foolproof. If the money is not invested wisely, then ELDCs simply end up with extensive debts. This is the origin of the 'international debt crisis'. In essence, African and South American countries borrowed money in the late 1970s to early 1990s that they could not effectively use — much was stolen by the country's ruling elites. The same corruption that has rendered them unable to pay their debts also helps to keep them poor. Much of this **development finance**, whether owed to foreign governments or to foreign banks, has now been written off. Although this helps the countries in the short term, it also destroys their credit rating. They are unlikely to be able to borrow in the foreseeable future.

However, the same approach can be a key to rapid economic growth. China, which enjoyed a growth rate of 7% p.a. through the 1990s, has been a major beneficiary of **inward investment**. By joining the WTO in 2001, it hopes to receive a lot more in the coming years. Within Europe, the UK has been the biggest recipient of inward investment. The UK has the advantages of speaking English, the international language of business;

having low wages relative to its skill base; lying within the EU tariff wall — and having employment legislation that makes it relatively cheap and quick for a company to fire workers when it wants to.

Inward investment is a key part of the global free-market system. Just as firms within an industry are forced by competitive pressures to be efficient, so also whole countries are forced to adopt business-friendly policies if they want to benefit from inward investment. If they destabilise politically or for some other reason fail to retain their attractiveness to the international investor, then a 'capital flight' develops as money leaves the country. At the time of writing, this is all too apparent in the case of Zimbabwe. Such **capital flows** can destabilise a country (and its currency) in a matter of a few days.

One of the arguments against further EU integration is that, in seeking to impose common employment legislation and common tax rates across Europe, the EU is restricting competition for inward investment in these areas.

Conclusion

The theory of comparative advantage demonstrates conclusively that globalisation is a powerful force for economic growth. However, as is so often the case, the benefits are not spread around evenly. Countries that can attract inward investment, and those that are fortunate in the movement of their terms of trade, are likely to gain more than others.

GLOSSARY

absolute advantage: lower costs in an industry in one country
capital flow: international transfer of financial or physical capital
comparative advantage: relative superiority, relative cost advantage
development finance: finance for economically less developed countries, normally from outside
inward investment: investment coming into a country from another one
law of one price: principle that traded goods cost the same everywhere
relative factor endowment: relative profusion of inputs
terms of trade: price of a nation's exports relative to imports
transport costs: freight and insurance costs, especially in international trade

How and why is globalisation regulated?

At the end of this section, you should be able to:

1 Explain the benefits of global financial stability, and some of the methods of achieving it.

2 Comment on the arguments put forward for restricting free trade.

Global stability: the international financial system

Many current international institutions have their origin in the severe global recession of the 1930s that followed the Wall Street crash of 1929. The USA tried to get out of recession by restricting imports, so that there was more work for domestic US industry. This merely spread the recession to European countries, which were now unable to export to the USA. Europe responded by restricting imports itself — which made the US recession much

worse. This domino effect created a global recession that was far worse than would have been caused by the initial stock market crash on its own.

It was a determination to avoid similar events in the future that led to the creation of many international institutions after the Second World War. We have already discussed the EU and the WTO, both of which were founded in their original form in the immediate postwar period. The main political creation of this time was the **United Nations**. And two new economic institutions were formed: the International Monetary Fund and the World Bank.

The main aim of the **International Monetary Fund** (**IMF**) is to promote **international financial stability** by collecting money from the world's major nations that can then be lent to any government facing severe financial difficulties. Normally the loans have been made conditional on 'structural adjustment': that is, on the government in question taking steps to cut its spending and/or encourage competition within and across its boundaries. The IMF is frequently criticised for lending with strings attached. This, it is asserted, amounts to bullying poor countries in their hour of need. However, much of this criticism is misplaced. The conditions that are laid down are those which, on the basis of the IMF's past experience, are necessary for tackling the underlying causes of the crisis.

The IMF has been kept busy ever since its inception. The **international debt crisis** of the 1980s and early 1990s involved the IMF in the provision of several emergency loans in Africa and Latin America. However, international debt is not just the concern of official-dom in its various forms. In 2001, the UK agreed to write off the debts of the poorest countries following a campaign by the major development charities. **Non-governmental organisations** such as these also have their part to play.

More recently, Korea has needed emergency aid following a lengthy period of slow growth in Japan and its neighbours during the 1990s. The UK, too, has not been immune, requiring an emergency loan in 1976. The top five recipients of IMF aid from its inception in 1947 up until 2000 have been Mexico, Korea, Russia, Brazil and Argentina.

The **International Bank for Reconstruction and Development** (the IBRD or **World Bank**) was set up to provide **soft loans** and **multilateral aid** to developing countries. This aid is in addition to the **bilateral aid** (often **tied aid**) that is also provided on a country-to-country basis. The World Bank works in more than 100 developing countries with the primary focus of helping the poorest people and the poorest countries. To this end, it has become the largest funder of education and health programmes in developing countries.

The two issues of global financial stability and poverty are closely linked. There can ultimately be no global stability while some members of the global community are desperately poor. This linkage has been brought home in sinister fashion by the terrorist attacks on the World Trade Center in September 2001. The countries in which the terrorist organisation al-Qa'eda flourished were Afghanistan, Sudan and Somalia, all of which are both impoverished and chaotic.

Trade negotiations

The basic issues surrounding trade negotiations can be summarised as follows:
- Each country stands to gain from free international trade, as shown by the theory of comparative advantage — and supported by the observation that free trade results in more competitive market structures.

- Nonetheless, free international trade creates specific groups of losers within each country — that is, the stakeholders in those industries that lack a comparative advantage. These potential losers campaign — often successfully — to restrict trade through tariffs and quotas.

The outcome of these two effects is termed **diffuse benefits, concentrated costs**.

The WTO, as Chapter 24 explained, is engaged in a never-ending series of negotiations aimed at reducing trade barriers. Nevertheless, a number of arguments are put forward for maintaining these barriers and restricting free international trade. Ask yourself: how convincing do you find them? How might they be abused?

- *Helping the losers.* The sudden removal of protection from an uncompetitive industry that has hitherto sheltered behind a tariff wall will result in widespread hardship as the industry folds. It may therefore be argued that transitional arrangements should be put in place to soften the blow. Rather than removing protection all at once, it should be phased out over a number of years. This line of reasoning is known as the **sunset industry** argument.

- *Helping the potential winners.* It may be that a country has a *potential* comparative advantage in an industry, but that it needs time to establish itself against existing competition. The classic example of this is the Japanese car industry after the Second World War. The Japanese government made it very difficult for other countries to export cars to Japan. Behind this protection, the Japanese car industry flourished — and soon developed into the most successful car manufacturers in the world with an undoubted comparative advantage. This reason for restricting trade is known as the **infant industry** argument.

- *The strategic argument.* One of the problems with any form of specialisation is that it works only if countries can guarantee that they will be able to trade subsequently. The **strategic argument** for protection is based on the possibility that, in an uncertain world, trade may be disrupted through war or other disputes. The argument goes that it is better to protect an uncompetitive domestic industry than to rely on a foreign one, which may one day not be available. The argument is strongest for the armaments industry — can anyone be relied upon to sell you munitions in time of war? It is also strong in the energy industry: first, because power is essential to all other industries and, secondly, because the Middle East, from which most of the world's oil supplies come, is a notoriously unstable region.

- *Market failures.* A separate group of arguments revolves round market failures, notably external costs, monopoly and inequality. It might be considered desirable to ban hardwoods exploited from forests that are not replaced (an 'external cost' argument); or to ban products manufactured by slave labour in Chinese prison camps (an 'inequality' argument); or to ban products from firms using predatory pricing methods to drive existing UK-based firms out of business — this is known as **dumping**.

GLOSSARY

bilateral aid: gifts from one government to another, often an economically less developed country
diffuse benefits, concentrated costs: many people gain a little, a few lose a lot
dumping: exporting goods at prices below the cost of production
infant industry: industry new to a specific country
International Bank for Reconstruction and Development (IBRD), World Bank: provider of 'soft' development loans to economically less developed countries
international debt crisis: inability of many poor countries to repay debt in the 1990s
international financial stability: safety and security of the global banking system
International Monetary Fund (IMF): provider of loans to countries in crisis

GLOSSARY

multilateral aid: gifts sent by an international organisation (e.g. EU, UN)

non-governmental organisation: private charity, often providing aid to economically less developed countries

soft loan: loan on favourable terms (e.g. to economically less developed countries)

strategic argument for protectionism: the 'what if trade breaks down?' argument

sunset industry: industry dying in a specific country

tied aid: conditional gifts (e.g. money which must be spent with the donor)

United Nations (UN): world debating chamber in New York, whose aim is to promote harmony and peace among nations

What ethical issues arise from globalisation?

At the end of this section, you should be able to:

1 Explain why some external costs can be properly addressed only within an international framework.

2 Discuss one or more international environmental agreements.

3 Discuss the issues raised by ethical trading.

4 Explain the impact of globalisation on income distribution.

Introduction

At the World Trade Organisation's meeting in Seattle, USA in 1999 there were widespread violent scenes from several thousand protestors on the streets outside. The protestors represented many different viewpoints: trade unions, environmentalists and anarchists were all well represented. But all saw the process of globalisation as their chief enemy, even if their demands were often contradictory. Since then, a travelling circus of protestors has gathered not only outside meetings of the WTO, but also at summits of world leaders.

This section will examine some of the issues surrounding globalisation that arouse such passion.

External costs and globalisation (see also Chapter 10)

It may well be asked why an increasingly global economy makes any difference to the analysis of external costs given in Chapter 10. There are basically two extensions to the observations made so far.

First, globalisation increases the economic activity of relatively poor countries. This is, of course, very much to their advantage in broad terms. However, ELDCs often lack the administrative and financial capacity to regulate the external costs that their new-found wealth generates. For example, illegal logging in the Amazon basin or in Borneo is generating significant negative externalities. Hardwoods are being cut down much faster than they are being replaced, leading to unsustainable development for these countries in the future. The 'genetic pool' of trees is also being reduced for ever, as species become extinct. In the absence of a government able or willing to deal with these externalities, there is a

good case for saying that international aid from rich countries should be made available — especially as their demand for the hardwoods is one of the root causes of the problem.

Second, many of the external costs generated by globalisation affect not only the countries directly responsible for the damage, but also the planet *as a whole*. In these circumstances, no single country, however well organised, can deal with the problem on its own. For example, the loss of rainforest is creating **global warming**, which may, through a rise in the sea level, affect countries thousands of miles away from the original forests. And the loss of genetic diversity as species become extinct is a loss for everyone. It is not, therefore, surprising that campaigns to save the tiger, the gorilla and the panda are partly led and almost wholly financed by OECD countries — rather than the countries in which the animals are found.

If a global problem such as global warming is to be tackled effectively, certain principles need to be established from the start:

- There will be no solution without an **international environmental agreement**. If countries are left to their own devices, the **free rider** problem will surface. Countries that try hard will benefit no more from their efforts than those that do not try at all. So there is little incentive for *anyone* to try. In effect, the global climate is *non-excludable* — like a conventional public good. A joint agreement will be needed on a global scale, just as societies make a joint agreement to fund public goods, such as defence, through taxation.
- There must be a recognition that rich countries will pay more than poor ones because they are better able to do so — and because it is their industrialisation over the past 150 years that has created the problem.
- As with the correction of any market failure, there will be an overall net gain to society — but specific groups of losers. There is a vital role for pressure groups in raising public awareness of the issues, and winning the democratic debate in OECD countries against the lobbying of potential losers. For example, oil companies stand to lose if their ability to extract this **non-renewable resource** is limited by environmental concerns.

The United Nations Framework Convention on Climate Change (UNFCCC)

The UNFCCC originated at the **Rio Summit** in late 1992. Its ultimate objective is to 'stabilise greenhouse gas concentrations in the atmosphere at a level that would prevent dangerous human interference with the climate system'. Since then there have been conferences at regular intervals. It is anticipated that such meetings will be needed into the indefinite future as the rate of global warming increases. In this respect, the UNFCCC is rather like the WTO — a long-term global institution set up to manage a long-term global problem.

The most significant result after Rio was the **Kyoto protocol** of late 1997, whose target was to reduce global greenhouse gas emissions of rich countries by 5% by 2008–12. This protocol showed how the principles outlined above were to work out in practice:

- *The principle of international agreement*. Countries cannot be compelled to do things that they do not wish to. But the signatories to Kyoto agreed to the target on condition that at least 55 countries signed up to it, including rich countries accounting for at least 55% of all CO_2 emissions — the main greenhouse gas. Furthermore, the 5% reduction target was negotiated between the rich countries. The EU ended up with a –8% target, the USA –7% and Japan –6%. Some countries, such as Norway and Australia, that already have relatively low emissions, negotiated themselves an increase.

- *The recognition that rich countries should pay more than poor ones.* ELDCs are not subject to any greenhouse gas cuts: if they can merely maintain their existing levels, that will be an achievement. But they cannot and should not be prevented from following the path of industrialisation just for the sake of reducing greenhouse gases. The countries that have created the problem have to take the lead in solving it. One way of easing the pain for the rich countries might be through *pollution licences* (see also Chapter 10). This part of the Kyoto protocol has not yet been put into practice. But the protocol agrees in principle that countries finding their targets difficult to meet should be able to buy *emission credits* from countries that have achieved their target with something to spare. The USA had hoped to achieve its own target by buying emission credits from other countries. However, in early 2001 the USA announced it was not going to sign the Kyoto protocol — perhaps calculating that there was no easy way to achieve its 7% reduction target, even if it bought up a few spare emission credits from other countries.

- *The need for public pressure on governments to take the issue seriously.* There is little that the UN can do to achieve this, but the protocol does emphasise the need for education. The hope is that increased public awareness will eventually feed through to stronger government action.

Ethical trading (see also Chapter 11)

In a market-orientated society, the views of 'the market' (customers) are crucial. The extent to which multinationals care about the ethical issues that their activities raise therefore depends on the level of **consumer awareness** about these issues. This in turn depends on the success of pressure groups in getting these issues discussed in public debate.

At its most successful, consumer power can alter the policies of the market leaders of industry. One notable success is the decision by the UK's major supermarkets to ban genetically modified (GM) foodstuffs in response to customer demand. Although at the time of writing there is no evidence to suggest that GM foods do any harm to humans, from the supermarkets' point of view customer perception is just as important as the underlying science, and perhaps more so. The decision was taken with profitability in mind rather than out of any sense of **corporate responsibility**.

Ethical issues also generate a niche market, which caters for those consumers for whom the ethical issues involved are of major personal importance. Traidcraft, Oxfam/Fair Trade and Out of this World (OOTW) are examples of companies for which methods of manufacture and trade are as important as the actual goods themselves. Customers pay more on the understanding that the ELDC workers who produce the goods have themselves been paid more than the going rate in their locality. This concept is known as **ethical pricing**. It has to be said that such enterprises, while praiseworthy in concept, have enjoyed limited commercial success.

More profitable have been conventional companies that have added a strong ethical stance to their image. The Body Shop, for example, does not allow animal testing of its products and takes pride in its treatment of its ELDC suppliers. Again, the Co-op has established itself as the 'ethical bank', notably by refusing to do business with companies involved in areas of business about which the majority of its customers have expressed reservations. These include arms dealing and fur farming. This general approach is known as **ethical trading**. In both companies, their ethical stance forms an important part of their marketing strategy.

The effect of globalisation on income inequality (see also Chapter 14)

The best recent examples of the effect of globalisation on income inequality are provided by the collapse of the Communist bloc in 1989, and the subsequent adoption by eastern Europe of free-market economies open to international trade. In a parallel development, China has also opened its borders to international trade in the 1990s, while retaining a communist, one-party government in domestic politics.

The immediate effect of globalisation is to create new winners — and new losers. The winners are those who grasp the new opportunities. Poland embraced globalisation most enthusiastically after 1989, and soon developed a class of millionaires who scoured Europe's warehouses looking for cast-off goods to sell at huge mark-ups to a population hitherto deprived of western consumer goods. The new losers were workers in Polish factories, manufacturing goods that could not hope to compete on quality with western substitutes. Therefore, the immediate effect of globalisation is to *widen* the gap between rich and poor.

As the years pass, the increased competition that globalisation creates leads to faster economic growth and a general increase in living standards. The increased demand for labour creates higher wage levels for all sections of society. The poor become richer and the rich become richer too; hence the gap between rich and poor remains wide. However, the alternative of isolating a country from contact with the outside world is normally a recipe for economic collapse and widespread hardship, as is evident in North Korea and Afghanistan today.

Globalisation may not solve deep-rooted problems in a country's economy. In the case of much of sub-Saharan Africa, war, AIDS, rapid population growth and a lack of management skills have led to *declining* standards of living since the 1970s. Widespread borrowing in the 1970s and 1980s was wasted — and led to a debt crisis that has only widened the gulf between these countries and the rest of the world. The discussion at the end of Option 3 on the 2002 Earth Summit in Johannesburg is also relevant here.

Thus there is no guarantee that globalisation will reduce income inequality. What it does offer is *opportunity* — if not for all, then for many. The world's two most populous countries, China and India, are doing very well out of globalisation. Their economic growth rates over the 1990s were 10% and 6% p.a. respectively. This has enabled them to diminish substantially the gap between themselves and the rich, OECD countries. But while globalisation has provided a powerful mechanism for raising global living standards, such improvements also highlight the tragic exceptions of countries that have been left behind.

GLOSSARY

consumer awareness: consumer knowledge about products and markets
corporate responsibility: ethical obligations of a firm to all its stakeholders
ethical pricing: pricing with due regard for moral standards
ethical trading: trading with due regard for moral standards
free rider: person benefiting from the actions of others without paying
global warming: increase in global temperatures caused by CO_2
international environmental agreement: necessary part of dealing with global externalities
Kyoto protocol (1997): international agreement to reduce CO_2 emissions
non-renewable resources: inputs whose global quantity is finite (e.g. oil)
Rio Summit: world environment conference in 1992

Chapter 26
Option 2: can there be certainty?

Introduction

This option is based on the theme of the uncertain future: an uncertainty that affects every economic agent from households to businesses to government. This guide concentrates on investment planning, for which you need to revise the balance sheet, covered in Chapter 7. The second main theme is the business cycle, which was first dealt with in Chapters 12 and 13. These chapters should be treated as an integral part of your revision for this option.

The uncertain future will be looked at in four sections:
- *How do companies plan for and finance growth?* This looks at issues associated with the money side of expanding a business, and briefly returns to strategic planning.
- *How do companies cope with the business cycle?* This examines the business response to booms and slumps.
- *What are the causes of the business cycle?* This looks briefly at explanations for this universal phenomenon.
- *How does government respond to the business cycle?* This examines a range of macroeconomic issues, and particularly government responses to recession.

How do companies plan for and finance growth?

At the end of this section, you should be able to:

1 Discuss strategic planning models, including Ansoff's Box.

2 Discuss the sources of finance, with particular reference to the gearing ratio.

3 Explain the payback period and the average rate of return.

Strategic planning: Ansoff's Box (see also Chapters 8 and 20)

Chapter 20 discussed SWOT analysis, the Boston Matrix and Porter's four generic strategies as tools for long-term thinking about a company's future. You should revise these as part of your preparation for Option 2.

Ansoff's Box (or Matrix) is a strategic planning model for analysing the four expansion options facing any company. It can simply sell more of its existing products to its existing markets (i.e. achieve increased market penetration). This approach is relatively risk-free. Alternatively, it can seek new markets for existing products (market development), perhaps seeking export markets. Or it can produce new products for existing markets (product development). Finally, it can develop new products for new markets. Known as **diversification**, this is the riskiest option of all.

The various options are illustrated by Figure 26.1. Any firm starts in the top-left segment and may either stay there or move into the other three segments.

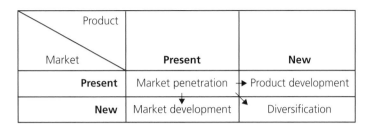

Figure 26.1 Ansoff's Box

Multinationals commonly develop *both* new products *and* new markets. Microsoft and Coca-Cola are developing new versions of their basic products all the time, but are also constantly seeking to break into new markets. Smaller companies may be well advised to concentrate on one or the other. The Korean inventor of a drinks can that automatically chills when you open it is concentrating on marketing the invention worldwide. He has made the strategic decision to invest what time and money he has on this one project, before he considers widening his product range.

Does expansion need financing? (see also Chapter 7)

Every asset on the balance sheet, whether a fixed asset (e.g. buildings and equipment) or a current asset (e.g. stock, debtors and cash), needs to be financed. In other words, a *source* has to be found for this cash and all other assets. The possible sources are examined below, but first it is necessary to ask whether a programme of expansion inevitably means that more assets will need to be bought and paid for.

It is possible to economise on the need for assets in a variety of ways. Extra office space can be found by putting Portacabins in car parks, or the extra space can be rented or leased rather than bought outright. It might be possible for an expanding company to contract out some manufacturing rather than invest in the extra factory space.

However, it is difficult to achieve a major expansion without putting down some cash up-front. New products have to be developed and launched with cash, entering new markets will require initial marketing expenditure, and any acquisition of another company has to be paid for. Even renting property normally entails paying 3 months' rent in advance.

Sources of finance (see also Chapter 7)

Current assets can often be financed through a variety of short-term solutions. For example, debtors can sometimes be financed by short-term creditors. Stocks can be financed through trade credit. And cash may not be necessary at all if the bank is prepared to offer a substantial overdraft on the firm's current account.

But when it comes to fixed assets, there are essentially only two sources of finance. Either the money can be borrowed or the shareholders have to find it. Shareholder finance takes place either through the issue of new shares, including **venture capital**, or through the use of retained profits that have not already been spent (i.e. its existing cash and possibly investments, although investments are not usually shown in A-level balance sheets).

The *proportion* of capital employed that has been borrowed is known as the **gearing ratio**. This is a crucial percentage for any company. A high gearing ratio indicates a risky position for the company concerned. It has been financed on borrowed money, on which interest must be paid. This fixed cost raises the break-even level of sales, and may bankrupt the company if this level is not achieved. However, if the company is successful, the relatively few shareholders stand to gain a very high reward.

$$\text{Gearing ratio} = \frac{\text{Long-term liabilities} \times 100}{\text{Capital employed}}$$

For example, suppose BT decides to buy up the Austrian national telephone company for £1 billion, financed through a combination of borrowing and new share issues.

Table 26.1 shows that, if the new subsidiary only makes a £50 million operating profit, a low gearing ratio is the only way to avoid a loss.

	Option A 0% gearing	Option B 40% gearing	Option C 80% gearing
Loan raised (£m)	0	400	800
Equity raised (£m)	1,000	600	200
Turnover (£m)	100	100	100
Operating profit: 50% margin (£m)	50	50	50
Interest @ 10% p.a. (£m)	0	40	80
Net profit (loss) (£m)	profit 50	profit 10	loss (30)
Earnings per £1 share	50/1,000 = 5p	10/600 = 1.7p	(30)/200 = 15p loss

Table 26.1 Effect of high gearing on a company making a small operating profit

However, if the subsidiary makes a £150 million operating profit, then Table 26.2 shows that the shareholders would do better to go for a high gearing ratio. Since the company now generates enough profits to cover interest payments easily, the shareholders would not want to dilute their ownership of the company by issuing new shares.

	Option A 0% gearing	Option B 40% gearing	Option C 80% gearing
Loan raised (£m)	0	400	800
Equity raised (£m)	1,000	600	200
Turnover (£m)	300	300	300
Operating profit: 50% margin (£m)	150	150	150
Interest @ 10% p.a. (£m)	0	40	80
Net profit (loss) (£m)	150	110	70
Earnings per £1 share	15p	18.3p	35p

Table 26.2 Effect of high gearing on a company making a large operating profit

Thus the issue for a firm seeking to expand is this: if it is confident that the expansion will work, the company should finance it by borrowing money. The owners' profits will be greater if the company prospers as anticipated. If, on the other hand, expansion entails significant risk, the company stands more chance of surviving if its owners are prepared to sell a proportion of the company to outsiders through the issue of more shares.

Investment appraisal (1): the payback period

This simple method looks at the amount of time an investment needs before the cash it generates pays for the initial outlay. Suppose a travel agent pays £50,000 for a piece of software enabling it to search for the best available flight deals. It calculates that the equipment will generate £2,500 additional net cash flow each month. It therefore takes 20 months to pay for the software (excluding any interest payments meanwhile). This is known as the **payback period** of the investment. Obviously the shorter the payback, the better for the company.

$$\text{Payback period in months} = \frac{\text{Initial capital outlay}}{\text{Monthly additional cash flow}}$$

In this case, the payback period (in months) is £50,000/£2,500 = 20

This method of assessing investments is commonly used by small companies for which cash flow is likely to be particularly important. A short payback period also reduces risk. A project that takes a long time to pay back may never make it, if changes in customer demand or competitors' products undermine the assumptions on which the initial investment was undertaken.

However, the payback method of investment appraisal does not consider what happens *after* the sum invested has been recouped, so it is of limited value when considering long-term investments.

Investment appraisal (2): the average rate of return (see also Chapter 7)

Suppose the travel agent calculates that the software costing £50,000 will generate £2,500 net cash each month for 4 years — before a better system comes out that renders the purchase obsolete. The operating profits from the investment will then be (£2,500 × 48) – £50,000 = £70,000. This works out as £17,500 p.a. over the lifetime of the software. Given that it cost £50,000 in the first place, this amounts to a return of 35% p.a. This figure is known as the **average rate of return** (ARR).

$$\text{Average rate of return} = \frac{\text{Average annual operating profit}}{\text{Initial capital outlay}} \times 100$$

In our example, we lay out the figures as follows:

Initial outlay	**£50,000**
Net cash, Year 1	£30,000
Net cash, Year 2	£30,000
Net cash, Year 3	£30,000
Net cash, Year 4	£30,000
Total net cash	**£120,000**
Operating profit over 4 years	£70,000
Annual operating profit	£17,500
Annual rate of return (ARR)	**£17,500/£50,000 x 100 = 35%**

The formula for ARR is essentially the same as that for % ROCE in Chapter 7. Both measure the annual return a company receives as a percentage of the cash invested in the first place. The only difference is that % ROCE shows the annual return from *total* company operations, while ARR measures the return on one specific investment project. Otherwise the concepts are identical.

A word of caution is necessary about mathematical investment appraisal techniques. They are only as accurate as the figures put into them in the first place — and these figures are often no better than informed guesses. To use the previous example, the *cost* of a piece of software can be known with some certainty, but the *returns* that it will subsequently generate can only be guessed at. Business history is full of disastrous investments — from Concorde to the Channel Tunnel to the dot.com crash. In the first two cases, the costs of construction were wildly underestimated. In the final case, the turnover that could be generated from visitors to websites was wildly overestimated. So mathematical appraisal needs to be balanced with business experience before a company can sensibly invest large sums of money.

GLOSSARY

Ansoff's Box (Matrix): analysis of a firm's expansion options
average rate of return (ARR): percentage of initial investment received annually
diversification: widening the product mix and/or markets
gearing ratio: loan capital as a percentage of total capital employed
payback period: time taken to restore cash to its initial position
venture capital: high-risk equity, often committed to a new start-up

How do companies cope with the business cycle?

At the end of this section, you should be able to:

1 Discuss company responses to a recession.

2 Discuss the need for good-quality information in a climate of uncertainty.

3 Comment on the effect of booms and slumps on the labour market.

Company responses to a recession (see also Chapter 12)

Any company should be constantly re-evaluating its operations, with or without a recession. However, a downturn often forces a company that has been unwilling to change to reopen the debate about its future. This is one reason why recessions have been called 'creative gales of destruction'. Some companies do not survive the time of hardship; few are left unchanged by the experience.

Every aspect of the company's business needs to be considered. Are there **cost-cutting** procedures that will not damage the firm? Should the product portfolio be slimmed down? Do its products need to become more innovative? Do its strategic plans (discussed in the previous section) need to be updated in the light of new conditions? Is its market research sufficient to enable it to identify its opportunities and threats?

The paragraphs below examine the impact of recession on two particular areas: production planning and human resource management.

Production planning at a time of uncertainty (see also Chapter 5)

Changes in demand for a company's products, whether caused by the business cycle or any other reason, create a need for a constant flow of information from all its stakeholders. What are customers buying? Do they like it? What are stock levels? Are they neither too high nor too low? Are suppliers reliable? Will they meet orders? Can the firm's own production facilities meet their orders in turn? What is cash flow? Is the set overdraft limit likely to be breached? Is the company employing too many people or too few? Are they properly trained and motivated?

In the following extract from *Business @ the Speed of Thought* (quoted in the *Nuffield Economics and Business Students' Book*, p. 479), Bill Gates suggests it is those companies that are best able to manage information flows that are likely to be the most successful: 'McDonald's is well on the way to installing a new information system that uses PCs and web technologies to tally sales at all its restaurants in real time. As soon as you order two Happy Meals, a McDonald's marketing manager will know. Rather than superficial or anecdotal data, the marketer will have hard, factual data for tracking trends.'

Indeed, **trend analysis** is an important way of reducing future uncertainty. The future rarely arrives completely unannounced. Its seeds lie in the present, and those companies that are quickest in reading the present will be best positioned for exploiting the future. For example, an up-to-date time series on sales of every item on the McDonald's menu will indicate which dishes are growing in popularity, which are losing appeal and need to be repackaged — indeed, where every item is in its product life cycle.

The same idea has also been popularised by Charles Handy through his concept of the **learning organisation**. Many of the ideas met in the AS section of the course, such as informal communication, democratic management styles, market research and total quality management, are based on the idea that companies need fast and accurate communication flows both within themselves and outside their own boundaries.

The effect of the business cycle on the labour market (see also Chapter 6)

As the AD curve shifts outwards during a boom, so also does the demand for labour. An increased demand for output is translated into an increased demand for inputs. Workers find their bargaining position improves as a **skills shortage** develops. Increased wages may be available as rates on **national pay scales** increase, but it is likely to be up to the individual worker to negotiate increases without the support of **collective bargaining**. Employers may consider offering **profit-related pay** or discretionary **bonuses** on the grounds that these do not have to be maintained if the volume of work slackens off in the future.

Skill shortages will also make it easier to negotiate favourable terms of employment. Employers will be more willing to offer part-time work, or explore the possibility of **job shares**. For those with commitments at home, employers might consider **flexitime** or, in some jobs, see if **teleworking** some of the week would provide an alternative.

In a recession, the balance of power shifts back to the employers. They can drive a harder bargain on wages, and be less accommodating to individual preferences. However, it is

still comparatively difficult to push through actual wage *reductions*. This is one reason for paying staff **piece rate** rather than **time rate**. With piece rate (e.g. the commission paid to a sales force), it is far easier for the employer to share the pain of a recession with the employee. As the company's sales fall, so too does the commission received by the salespeople.

Another method that firms use to cope with volatile trading conditions is **fixed-term contracts**. By employing someone on, say, a 2-year contract, there is no obligation to use them after the time is up. In return for the lower level of security, someone working on these terms normally needs to be offered a higher rate of pay. A variant on this is the **fixed-hours contract**, where the worker agrees to work for so many hours a year, but is given no guarantee as to when those hours will be. Alternatively, some jobs can be **outsourced** altogether. Cleaning and catering services are often outsourced, and IT support is increasingly outsourced as well.

GLOSSARY

bonus: flexible payment when workers or firms do well
collective bargaining: trade union negotiating on behalf of workers
cost cutting: emphasis on cost minimisation/reduction
fixed-hours contract: workers turn up as required, within total annual hours
fixed-term contract: work contract whose length is specified in advance
flexitime: situation where a worker has some discretion when to put in the hours
job sharing: situation where one job is shared by two part-timers
learning organisation: firm committed to continuous improvement
national pay scale: wage level decided by national arrangement
outsourcing, contracting out: buying in services previously done in-house
piece rate: payment per item (e.g. sales commission)
profit-related pay: pay that rises to some extent if a firm's profits rise
skills shortage: situation where skilled labour is in short supply
teleworking: working from home, connected by telephone
time rate: payment for each hour worked
trend analysis: examining a trend to predict future changes

What are the causes of the business cycle?

At the end of this section, you should be able to:

1 Explain in outline how the multiplier, investment and expectations magnify the business cycle.

2 Explain in outline how the tax-and-benefit system, international trade and savings dampen the business cycle.

Magnifying the business cycle (see also Chapter 12)

Chapter 12 showed that recessions are normally caused by 'shocks' — events that create major macroeconomic movements. These may be political, economic, social or technological in origin. These four causes of shock can be summarised in the useful acronym, **PEST**. The terrorist attack on 11 September 2001 was a political shock. The bursting of

the dot.com bubble in 2000 was an economic shock. The internet-inspired boom of the 1990s was a (benign) technological shock. The **new paradigm** (new model) of economic growth is based on the assertion that advances in IT have permanently raised the long-term economic growth rate.

Social shocks tend to be slower moving, and feature much less in traditional economic analysis — even though they may be the most important factor in the long run. The collapse in Christianity's influence in the UK over the past 20 years and the corresponding rise in cohabitation, births outside marriage, and divorce is probably the best recent example of a social shock.

The postwar recessions have all been caused by economic shocks. Those in 1974–75 and 1980–81 were caused by enormous increases in oil prices as the OPEC cartel raised prices. The recession of 1990–92 was caused by deliberate government action: an increase in interest rates to 16% p.a. This increase was designed to reduce inflation — which it did, but only at the cost of pushing the economy into recession.

However, while shocks have the ability to reduce aggregate demand, the *extent* and *duration* of recessions cannot be explained by a single event. Rather, the single event 'starts the ball rolling' — creating a snowball effect that turns an initial reduction in AD into something much more serious. The three mechanisms that cause this leveraging-up of the original shock are as follows:

The **multiplier**. Suppose the atrocity of 11 September 2001 led to 200,000 lost jobs in the airline industry. That equates to 200,000 fewer salaries being paid — and subsequently spent. A knock-on effect will be some job losses in retailing, and in the other areas of the economy where those 200,000 salaries were spent. This in turn will lead to further job losses, and so on, in a series of diminishing ripple effects. If the *final* loss in jobs created by this process was 400,000, the multiplier would have a value of 2: that is, the total job loss divided by the initial job loss.

The operation of the multiplier is most apparent at a regional level. The closure of a town's major employer can have a devastating effect on the local economy, as the loss of spending power among former employees leads to a knock-on effect that closes down many other businesses too. In this context, the multiplier is known as the **regional multiplier**.

The effect on investment. Suppose 11 September 2001 led to a 10% reduction in the demand for air travel — and suppose the average aircraft has a lifespan of 20 years, leading to a 5% replacement of the global airline fleet every year. Since demand for flying has fallen by 10%, it will not be necessary to replace *any* aircraft for 2 years. In other words, the 10% decline in demand for air *travel* has led to a 100% decline in demand for new *aeroplanes*. This explains why investment goods industries are so volatile. A relatively minor reduction in the demand for consumer goods can lead to a devastating collapse in demand for the investment goods needed to produce those consumer goods. This phenomenon is known as the **accelerator**, but is not explicitly mentioned in your specification.

The role of **expectations**. While the population at large are not familiar with the technical language of the multiplier and the accelerator, they are all too aware of the reality of recessions. Therefore, one result of a shock is to make the population guess, on the evidence of their past life experience, that a recession is on the way. Many will cut back

on personal consumption in order to build up their savings in case they lose their jobs. This very action has the effect of throwing other people out of work, and so bringing on the recession that was feared. This is just one example of a self-fulfilling prophecy — an occasion where the anticipation of an event actually brings on the event itself. Governments are aware of this psychological herd instinct and may try to counteract it by assuring people through the media that a recession is *not* on the way. Whether this tactic works or not depends on whether anyone believes the government. As you may guess, the government's credibility is not necessarily very good.

Dampening the business cycle

Happily, there are also forces at work which have the opposite effect to that described above. These forces *dampen* the business cycle, making recessions less severe than they would otherwise be. These forces are known as **automatic stabilisers**.

The most powerful automatic stabiliser is the tax-and-benefit system. People in work on an average wage take home roughly 75% of their gross salary, the rest going in taxation and pension contributions. If they lose their jobs, then jobseekers' allowance, housing benefit and income support may pay them anything from 25% to over 50% of their gross wage. So their actual loss of spending power is much less than their gross wage. The fall in consumption during a recession is therefore much less than might have been supposed. On top of this, consumers will often run down their savings during a period of unemployment, again minimising the reduction in actual consumption spending.

Additionally, government spending on health, education and so on is another automatic stabiliser. These expenditures are usually maintained at normal levels during a recession. So a whole major area of aggregate demand is almost immune to the business cycle.

International trade may also work as an automatic stabiliser. Provided the initial shock causing the recession was domestic in origin, export demand will not be affected.

Conclusion

While there has been no recession at the time of writing for 10 years, it is all too probable that there will be recessions in the future. Businesses have to be prepared for them, as do governments. In the final section, we look at a range of government responses to recessions.

GLOSSARY

accelerator: effect on investment of changes in aggregate demand
automatic stabiliser: tax/benefit system dampening aggregate demand shocks
expectations: economic agents' beliefs about the future (e.g. inflation)
(national) multiplier: snowball effect on consumption of changes in aggregate demand
new paradigm: belief, for example, that IT has raised long-term economic growth
PEST analysis: political, economic, social and technological causes
regional multiplier: operation of the multiplier within one region

How does the government respond to the business cycle?

At the end of this section, you should be able to:

1 Explain the uses and limitations of economic forecasting techniques.

2 Discuss the causes of and solutions to unemployment and inflation in the context of the business cycle.

3 Discuss the welfare effects of a recession, and the impact of welfare benefits on incentives.

Anticipating the business cycle through economic forecasting

Forecasting describes the activity of trying to predict the future. In an economic context, it describes the attempt to predict economic variables in the years ahead. Forecasting is carried out so that economic agents can plan for the future. In the case of the government, such forecasts may enable it to prevent a recession, or at least to prepare for it.

So each year the government's budget includes a forecast of the major macroeconomic variables — inflation, unemployment, economic growth and the PSBR. Of course, the government's own tax and spending proposals will themselves have a strong influence on the size of the PSBR. Equally, the Bank of England produces its own economic forecasts, and has a particular interest in (and responsibility for) the inflation rate. If it thinks the inflation rate is likely to fall outside the 2.5% p.a. target by more than 1%, then interest rates will be adjusted to help hit the target.

International organisations such as the WTO, the OECD and the EU also produce economic forecasts, so that they can better plan for the aspects of the world economy for which they have a responsibility. Large companies, too, have their own forecasting units, specialising in the industry in which they are involved. For example, builders need to know population trends, regional mobility and trends in new household formation (including graduation, marriage and separation) before deciding what land to buy and what types of housing to build.

How is forecasting done?

The basic tools are macroeconomic models. These consist of a series of mathematical equations that seek to explain how the main variables interrelate. The models themselves are based on **extrapolation**. If, for example, it has been observed over the past 10 years that an x% increase in income results in a $0.7x$% increase in spending the following year, then one possible equation would be: $C_t = 0.7Y_{t-1}$ (i.e. consumption is 70% of last year's income). A whole set of such equations based on past time series can be used to predict the effect of, say, a 50% increase in the price of oil or a penny-in-the-pound reduction in income tax.

Of particular usefulness are **leading indicators**: that is, variables that change in advance of economic activity. So investment plans of companies give a good indication of what they *will* invest — and so how aggregate demand itself might change. Of course, any one figure might just be a one-off with little significance. To get round such 'bumps', forecasters

often base their predictions on **moving averages**: for example, taking the average of the last three or five figures.

Lagging indicators are of less use. For example, unemployment normally only starts to rise *after* an economy has entered a recession, and is therefore of little use in predicting one.

Why are forecasts inaccurate?

For one thing, *any* forecast has to be inaccurate because the future is essentially unknowable. Extrapolation can never be relied upon. Even if the formula $C_t = 0.7Y_{t-1}$ has worked for the past 10 years, there is no guarantee that the relationship will be stable for all time. Any social science, the study of human beings, has to contend with the changeable nature of its subject — a problem that does not affect the natural sciences.

On top of this, the prediction itself will change outcomes. Imagine that a fall in real GDP of 1% is predicted (i.e. a recession). Many firms will *respond* to that prediction by cutting back investment plans. This will, of course, make the recession worse. An alternative possibility is that the government will respond by adopting expansionary policy of some sort — and so the predicted recession never happens. The original forecast then appears inaccurate.

In a different context, the same points could be made about A-level predictions. The predictions themselves change the future as students respond to them by working harder (or giving up), and as universities make or withhold offers on the strength of them.

However, just because economic (and A-level) predictions are bound to be inaccurate is no reason for not making them. An imperfect guide to the future is better than no guide at all. In fact, the Bank of England responds to this uncertainty by producing a *range* of predictions in the form of a fan chart, with each section of the fan representing a different possible outcome.

Responding to unemployment and inflation associated with the business cycle (see also Chapter 13)

Chapter 13 discussed the causes of and solutions to both unemployment and inflation. You should be thoroughly familiar with this material when revising for Option 2. Two key themes are worth re-emphasising here.

First, a government cannot use demand management to spend its way out of a recession (and so reduce unemployment) *if* it also wishes to stick to an inflation target. The same outward shift in AD that increases output and employment *also* increases inflation. This could be illustrated by reversing the shift in Figure 12.3. As it happens, there has not been a recession since the introduction of formal inflation targets in the 1990s, so it has not yet been seen how the government will cope with this dilemma. When these circumstances arise, the government is likely to come under strong pressure to abandon its inflation target in order to limit the depth of the recession.

Second, it is not currently possible for the government to use demand management to reduce unemployment, because demand management is now used to hit the 2.5% p.a. inflation target. Another tool must be found to reduce unemployment. The key is a flexible

labour market. At the time of writing, significant increases in the minimum wage and a newly powerful trade union movement are both creating concern that the labour market is not as flexible as it was 5 years ago. In the event of an economic downturn, it will be interesting to see whether rising unemployment is quickly reversed — or whether employees have lost the capacity to adapt to harsher conditions.

How does the government cope with the welfare effects of a recession? (see also Chapter 14)

In the last recession of 1990–92, unemployment rose from 1.5 million to 3 million. The welfare effects of such an increase are severe. Typically, the number of people on the unemployment register rises during a recession because the *duration* of unemployment rises. Rather than taking a month to find a new job, too many of the unemployed take a year or so instead. Of course, the **welfare policy** of the government (see Chapter 14) reduces the actual economic hardship faced, but the psychological toll is still significant. Additionally, the unemployed quickly use up their savings. As a result, not only does income distribution become more unequal in a recession, but so does **wealth distribution**.

Furthermore, because unemployment tends to be concentrated in regions distant from the southeast, regional differences become greater too. In this area, the EU has responded with its own regional policy, which is aimed at all areas of the EU whose GDP per head is less than 75% of the EU average. Such areas are eligible for Objective 1 funding to promote economic development. For those regions seriously affected by industrial decline as heavy industries such as steel close down, there is additional **Objective 2 funding.** Such budgetary expenditure will be put under strain if the EU goes ahead with plans to include eastern Europe. The current major beneficiaries, such as Scotland, Portugal and Greece, will be less eligible if their status as relatively poor members of the EU is taken by Poland, Latvia and Estonia.

The welfare state and incentives

One of the hardest questions for any society to answer is the extent to which the richer members should help the poorer members through the tax-and-benefit system — and what price society as a whole is prepared to pay to offer this help. Since the collapse of communism in 1989, the extreme socialist position has become untenable. 'From each according to his ability, to each according to his needs' is a fine ideal, but the attempt to impose such a redistribution of wealth has failed. The last bastions of this approach, Cuba and North Korea, are both desperately poor. The reasoning is simple: if each family receives 'according to its need' *regardless of the amount of work done*, then there is little incentive to work. It will become impossible in practice to get each household to contribute 'according to its ability'. Not surprisingly, extreme socialist states become dictatorial. While it may be possible to compel people to turn up at the factory gate, it is not so easy to compel people to use their initiative and enthusiasm — and no modern economy can flourish without these characteristics among its workforce.

The same problem of a lack of incentives exists in less acute form in the mixed economies of Europe. Incentives for the well-off are more attractive than they were. The top marginal rate of tax in the UK of 40% enables the well-off to keep more than half of extra earnings. This is a significant improvement on the *83%* top marginal rate that existed before the Thatcher premiership of 1979–91.

However, at the bottom end, incentives are much less secure. The combination of relatively generous **transfer payments** for the poor, and marginal tax rates of around 32 % for those in low-paid work (i.e. the income tax rate of 22 % and National Insurance contributions of 10 %) creates a **poverty trap**. The unemployed household moving into low-paid work may find that the loss of benefits and the requirement to pay tax actually leaves the household either worse off or only very slightly better off. In these circumstances, the temptation to remain unemployed (perhaps doing casual, undeclared jobs for cash at the same time) is very real.

The UK government has attempted to avoid the worst effects of the poverty trap in a number of ways. For example, after six months of receiving **jobseekers' allowance**, the unemployed are compelled to attend an interview if they are to continue to receive benefits. The hope is to confine the benefit to those who are genuinely seeking work. Or again, **working families tax credit** (WFTC) is given to low-paid workers with children. The purpose of the benefit is to ensure that work pays. Given that welfare benefits are greater for those with children to support, without this benefit many families would be better off out of work than in.

GLOSSARY

extrapolation: predicting the future by using the past
forecasting: predictions, both for firms and for the whole economy
jobseekers' allowance: current name for unemployment benefit
lagging indicators: variables following changes in output
leading indicators: variables foretelling changes in output
moving average: average of the last n readings of a variable
Objective 2 funding: EU help for areas suffering industrial decline
poverty trap: effective marginal tax rates of nearly 100% for the very low paid
transfer payment: gift or benefit (e.g. a welfare payment from government)
wealth distribution: the degree of wealth equality in a population
welfare policy: expression of government principles with respect to poverty
working families tax credit (WFTC): benefit to low-paid families, to overcome the poverty trap

Chapter 27
Option 3: competition, conflict or consensus?

Introduction

This option is based on the relationships between the corporation and its various stakeholders. The fundamental question is: how can stakeholders be protected from the power that the large corporation wields?

This option will be looked at in four sections:
- *The corporation: a force for good?* This reminds us of the fundamental benefits and drawbacks of profit-seeking companies in a free market.

- *Protecting suppliers, employees and consumers.* This looks at the relationships that the corporation has with these groups.
- *Protecting shareholders.* This examines the legal defences that shareholders have, and the interpretation of accounts.
- *Protecting the community and the wider environment.* This looks at the themes of social and environmental responsibility.

This option makes wide-ranging use of earlier content. Chapter 11, in particular, forms an introduction. Additionally, the final section of Option 1 on the ethical issues of globalisation should also be considered part of Option 3.

One aspect of corporate power that is marginal to this option is monopoly power. This has already been covered in Chapters 21 and 22 of the A2 core, and Chapter 9 from the AS specification. Equally, there is only limited reference to specifically global issues right at the end of this option. They have also been covered in Chapter 24 of the A2 core and Chapters 15 and 16 of the AS course.

The corporation: a force for good?

At the end of this section, you should be able to:

1 Summarise the benefits and drawbacks of corporations working in a free market.

2 Explain the purposes of patents and copyright.

Introduction (see also Chapter 1)

Every modern industrial economy is powered by the activities of private sector, profit-seeking companies. They are the economic agents that organise production, specialise in every conceivable field, respond to customer demands, innovate to survive — and have generated standards of living unimaginable in previous generations. Chapter 1 showed how, in response to the price mechanism, companies are driven to produce the very goods consumers want, and in the right proportions. In other words, companies are the agents by which allocative (Pareto) efficiency is achieved. Competitive forces also compel firms to be technically efficient, raising the productivity of their inputs with the result that a country's output, its real national income, is maximised.

The benefits of the free market are also dynamic in nature. Competitive pressures lead to continuous improvements in quality, and to the invention of new products. Firms are compelled to invest some of their profits in innovation — in new and better products and new and better production processes. Otherwise they will fall behind in the never-ending race for business survival. These pressures are the main forces behind economic growth. The UK's long-term growth rate of 2.5% p.a. may not sound spectacular, but it leads to a doubling of living standards every 28 years: in other words, in every generation.

Of course, not everything is rosy in the capitalist world. Chapters 9, 10 and 14 looked at examples of market failure caused by monopoly, externalities and the extreme inequality generated by the free market. And this option will examine the need for protection of the less powerful economic agents in their dealings with the corporation. However, the

undoubted defects of free-market capitalism should not blind us to its enormous successes. Since the collapse of communism in 1989, there is no other economic model that commands serious attention.

Property rights

One of the cornerstones of the way the free market works is the concept of private property. Economic agents with the necessary resources are free to buy any good that has not been declared illegal, and use it in a manner they think fit. If people were not allowed to *keep* the things they work for, there would be little incentive to work for them in the first place.

The importance of private property to the effective functioning of the free market then raises the question of whether *ideas* have **property rights** attached to them as well. It is impossible to prevent people copying very general ideas — workers switch between companies carrying ideas with them, the media disseminate ideas and we all gather information from our environment every hour of the day. But very specific ideas — a new product, a new production method, a film or book or song — can be protected by law. There are two main avenues by which such ideas are protected.

First, new products and new processes (production methods) are protected by **patents**. A patent has to be applied for through the Patent Office. The idea must be considered genuinely new, not merely a variant on an existing product. If successful, the patent grants an exclusive right to the product for 20 years, after which anyone may exploit it. A variant on a patent is a **trademark**. Trademarks are the particular brand names or motifs under which businesses trade. They may also be registered with the Patent Office.

However, under UK law there is no right to the general appearance of a product. For example, the makers of Penguin biscuits were unsuccessful in their attempt to prevent ASDA from selling a very similar type of biscuit that they called a Puffin. And many own-brand colas use packaging that looks remarkably similar to that of Coca-Cola. Only if the courts think there is a real risk that customers will confuse the two products will they defend a general design. So the makers of 'Oxford' marmalade managed to persuade the courts to prohibit a rival from selling 'Oxford and Cambridge' marmalade on the grounds that this amounted to an attempt to 'pass off' one product as another.

The second means of protecting ideas is **copyright**. Authors, composers, artists and computer programmers have automatic ownership of their work, which prevents others from copying it without permission. The owners of copyright can, if they wish, give permission for it to be used on any terms they think fit. Copyright lasts for 70 years after the owner's death.

The **intellectual property rights** granted by the patent and copyright system seek to remedy a defect in the free market. It is important that they do so. In Hong Kong, the movie industry has been virtually destroyed by widespread piracy that enables consumers to watch pirated copies of new films before they have even been launched. At the same time, the 20-year limitation on patents recognises that there is also a public interest in ideas becoming freely available after inventors have had the chance to exploit their idea.

Patents can be registered internationally, but the reality is that it is virtually impossible to protect a patent in most ELDCs. Laws are usually in place to protect intellectual property

rights, but in practice they are unenforceable. While on holiday in Sri Lanka, the author was unable to find a single legal copy of Microsoft software in the capital's department stores.

On a global level we have ended up with a rather messy solution whereby intellectual property can be defended in rich countries, but where it has been effectively abandoned (some would say 'stolen') in poor countries. Whether we should deplore the theft, or applaud the reduction in inequality, is a difficult moral issue.

Nor is this dilemma unique to poor countries. In the 1980s virtually every UK school was engaged in widespread photocopying of copyright material, which at the time was illegal. Since then, the reality of what was going on has been recognised and a licensing system has been introduced enabling schools to photocopy material for classroom use. On a personal level, readers may be aware of illegal copying of music, videos and computer programs. The technical developments of CD-writers, video recorders and the internet have made it very difficult to prevent households from carrying out these activities. The price of such activity is the slower development of creative work than would be the case if the political will existed to enforce copyright law in the home.

GLOSSARY

copyright: ownership rights of an author or artiste
intellectual property rights: right to ideas (e.g. patents, brands, software)
patent: exclusive rights to an invention for 20 years, protected by law
property rights: rights of ownership
trademark: logo or design representing a company or product

Protecting suppliers, employees and consumers

At the end of this section, you should be able to:

1 Discuss business relationships along the supply chain.

2 Discuss the changing relationship between employers and employees.

3 Discuss the role of trade unions, and of employment law

4 Explain why and how consumers are protected from sellers.

Protecting small businesses in the supply chain (see also Chapter 5)

The **supply chain** describes the stages through which a product passes on its way to the final customer. Also known as the *chain of production*, it is of particular significance to manufacturers. They have to buy in raw materials 'upstream' and then find distributors (i.e. retailers) to whom to sell their output. This concept was touched on in the discussion of supplier relationships in Chapter 5 and of vertical integration in Chapter 20. Relationships up and down the supply chain are essentially buyer/seller relationships. But instead of the firm being the seller and the household being the buyer, both the seller and the buyer are firms. In other words, their transactions are 'B2B', rather than 'B2C'.

Like any buyer/seller relationship, B2B relationships exhibit interdependence. Both parties to the transaction rely on each other. If bicycle manufacturers rely on ball-bearing suppliers, so also do the ball-bearing suppliers rely on bicycle manufacturers. Given this mutual reliance, why should either party need protecting from the other? Often negotiating strengths are not equal: big companies in oligopolistic industries tend to have more power than small companies in competitive structures. And buyers normally have the advantage over sellers in the B2B context. For example, they can improve their cash flow by delaying payment to their suppliers. There is not a great deal that their suppliers can do about it.

Specifically, major retailers often wield enormous power over their suppliers, as the retailers control the chain of distribution — the route to the customer. For example, in 2001 the new chief executive of Sainsburys wanted to increase company stock levels of a range of products to back up a guarantee never to run out of them. The suppliers involved were sent a letter asking them to pay Sainsburys for the increased stock level it was proposing to carry. The letter was sent with an invoice attached! More commonly, retailers run price promotions and demand that their suppliers pay for them by providing the goods at a reduced price.

None of the above tactics is illegal, although in the case of unreasonable delay of payment, it *might* be possible to recover interest on the sum if the supplier was determined enough. A more realistic sanction would be a refusal to supply that particular customer again — assuming the supplier can afford to follow this course of action. The bigger the customer, the harder it will be to do this — and the big customers know this only too well. By contrast, it *is* illegal for a manufacturer to refuse to supply a particular retailer. A manufacturer with a luxury brand image might seek to maintain its exclusivity by not supplying discount retailers that would sell the product at a low price. As described in Chapter 22, such behaviour is illegal under the 1998 Competition Act.

The changing employer/employee relationship (see also Chapters 6 and 20)

Chapter 20 explained that UK companies are tending to move away from autocratic management styles, and towards the delegation of decisions to employees. As the number of unskilled jobs in the UK has declined, so the general skill level of workers has increased. Employees increasingly expect to make decisions, and have the capacity to do so. Many companies aspire (as mentioned in Option 2) to become *learning organisations* — communities where all stakeholders are communicating effectively with each other.

One method that has been used to try to move employees closer to their companies is encouraging **employee share ownership**, by either giving employees shares every month or offering them at a reduced price. The idea is that this gives the employee a direct financial stake in the success of the company. If the company does well, there will be an immediate financial benefit to the workers themselves. They therefore have an incentive to do their best. The government has sought to encourage this by offering tax concessions to firms that offer shares to their staff.

However, the connection between the performance of any individual employee in a large company and that company's share price is slender. So as a means of motivating a workforce, this method will have limited success. Indeed, the purpose of employee share ownership schemes is more symbolic than real. It speaks of an *aspiration* on behalf of

management that their employees should identify with the company, and should share in its success.

Employee share ownership flourished briefly during the internet boom in the years leading up to the crash in 2000. Many new start-ups were short of cash, but had great prospects — or so they thought. Often employees were persuaded to work for small amounts of cash and generous numbers of shares — shares that in all too many cases became worthless shortly afterwards.

At a different level of the company, it may make more sense to pay directors in part in shares. The directors really do have the ability individually to influence the share price, and so the incentive provided by offering them shares is very real. Normally these are provided in the form of **share options**. So a director might be granted 100,000 share options giving the right to buy shares in 2 years' time at today's price. For every £1 the share price rises, the director stands to gain £100,000.

Trade unions

Even though many companies aspire to foster good relationships with their employees, the reality is that employees still need protection from their employers. Trade unions provide one form of help. As mentioned in Chapter 6, collective bargaining has become less important as so many employment contracts are now negotiated individually. With the decline of collective bargaining, the strike has become less important too, because workers will normally only go on strike in pursuit of a joint, collective grievance — typically, low pay.

The changes in unions' legal position forced through parliament by Margaret Thatcher in the 1980s have also made **strikes** more difficult. The **closed shop** has been effectively abolished. **Sympathy strikes** and **political strikes** are now illegal. And no strike may be held unless union members have first voted for it in a **strike ballot**. Furthermore, trade union leaders have to be elected by a **postal ballot**, rather than by a show of hands at a meeting. This has resulted in more representative union leaders emerging. On top of this, there has been a general decline in male, manufacturing employment in the UK where unions were traditionally strongest.

Recent developments within the trade union movement are a response to its much weakened role — weaker numerically (membership is roughly half its peak figure of 13 million in 1979), weaker legally, and weaker in public perception of its place in society. They include:

- **Defensive mergers**. The actual number of unions has been considerably reduced, with dozens of smaller ones eliminated.
- **No-strike agreements**. Pioneered by the electricians' union (EETPU), these deals give up the right to strike in return for concessions from employers. Sometimes the company agrees to settle disputes by going to *arbitration* — an arrangement whereby a third party is asked to settle the disagreement. A government organisation called the Advisory, Conciliation and Arbitration Service (ACAS) is the main provider of this service.
- **Single-union agreements**. Employers agree to negotiate with just one union. This helps to avoid **demarcation disputes**: that is, different unions arguing over whose members should do which jobs. It often leads to closer, friendlier relations between the two sides as well.
- **The Japanese approach**. Workers offer total flexibility in return for job security. Workers

will do any job, retraining as necessary. In return, the firm will go to almost any lengths to avoid compulsory redundancies.

- **Fringe benefits**. Like other clubs, unions try to attract members with a range of extras, such as lower-cost insurance and other marketing ploys negotiated with major national companies.

Despite their general decline in membership and influence since 1979, in 2002–03 trade unions have shown signs of a modest revival. Since 2000, numbers have shown a slight increase. And the one-day strike by the large trade union Unison in July 2002, followed by firemen's strikes in November, may indicate a rise in trade union militancy — at least in the public sector, where unions remain strongest.

Employment law

The purpose of **employment law** is to even up the balance of power between workers and their more powerful employers. At the same time, there is widespread recognition that *too much* protection for workers may, paradoxically, make companies more reluctant to employ people in the first place. So the continental model followed by France and Germany, where it is both time consuming and expensive to make workers redundant, is not one that recommends itself to either the Labour Party or the Conservative Party.

Employment law is based on the idea of *fairness*. Workers should be treated in a reasonable manner. So, for example, workers who are dismissed can, if they have been with their employer for at least a year, appeal to an **industrial tribunal**, claiming **unfair dismissal**. If they were made **redundant**, they could appeal on the grounds that they were not selected fairly. Or if they were dismissed for misconduct, they could appeal on the grounds that they were not given the warnings to which they were entitled under the **disciplinary procedure** laid out in their contract of employment.

Another section of legislation is designed to ensure that workers are treated equally, regardless of gender, marital status, race or disability. Gender issues are overseen by the **Equal Opportunities Commission** (EOC), and race issues by the **Commission for Racial Equality** (CRE). Both were set up following equal opportunities legislation in the 1970s and were initially concerned to protect the rights of women and ethnic minorities. As society has changed, so a small but increasing proportion of their caseload has been concerned with ensuring that men and whites are treated equally — not just women and ethnic minorities.

Disability discrimination was made illegal in 1995, and is supported by the **Disability Rights Commission** (DRC), set up in 2000. Employers have a duty to treat disabled people equally unless they can show that the disability makes it impossible to do the job. Employers also have a duty to make reasonable adjustments to accommodate a disabled person. These adjustments might include improving access to premises, modifying equipment or providing extra training.

At the time of writing in 2003, the government is proposing to replace the EOC, CRE and DRC with one super-watchdog designed to combat all forms of discrimination. This proposal has been put forward in response to an EU directive that will also outlaw discrimination on three further counts: sexual orientation, religion and age.

In conclusion, while both trade unions and employment law have their place in helping workers deal with their employers on equal terms, they cannot in the end provide anyone

with **job security**. This elusive benefit must be found in the skills and talents of the individual, rather than through legislation. It remains the case that 'to be employed is to be at risk, to be employable is to be secure'.

Protecting the consumer (see also Chapters 4 and 11)

Consumers begin their relationship with companies with one significant advantage: they are buyers, not sellers. Successful firms therefore spend a great deal of effort finding out precisely what it is that their customers (and potential customers) want — and then trying to sell it to them. As Chapter 4 showed, most market research, whether primary or secondary, quantitative or qualitative, is aimed at all of us in our capacity as consumers. The relationship between firms and households is therefore of enormous benefit to both parties.

Nonetheless, as mentioned in Chapter 11, the individual customer knows less about the product than the seller and normally has less money to pursue a court case to a satisfactory conclusion. For this reason, there is a body of consumer law designed to redress the balance of power. As with employment law, the key theme is *fairness*. So, for example, customers do not have the right to return a product just because they decide after the purchase that they do not want it. Individual companies may offer such a returns policy, but that is a commercial judgement that each company makes for itself. However, there *is* a legal right for customers to return products that they bought after a salesperson called at their house. The reasoning is that the buyer might have felt under pressure to agree a sale just to get rid of the seller.

Examples of consumer legislation include:
- The **Sale of Goods Acts (1979, 1994)**, which state that goods must correspond with their description, be of satisfactory quality and be fit for their intended purpose.
- The **Consumer Credit Act (1974)** states that sellers offering credit must make clear the interest rate paid (known as the APR), the price without credit and the additional interest payable.
- Under the **Unfair Contract Terms Act (1977)** the courts will not support 'small print' in a contract where the terms are plainly unfair. For example, consumers cannot sign away their rights under existing consumer law.

Another way that government has protected the consumer is in the setting up of the **Food Standards Agency** (FSA) in 2000. Its brief is to advise on food safety issues, from the viewpoint of the consumer. Previously this had been handled by the Ministry of Agriculture, Fisheries and Food (MAFF). However, it was thought that MAFF had too close links with the sellers (i.e. farmers), and was therefore unable to give impartial advice to the buyers (i.e. consumers).

Finally, the **Consumers' Association** is a pressure group that, for many decades, has promoted consumer interests. One way it has done this is to publish the monthly **Which? magazine**. It regularly compares the goods and services of firms in the same industry — from gas suppliers to jam makers to washing machine manufacturers — and comes up with its recommended best buys. To ensure its independence, it never accepts advertising. Like any pressure group, it also runs campaigns. In 2002, its campaigns included scrapping the common agricultural policy (see Chapter 16), aiming for open competition throughout the EU in the sale of cars, and full labelling of genetically modified foods.

GLOSSARY

closed shop: restriction of work in a firm to union members

Commission for Racial Equality (CRE): body enforcing UK law on race discrimination

Consumer Credit Act (1974): law governing firms wishing to sell on credit

Consumers' Association: charity that champions consumer interests

defensive merger: merger motivated by falling sales

demarcation dispute: competing trade unions fighting for available work

Disability Rights Commission (DRC): body set up to enforce the Disability Discrimination Act

disciplinary procedure: formal response to employees considered unsatisfactory

employee share ownership: giving workers shares in their own company, or selling them cheaply

employment law: those laws governing the employment relationship

Equal Opportunities Commission (EOC): body enforcing UK law on gender discrimination

Food Standards Agency (FSA): government body advising on food safety

fringe benefit: perk going with a job, or with membership of a club

industrial tribunal: court hearing employment disputes

'Japanese' industrial relations: workers give flexibility and receive job security

job security: the situation where workers are safe in their jobs

no-strike agreement: right to strike given up for concessions

political strike: strike designed to influence government policy

postal ballot: vote conducted by post (e.g. for a union leader)

redundancy: worker dismissed due to a shortage of work

Sale of Goods Acts (1979, 1994): state that goods must be of 'merchantable quality'

share option: option to buy shares in the future at a price fixed today

single-union agreement: employer negotiates with just one union

strike: collective withdrawal of labour

strike ballot: vote of trade union members about strike action

supply chain: firms through which inputs go; chain of production

sympathy strike: strike supporting another firm's workers

Unfair Contract Terms Act (1977): unreasonable 'small print' is not enforceable

unfair dismissal: sacking of a worker without sufficient cause

Which? magazine: magazine of the Consumers' Association

Protecting shareholders

At the end of this section, you should be able to:

1 Explain the importance of corporations providing accurate accounts.

2 Explain the legal protection available to shareholders.

3 Interpret balance sheets and profit and loss accounts, with particular reference to the asset turnover and acid test ratios.

Introduction

It was explained in Chapter 3 that firms take a variety of legal forms. In the case of sole proprietors, partnerships and private limited companies (Ltd), the owners normally run the companies themselves and have little interest in falsifying the accounts — other than possibly to deceive their bankers, suppliers or the tax authorities. But in the case of the

public limited company (plc), the owners are thousands of individual shareholders who have no direct role in running their company. They rely entirely on published accounts and other publicly available information to tell them what their company is worth, and therefore what a reasonable share price is.

The importance of accurate accounts was brought home with increased force in 2002, when two major US companies went bankrupt after falsifying financial information. Enron was originally an energy company that diversified into the much riskier business of energy trading. It concealed its debts by setting up subsidiary companies to carry those debts, while keeping secret the fact that it owned these **off-balance-sheet vehicles**. Shortly afterwards WorldCom, a telecommunications company, went bankrupt after billions of dollars of running costs were falsely classified as capital investment. These then appeared as assets on the balance sheet — and falsely inflated the profits on the profit and loss account by reducing the costs.

These two scandals caused significant falls in the US stock market, as investors wondered which other companies might have lied about their true financial position. We look now at what shareholder defences are in place in the UK.

How UK shareholders are protected

There are a number of safeguards for UK shareholders:

The legal requirement to publish accounts. All limited companies must lodge their accounts with Companies House every year, where they are available for anyone to inspect. They can also be inspected over the internet. An annual report must be made available to all shareholders.

The legal requirement to hold an annual general meeting. The **annual general meeting** (AGM), to which all shareholders must be invited, gives them an opportunity to ask questions, air grievances and vote on resolutions. Every vote is on the basis of one share, one vote. The AGM is the ultimate source of authority for any company. For example, the directors who run the company can be voted on or voted off at the AGM.

The legal requirement to appoint independent auditors. **Auditors** inspect accounts and say whether they give a true and fair picture of the company's financial position. They are firms of accountants and must have no financial interest in the companies that they inspect. One of the features of the Enron scandal was the too-close relationship between the company and Arthur Andersen, its auditors.

The legal ban on insider trading. Directors and other employees of the company are normally the first to find out **market-sensitive information**. This is any information that would influence the company's share price — for example, news of a big order, the departure of a key employee, a product development breakthrough or the collapse of merger talks. Employees are not allowed to buy or sell shares on the basis of this information — **insider trading** — which gives some protection to other shareholders who are not in such a privileged position. Directors are particularly likely to find out market-sensitive information first. As an additional precaution, all directors are required to publish details of any share trades they undertake in their own company. Although the rule against insider trading is difficult to enforce, there have been some successful prosecutions.

The role of non-executive directors (non-execs). Major companies are run by a board of directors. These include a group of full-time employees of the company known as executive directors. This group includes the managing director, the finance director, the marketing director and so on. Additionally, most boards have others who work only a very few hours a week for the company. They are appointed for the particular skills, experience or contacts that they possess and are known as non-executive directors. Non-execs should be able to offer an independent view, and act as a safeguard for shareholder interests.

It is often the case that the interests of shareholders diverge from those of the full-time directors. For example, the directors might be keen on a big takeover, which would give them the prestige of running a bigger company. The shareholders, meanwhile, might be more interested in whether the bigger company will give a greater return on the capital employed. This divergence of interests is sometimes called the split between **ownership and control**. The shareholders own the company, but the directors control it. The non-execs should ensure that there is no such split — that the board is at all times the servant of the shareholders in reality as well as in name.

One problem with the oversight of big business is that directorships are often inter-locking. The non-execs of company A may not want to upset the executive directors of company A, because in company B the roles could be reversed! This is one reason why executive pay is often disproportionate to the performance of the individual concerned. The non-execs who set the pay of the executive directors may incline to generosity in the hope that in another context the favour will be returned.

Interpreting accounts (see also Chapters 3 and 7)

Even if shareholders have full and accurate accounts, they still have to know how to interpret them if they are to come to a full understanding of how their company is performing. You will already know that the two main sets of accounts are the profit and loss account and the balance sheet. To complete this option successfully, you must understand them fully. This would be a good time to revise them from Chapters 3 and 7. These chapters also covered profit margins, percentage return on capital employed and the working capital ratio. All these concepts are crucial to interpreting accounts and should also be revised as part of this option. We now consider two more ratios.

The acid test ratio. This is a variant on the working capital ratio. It omits stock from the equation on the grounds that stock may not sell. The resulting ratio is known as the **acid test ratio** and compares the cash the company has plus the money it is owed, against the money that the company owes in the short term:

$$\text{Acid test ratio} = \frac{\text{Cash} + \text{Debtors}}{\text{Currrent liabilities}}$$

The definition of what is 'safe' depends on the overall financial health of the company. A large and profitable plc could ignore normal ratios, secure in the knowledge that banks would be only too happy to lend it more money if it were needed. But for a new start-up, the situation would be quite different. A temporary failure to keep sufficient cash could lead to its closure. But, as a rule of thumb, an acid test ratio of 1.0 or higher is normally considered sufficient.

One problem for the shareholder in interpreting this kind of information is that it is normally published only every 6 months or every year. And the cash position of any

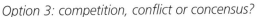

company can deteriorate very quickly. In a fast-changing business environment such as computer sales, a decline in turnover can quickly lead to the position where the **overdraft ceiling** is reached, and the firm's bankers cease to honour company cheques with very little warning.

The asset–turnover ratio. The **asset–turnover ratio** measures turnover relative to the assets of the company (less current liabilities).

$$\text{Asset–turnover ratio} = \frac{\text{Turnover}}{\text{Total assets less current liabilities}}$$

Since total assets less current liabilities are also equal to capital employed, this formula is not very different from % ROCE. Instead of measuring *profit* relative to capital, it measures *turnover*. Of the two formulae, % ROCE is far more important. Suppose you compared two supermarkets with the same capital investment, but one was charging rock-bottom prices (and therefore selling more) while the other was charging average prices. The price discounter would have a higher asset–turnover ratio, but might well be making less profit because its profit margin is so low. This highlights the fundamental problem with this ratio. Unless a firm's profit margin is known, information about its turnover is of limited value in assessing financial performance.

To conclude, it is important to remember that shareholders are engaged in entrepreneurial activity whenever they buy shares. In return for their share of the profit, they also have to accept the risk that goes with it. Shareholders may lose out through theft or failure to disclose relevant information — but more commonly they will lose out because their directors do not perform as well as directors in rival companies, or simply because market conditions turn against their line of business.

For example, BT sustained enormous losses in 2001/02 when it was forced to **write down** the value of intangible assets from its recent acquisitions of foreign telecommunications companies. When it became obvious that the goodwill owned by these companies was worth far less than had previously been thought, the new owner simply had to take the loss.

GLOSSARY

acid test ratio: measure of short-term liquidity
annual general meeting (AGM): meeting of shareholders each year, the ultimate authority in the company
asset–turnover ratio: turnover expressed as a multiple of assets
auditor: person or company that checks up on others, especially accountants checking a firm's accounts
insider trading: illegal dealing in shares by employees of a company
market-sensitive information: information that could change a company's share price
non-executive director: director giving a few hours a month to the role
off-balance-sheet vehicle: dummy firm set-up, taking debt off the parent firm's records
overdraft ceiling: maximum overdraft allowed by a bank
ownership and control: theory that managers, not owners, often control a firm
write down: decision to reduce the stated value of a firm's assets

Protecting the community and the wider environment

> **At the end of this section, you should be able to:**
>
> **1** Discuss the purpose and limitations of social audits.
>
> **2** Discuss the concept of sustainable development with reference to the 2002 Johannesburg Earth Summit.

Protecting the community

Chapter 11 discussed the issue of corporate responsibility, extending the basic idea with reference to ethical trading at the end of Option 1. One way of measuring a corporation's ethical stance is to undertake a **social audit**.

The idea stems from the regular financial audits that all companies are compelled by law to undergo. If it is so important, the argument goes, to have a company's *financial* health externally checked, then why shouldn't its broader impact on society also be externally checked? The term first emerged in the 1970s to describe evaluations that focused on the likely impact of a firm's activities on jobs, the community and the environment. It was taken up by the Co-op in the 1980s and by The Body Shop in 1993 and Ben and Jerry's ice cream in 1995. In the words of Anita Roddick, founder of The Body Shop: 'Auditing shouldn't just be for accountants. A company should open its heart as well as its books.' Similar ideas are expressed by the term **social accounting**, or sometimes more specifically **environmental accounting**.

These few companies take social auditing very seriously, even appointing an external social auditor who produces reports on some or all of the following questions:

- Do stakeholders believe the company lives up to its stated objectives and values?
- Does the company minimise resource consumption to the benefit of the environment?
- Does the company implement equal opportunities, encouraging social inclusion?
- To what extent have specific performance targets been met?
- Has external certification been achieved in this area: for example, the quality standard AA1000, offered by the Institute of Social and Ethical Accountability?

Social audits have now spread out beyond this small band of enthusiasts and have been embraced by many large companies. For example, PriceWaterhouseCoopers, an internationally known accounting firm, conducted over 6,000 social audits in 1999 mainly examining labour and environmental practices. Among its clients were Nike, Disney, Wal-Mart and Gap.

It is open to question how many of these large companies really believe in social accounting, and how many are simply trying to avoid the bad publicity that, for example, accompanies using sweatshops in Asia. But either way, if companies are being forced to recognise their social responsibilities, that can only be a good thing. It is also an indication of the success of pressure groups that have campaigned on these issues.

The campaign to force corporations to behave responsibly is never-ending. Just as Arthur Andersen, the auditors of Enron, have been found negligent in their financial audits, so

also there is suspicion that commercial companies doing social audits are not always doing the job properly.

Protecting the environment

Chapter 10 explained how environmental damage was an example of market failure, in this case caused by externalities. At the end of Option 1 the world's response was discussed, notably the Rio Summit of 1992 and the Kyoto protocol of 1997. *These should be revised for Option 3 as well.* Our examination of environmental issues concludes with a look at the 2002 Earth Summit in Johannesburg, South Africa.

Sustainable development has been defined as 'meeting the needs of present generations without compromising the ability of future generations to meet their own needs'. The Johannesburg Earth Summit in August/September 2002 was based around this theme. With some 65,000 delegates in attendance, it was the biggest ever international convention. Over 100 Heads of State attended (though the US President, George Bush, was notable for his absence), together with numerous environmental and Third World charities. There was also a strong presence from multinational firms such as McDonald's, Nike, Nestlé and Rio Tinto.

Targets were set to halve the number of people living without clean water and sanitation, to restore depleted fish stocks and to reduce species loss — all by 2015. The proposals to open the EU's and USA's domestic markets to agricultural produce from poor countries, and to set targets for the use of renewable energy sources, were defeated.

The relatively modest achievements of the Summit were hailed by business and government as a success — and condemned by charities for not going nearly far enough. The proposal to set targets for the use of renewable energy illustrates the horse trading involved. On the one hand, environmental pressure groups and the EU were anxious to establish them. On the other hand, oil-producing nations naturally resisted a proposal that would reduce the value of their oil. Many of the poorest countries also took the view that what they needed were more conventional power stations, which are the cheapest current method of producing electricity.

GLOSSARY

environmental accounting: producing accounts that include the external impact of a company
social accounting: recording a firm's ability to please its community
social auditing: checking up on a firm's general behaviour

Chapter 28
A2 papers (Units 4 and 5)

Introduction

Unit	Method of assessment	Comment	A2 weighting
4	Examination	1 hour 45 minutes, based around pre-release material	30%
5	Examination	2 hours, in which questions on two of the three options must be answered	40%
6	Coursework (see Chapter 29)	Two pieces: one from each of the chosen options in Unit 5	30%

Marking schemes

In looking at AS papers in Chapter 17, the four criteria of knowledge, application, analysis and evaluation were discussed. These also apply to your A2 examination papers. The general standard is higher at A2, and the 'analysis and evaluation' criteria are more important than they were at AS.

The layout of questions

This will not necessarily stay the same year by year, but changes should be well publicised. In 2002–03, A2 questions were designed as follows.

The Unit 4 exam contained around five sides of pre-released material made available around the beginning of the academic year. Your teacher will almost certainly give this to you well in advance of the actual exam. You then enter the examination in January or June and find a smaller amount of *additional* material to read as well as the original pre-released material. There are then three questions to answer for a total of 40, and finally a lengthy question for 40 marks that is not subdivided. Thus, there are 80 marks in total for Unit 4.

The Unit 5 exam contains all three options, of which every candidate should attempt just two. Each option takes an hour to complete, so the examination is 2 hours long.

Within each option, there are three data–response questions for which no choice is given. They carry 25 marks in total. Then the candidate has to choose one of two structured essays that also carry 25 marks. So 50 marks are available for each option, making 100 marks for Unit 5.

In 2002, all the essays began with a part (a), which started with the command 'explain' or 'examine', and carried 10 marks. Part (b) then started with 'evaluate' and carried 15 marks. This illustrates the increasing importance of analysis and evaluation in the A2 papers.

It is absolutely essential that candidates attempt the two options for which they have prepared, even if the questions in the other option look easier.

Issues arising from the Unit 4 pre-release style of examination

In 2002, the Unit 4 material was based on the purchase by Interbrew of Bass Brewers in 2000, and the competition issues that this threw up. The pre-released material contained a report from the Competition Commission later in 2000 concluding that Interbrew should be compelled to sell Bass Brewers. The government subsequently followed this recommendation. How can candidates prepare for this style of examination?

- You need to be very familiar with the pre-released material. Make sure you have summarised its key points. If there are any details in it that you do not understand, be sure to ask your teacher. Additionally, each year, an analysis of pre-released material is available on **www.geraldwood.com**.
- If you are sitting the unit in June, make sure you have seen the January exam paper. Although the additional material is different in the two exams, the January questions will provide you with excellent practice.
- Research the topic indicated by the pre-released material. So in 2002, for example, candidates could have looked at the Competition Commission website and studied everything there connected to the brewing industry. Web searches on Interbrew and Bass Brewers would also have kept students up to date with the unfolding story. Teachers may well do exercises like this with you in class. Of course, in your year the pre-released material will be on a different topic, but the principle is the same.

A2 past paper practice

All the A2 questions except one are similar in style to the AS questions, examples of which were discussed in Chapter 17. There is no need to look at further examples here. The exception is the 40-mark question in the Unit 4 examination. Below is a possible question that would fit in with the 2002 pre-released material. It is followed by some guidance notes and a suggested answer.

> **Evaluate the Competition Commission's recommendation to instruct Interbrew to sell off Bass Brewers.** (40 marks)

Guidance notes

Any lengthy question from Unit 4 will need:

- a clear plan — with over 50 minutes to spend on this long question, a good answer will stretch to three or four sides of handwriting; some sort of structure is essential
- frequent reference to the text, both to the pre-released material and to the additional material
- detailed demonstration of knowledge from the specification
- plenty of analysis and evaluation

The answer that follows is based on the following plan:

- an introduction to the issues that the Competition Commission has to consider when judging mergers
- a look at the Interbrew/Bass Brewers merger to see if competition would be damaged
- a look at alternative remedies proposed
- conclusion

Note: the word **(evidence)** in the essay that follows shows that the detail used was obtained from the material provided. As all the material provided ran to nine sides, it is not included here.

Suggested answer

One of the jobs of the Competition Commission is to advise government on recent mergers, and on proposed future mergers. The government has the power to prevent any merger that it considers to be against the public interest. This power should be used sparingly. Normally, if two firms wish to merge it is because there are 'synergies' (economies of scale) to be gained. The goods will be produced more cheaply, and some of this saving will, in a competitive market, feed through to the consumer in the form of lower prices. Everybody stands to gain from this sort of merger, except possibly the workers, some of whom may be made redundant.

However, if the merger results in a less competitive market, the customer stands to lose out. If the industry already had many large companies, two of them could merge without the level of competition being significantly affected. However, if there were only two or three large companies, a merger between two of them would undoubtedly reduce consumer choice. With the reduced degree of competition, companies tend to become technically inefficient. And as they raise their prices, so the industry contracts to below its optimal size, making it Pareto inefficient as well. The monopoly profits then gained by the lucky shareholders lead to a greater degree of inequality too. For all these reasons, monopoly power is an example of market failure. The Competition Commission is there to prevent monopoly power from forming through mergers that operate against the public interest.

One of the issues, therefore, in the purchase of Bass Brewers by Interbrew is whether the new company would wield significant market power. Interbrew, of course, stoutly denies this. It points out that in many European countries the market leader in brewing has a market share of over 30%. Since its own, new market share is only 33–38%, it argues that this is well within the EU norm **(evidence)**. However, we could equally well say that the EU average share for the market leader was too large, and that British brewing should not follow this poor example.

A more telling comparison is available from looking at the three-firm concentration ratio before and after the merger. Beforehand the figure was 64%, consisting of Scottish Courage (26%), Bass Brewers (23%) and Interbrew (15%). After the merger, the ratio rose to 76%. This consists of Scottish Courage (26%), Bass Brewers/Interbrew (38%) and Carlsberg (12%) **(evidence)**. In other words, the three-firm concentration ratio has risen from under two-thirds to over three-quarters. Although Interbrew claims that there is still vigorous competition between five major players, their list of five includes Anheuser-Busch with only 3.2% of the market **(evidence)**! We might wonder how much real competition a player of this size will be able to offer a company over ten times as large.

There is a further statistic that makes Interbrew's case very shaky. It paid £2.3 billion for Bass Brewers, even though independent analysts valued it at only £1.6–1.8 billion **(evidence)**. How could Bass be worth over £500 million more to Interbrew? The suspicion must be that Interbrew calculated it could still get a reasonable return on the extra £500 million of capital employed by exploiting its new market power and charging more for its beer. At the very least, this statistic casts doubt on Interbrew's claim that synergies will result in price reductions for the consumer.

The Competition Commission was, therefore, correct to say that the merger operates against the public interest. However, before the government can agree to the recommendation to force Interbrew to sell off Bass Brewers, it has to be convinced that there is not a less drastic remedy. It is impossible not to feel some sympathy for the anguished Chief Executive of Interbrew, Hugo Powell, who said the instruction to sell off Bass Brewers was 'disproportionate to the competition issues at stake' **(evidence)**. We do, therefore, need to consider some of the alternative remedies that the Competition Commission looked at.

First, Interbrew promised not to close any breweries or remove any brands until 2003 **(evidence)**. Since one of the first things a monopolist does is to cut back capacity to drive up the price, this was clearly an offer worth considering. But since the promise only extends for 3 years from the date of the purchase, the implication is that Interbrew is merely offering a stay of execution. Why should Interbrew be offered indefinite possession of monopoly power in return for 3 years of good behaviour?

Another possibility would be to force Interbrew to sell off some of the brands of Bass Brewers, or some of the brands Interbrew already owned. The Competition Commission rejected this on the grounds that it would be difficult to split Bass Brewers in two and that Interbrew's existing interest in beer was dominated by just one brand, Stella Artois **(evidence)**. There was, therefore, no neat division of either original company that could be brought about.

In conclusion, I would, therefore, advise the government to follow the recommendation of the Competition Commission and instruct Interbrew to sell off Bass Brewers. There is one further point to make. Interbrew probably stands to lose some hundreds of millions of pounds on the whole saga. It is unlikely that anyone else will be prepared to offer the inflated price of £2.3 billion that Interbrew originally paid. However, Interbrew only has itself to blame for this loss. It should have made its original offer conditional on receiving Competition Commission approval. This is the normal method of procedure. Interbrew has behaved like householders who build an extension first and then seek planning permission afterwards. If permission is not given and they have to knock down the extension, they deserve little sympathy.

Chapter 29
A2 coursework (Unit 6)

Introduction

Towards the end of the A2 year, your teacher has to submit *two* pieces of coursework from each candidate — just as at the end of the AS year. You will be studying two of the three options. On each option you study, you must write *one* project — making two projects in all. As in the AS year, the A2 projects count for 30% of the year's marks. It is well worth making a real effort on these projects. They can easily make a grade or two's difference to your examination result.

Differences from the AS projects

- The suggested maximum length is increased to 1,500 words, excluding appendices.
- The marking scheme indicates that a higher standard is expected. This is illustrated in the extract from the marking scheme below. Compare it with the marking scheme for AS projects in Chapter 18, and you will see the difference.
- Otherwise, the A2 projects are very similar to the AS ones. *All the advice given for the AS projects in Chapter 18 is, therefore, relevant here.*

Knowledge

13–18 Has demonstrated a good knowledge of relevant areas, selecting appropriately

19–25 Has demonstrated detailed, accurate and wide-ranging knowledge of concepts, theories and contexts, relevant to the investigation

Application

13–18 Has applied a selection of concepts, theories and methods, integrating economics and business terminology

19–25 Has applied a wide range of relevant concepts, theories and methods, integrated them and used them in a creative and original way

Analysis

13–18 Has used logical analysis of economic and business problems relevant to the investigation

19–25 Has used logical and perceptive analysis of economic and business problems as an integral part of the investigation

Evaluation

13–18 Has evaluated effectively and reached conclusions in an organised and coherent manner

19–25 Has evaluated convincingly, using independence of mind to reach conclusions that are logical, balanced and original

Some ideas for titles

Many of these titles reflect issues of current concern in 2001–02. You will need to find your own titles that reflect your personal interests and the current affairs of your year of study. The numbers in brackets after each title indicate the chapters in this revision guide whose content is most useful for the project concerned.

As at AS, the requirement for relevance to the option gives considerable freedom when parts of the course are interconnected. If, for example, some aspect of Unit 4 appeals to you, the topic is very likely to have relevance to one of your options too.

Option 1 project: what is the global future?

- How should Dyson decide where to locate its operations? (1, 5, 15, 25)
- What economic problems currently exist in Zimbabwe (or Argentina), and how might they be solved? (12–15, 25)
- To what extent did the Johannesburg Earth Summit of September 2002 increase the chances of an improvement in the standard of living of the world's poorest nations? (14, 15, 24, 25)
- Whose interests are served by globalisation? A critical examination of the work of the WTO, with reference to the dispute over X. (15, 16, 24, 25)

Option 2 project: can there be certainty?

- How does the internet start-up X intend to break even? (1, 3–8, 26)
- Why has the Bank of England been so successful in hitting its inflation targets since 1997? (13, 26)
- Comment critically on the way Matalan has managed to finance its expansion. (7, 20, 26)
- How to lose £13 billion: an assessment of Marconi's strategic planning errors. (1, 7, 8, 26)

Option 3 project: competition, conflict or consensus?

- Trade unions resurgent? A critical examination of the new militancy in 2002–03. (6, 20, 27)
- How effective is the Consumers' Association in protecting consumer interests? (4, 11, 22, 27)
- A force for justice, or an unnecessary generator of red tape? An analysis of the work of the CRE (or EOC or DRC). (6, 11, 27)
- To what extent can auditors safeguard shareholder interests? An analysis of the collapse of Enron (or Worldcom). (3, 7, 27)